Peter R. Senn

Social Science and
its Methods

Holbrook Press, Inc.,
Boston, Mass.

DEDICATION

For MARTHA and PAUL
in the hope that their generation
will use social science
better than mine has.

Library of Congress Catalog Card Number: 78-94339
Printed in the United States of America

Contents

Preface

Social science, in this book, is treated as a science, a truth-seeking endeavor, and a self-correcting system on a par with any other science. The text assumes that every educated person needs to understand science as well as to love the truth. It describes many of the most important methods used by social scientists. Each of the parts of scientific inquiry has methods associated with it. These methods are the practices of scientists in their search for truth.

The parts of the science system—problem formulation, hypothesis, observation and description, explanation, prediction, control—are discussed with their methods, and each method is analyzed in the context of its actual use wihin a social science discipline. In addition, each of the major disciplines is described in connection with its characteristic methods, methods which are useful as well in other disciplines.

This book is a departure from the usual introductions to social science in the rigor of its approach, in its close connection with what social scientists really do, in its coverage of the disciplines, its emphasis on the methods, and its consistent scientific-humanistic outlook.

Part 1 describes the scientific system of inquiry and how social science fits that system. In part 2, some of the widely-used methods of social science are described in connection with each of the central disciplines. Part 3 discusses specific uses of social science (in social work, planning and education), particularly in regard to scientific problems of prediction and control. Part 4 is devoted to placing social science into a humanistic frame of reference.

Appendix A, "How to Find It in the Social Sciences," is a cross-tabulated listing of hundreds of references, most of which are annotated. It should make easy the finding of reference material and will enable anyone to go as deeply into a subject as he wishes.

Foreword

TO THE STUDENT—This book is an introduction to social science. The core disciplines (history, sociology, geography, economics, political science, psychology and anthropology) are all described, as well as the applied social sciences of planning, education and social work. The description of each discipline covers also some of the main ways scientists try to approach the truth. Many of the examples and issues included are ones which pose problems to the social scientist at the present time.

TO THE TEACHER—Don't worry that social science is a big subject. If you feel, as we do, that our subject is of vital importance, then the problems of teaching are less significant than our attempts to do a good job. Where you disagree with interpretations or selections, use the book as an example of another viewpoint. Social science is still young, and there is much room for well-reasoned alternative viewpoints. If we left the student only with this knowledge, we would have accomplished something worthwhile.

TO THE PROFESSIONAL SOCIAL SCIENTIST—You know that experts in your own field are not of one mind on every question. Therefore some condensations and summarizations are bound to be less satisfying to some professionals than to others. What we have attempted to do is avoid any serious distortions and make our judgments on the basis of a careful review of the professional literature. But judgments remain in any case. Where you may disagree, please do so with charity. Imagine the job you would face if you attempted to cover all of social science for an introductory text.

TO THE GENERAL READER—This book is based more on what social scientists do than on what theoreticians think they do—but it includes that as well. The system of social science inquiry is not entirely a neat and logical package.

ACKNOWLEDGMENTS

Mary Senn, my wife, aided me during every part of the development of the book, with ideas, typing, criticisms, indexing and proof reading. Without her the book would never have been produced.

I was helped throughout the book by my editor, Mr. Edward Surovell. Mr. Barry Fetterolf of the Holbrook Press was more patient than I had any right to expect. I have borrowed and adapted freely from the vast literature of the social sciences in the spirit that what scientists publish they give to the world. This is an elementary text, and while it would be impossible to credit every original thought or example, I do wish to acknowledge my great indebtedness to that literature.

Mr. Richard Taylor, Chief Librarian of the Wright Campus of the Chicago City College, checked all the entries for Appendix A, "How to Find It in the Social Sciences," and made numerous corrections and suggestions. Mr. Fred Schlipf of the University of Chicago Graduate Library School pointed out several errors in the Appendix, drew attention to organizational, format and other problems and suggested additions and deletions for it. This Appendix was usefully criticized by Professors Michael Scriven, Harold Berlak, Jack Cousins, and Robert Stake. Professor Irving Morrissett did an outstanding job of editing an early version of it.

In the main text I am also indebted for a number of amendments and suggestions to Professors Fay-Tyler Norton, Thelma Peters, Joseph Olson, John A. Perry, and L. M. Winebrenner.

My thanks to all of the above. The faults that remain are mine.

PETER R. SENN
Professor of Economics
Chicago City College

Part **1**

Social Science Described

Part 1 introduces you to the system of scientific inquiry and shows you how social science fits into that system. The structure of scientific beliefs, the disciplines of social science, and the relationships of values to social science are some of the topics discussed.

Chapter 1

Methods In Science

TRUTH AND PROGRESS IN SOCIAL SCIENCE

Social science, as a part of science, shares science's goal of seeking the truth. Scientists think of truth as being something approachable but never quite reached. Scientists know that what men have accepted in the past as true has always been changed —enlarged upon or discarded—as time passed. In this way has knowledge grown and science progressed.

We are all familiar with certain aspects of the progress made by science through its pursuit of this goal of truth—space rocketry, computers, antibiotics that save lives, plastics, atomic power, and jet engines. The list that might be made is a long one and would likely concentrate on biological and physical sciences. The social sciences, true, have contributed to our well-being, but of these contributions we are often, and unfairly, less conscious. Consider, however, what life would be like with an economic system that did not function well. We can see the results in some underdeveloped countries. If our educational system fails to make young people into acceptable members of society, what will become of them—or of the society?

Although we are often less conscious of the contribution social science has made to our well-being, we are very conscious of the problems it is called upon to solve, which range from war, through race relations and urban renewal, to individual problems like loneliness. Unfortunately, social science is not developing rapidly enough to cope effectively with some of the most pressing problems of our time. There are various reasons for the failure to find solutions, but perhaps the dominant reason is lack of knowledge about the *methods* of social science. These methods are part of the methods of science, and only by knowing and using them can we improve the quality of our lives.

WHAT ARE METHODS?

Scholars have defined and used the term "methods" in many different ways. Each of their definitions and usages emphasizes one or another part of what the methods of science are. But today most social scientists would agree that methods are procedures, or ways of knowing, that involve systematic arrangement. For the social scientists this means setting up rules and proper practices to obtain specific answers to questions according to a plan.

The study of scientific methods has three parts. The first part concerns itself with the world and its phenomena. The second studies the logical relations of the symbols social scientists use to represent the phenomenon under investigation and the logical relations between the phenomena themselves. The third part concentrates on the correspondence between the phenomena and our representation and understanding of the phenomena.

This book is primarily concerned with the first part of the study of methods, where such questions are asked as: What happened? How? When? Where? Why? Who is involved? Ways of answering these questions that give reliable knowledge are part of the methods of science.

In studying society, there must be some concern with logical questions. We cannot directly represent social phenomena but must use symbols instead. And the symbols used— language itself is our primary symbol—cannot be put together haphazardly if they are to make sense. Numbers are another way to help us understand logical relations. All of science uses numbers, and we know that there are certain definite ways that they must be manipulated, as in the addition and subtraction of simple arithmetic.

The third part of the study of methods must also concern us to some extent. This is the relationship between the symbols we use to think about social events and the events themselves. For example, $1 + 1 = 2$ is a well defined and understood property of numbers. It does not follow that only the properties of numbers will be important when we represent social events with the numbers. If 1 stands for male and the other 1 stands for female and $1 + 1$ means a marriage, then $1 + 1$ might equal 3 or more depending upon the number of children the couple has. In other words, the logical way the symbols that stand for the event are related must be the same logical way that the events or phenomena themselves are related. The relationships between the symbols must correspond to the relationships between the phenomena or events.

No part of the study of methods is totally independent from any other part. In order to make the study understandable, we must concentrate on those methods social scientists use which work. This means emphasizing the first part of the study of methods, as we have defined it—*that part which concerns giving reliable answers to certain kinds of questions.*

Methods, Not Methodology

The study of methods differs from the study of methodology. Methodology studies the *rules* of methods. It is the science of method in the same way that theoretical physics is the science of engineering. The engineer builds things using the theories and knowledge of physics. Social scientists discover things by means of methods that are investigated by methodologists.

Why Study Methods?

Although philosophers can cast doubt on almost anything, and wise men have said that nothing in life is certain, men still must act as they live. In their highest development as men, they act as though they have knowledge even when they do not. Men have long known this—but how did they know it? The study of methods is one way to get more certain knowledge. Not perfect knowledge, but more certain knowledge. No single method will tell us all we want to know, and even several methods combined cannot give us ultimate truth— remember the way we said scientists think of truth. Yet we can know more only if we can improve the ways we find knowledge through the study of methods.

Thus, the main answer to the question "Why study methods?" is that we can know more certainly. And every man, by virtue of being human, wants to know, indeed must know if he is to survive, about himself and other men. It is true that not everyone wants to know the answer to every question social science methods can answer. But why should he? Thoreau put it well when he said, "I came into this world, not chiefly to make this a good place to live in, but to live in it, be it good or bad. A man has not everything to do, but something."

Whatever it is you wish to do, you will need to know. Is it to understand why you may be asked to die in a war you did not start? You may want to know something about international relations, a part of political science, or why some men have always seemed to like killing, a subject of psychology. Or perhaps you just want to make more money. To know how, you will have to use the methods of economics. Have you noticed your own feelings of elation, depression, anger, or fear? Perhaps you are interested in understanding these feelings because you want to know yourself. The methods of social science are the most certain ways we have for you to obtain this knowledge.

There are other reasons for wanting to know about scientific methods besides their uses. You may simply be curious about how social scientists arrive at their conclusions. Curiosity, especially about important subjects like those tests that determine so much of your place in the school world, is a healthy thing. Or perhaps you just have a simple desire to know things in order to determine what is arbitrary opinion of the kind that has held the world back so long. To be rational about your beliefs as opposed to basing them on temperament, for example, is another good reason for studying scientific methods. And these methods are often useful in settling differences. Scientists call this *the process of verification*. The study of methods has strengthened the love of truth for many people.

Induction—The Way of Science

By induction we mean a way of reasoning that allows general statements to be made from observing individual cases. For example, we make the general statement that the sun will come up tomorrow from a large number of individual observations that the sun has always come up after it has gone down. Inductive reasoning is based on probabilities resulting from observation of actual phenomena. The more observations we have, the more certain we can be and the greater the probability.

Deductive reasoning, on the other hand, is the process by which necessary conclusions must follow from accepted premises. In other words, the deductive process involves conclusions based on the meaning of the statements without any necessary reference to observation.

Scientists use deductive reasoning, as it is sometimes a very powerful tool. But all science must pass the test of being able to deal with the real world. Thus even when deductive reasoning is used, science must rely on inductive reasoning based on observation.

Methods and Demonstration

When Alice began her travels in Wonderland she had a discussion with the Cheshire Cat.

> "Would you tell me, please, which way I ought to go from here?"
> "That depends a good deal on where you want to get to," said the cat.
> "I don't much care where—" said Alice.
> "Then it doesn't matter which way you go," said the cat.
> "————so long as I get somewhere," Alice added as an explanation.
> "Oh, you're sure to do that," said the cat, "if you only walk long enough."

The study of methods alone cannot tell us where we want to go—but if we have some idea, methods can tell us much about how to get there.

The modern development of social science is scarcely two hundred years old. Yet it influences every moment of your life, conditioning the way your schools are supported through economics, telling you how you should raise your children, and even allowing fun to be made of burial habits. Such a young science in man's long history, although it has already accomplished much, has not yet begun to influence your lives the way it surely must. For, at the one extreme, there is the threat of atomic annihilation through the misuse or lack of social science knowledge. At the other extreme, if this does not happen perhaps overpopulation will make a better life impossible. Whatever problems we face, we find that social science knowledge is an indispensable prerequisite for their solution. Man has struggled long just to get the idea of social science. Now we must develop it and use it to fulfill its promise.

Chapter 2

The Structure of Science

SEEKING THE TRUTH

Science is one result of man's efforts to civilize himself. For over a thousand years, men of many cultures, as they contemplated what being a man meant, gradually came to the conclusion that knowing the truth is the highest goal of man. The development of science was and remains a response to man's desire to know the truth. But there is a great distance between the ultimate aim and our present position. Science comprises both knowledge and the ways that men have developed to reach their

9

highest goal. Both knowledge (the products of science) and the ways (the processes of science) include many separate steps and paths. The methods of science have been developed to guide us on our way.

But what is the truth? Like all fundamental ideas, the idea of truth changes. Like many other words, "truth" stands for different ideas. Today it has several connotations that are more or less important, depending on the viewpoint of the individual. Some men find truth in religion, others in art, some in literature. Most scientists admit that not all the realms of human experience are now able to be investigated scientifically. Scientists generally limit their inquiry to those areas of experience and the world where they may be objective, logical, and systematic in a way that will permit them to accumulate reliable knowledge.

For most scientists, the truth is known when they can predict what will happen under specific conditions. Obviously not all phenomena can be thought about in this way, and therefore scientists do not claim that this method of working can cover all fields. They are mainly content to follow the philosophy of "live and let live" in their work, leaving to others the exact specification of the ultimate goal toward which they strive. They know the general direction but also that it is far away. The rewards of the journey toward truth are great in themselves.

THE SYSTEM OF SCIENCE

Science can be thought of as a system for producing the truth. And like every system it has parts that are related to each other. The major parts of the scientific system are: (1) problem formulation; (2) observation and description; (3) explanation; (4) prediction and control.

Each of these parts of the scientific system has methods associated with it. What is sometimes called the scientific method is a brief way of referring to the scientific system of producing reliable knowledge and the specific methods that apply to each part of the system. A practicing scientist uses the whole system and the methods associated with each part with the same familiarity that others use a car. An introduction to science must begin by introducing you to the parts of the scientific system, just as when you begin to learn to drive, you learn the parts of a car, or in learning to sew, you learn the parts of the sewing machine. The system of science is much too complex to be grasped quickly and all at once.

It helps to understand the parts of the scientific system if you understand that one of the central characteristics of science is that it is self-correcting. Each part of the system has built into it what might be called error-detection elements. Over a long period of time errors made by one scientist or assumptions falsely held by scientists in general will fail to produce correct solutions to new problems, and scientists will then have to re-question their former concepts of truth. Thus when errors are detected the rest of the system operates to overcome them. No other way of knowing or truth-seeking has this characteristic. It is largely because of the self-correcting nature of science that most men regard it as the most powerful way to seek and to know truth. This is not to say that errors do not exist in scientific work. Of course they do. But the system of science is so constructed that the errors which do exist sooner or later will be discovered and corrected.

Problem Formulation

Scientific inquiry begins with problems. Why do people act as they do? What are the causes of mental illness? How shall we educate our children? How do minority prejudices begin? What can be done to prevent a third world war? Can we reduce the growing gaps between the richest and the poorest nations? Why does water freeze at 32°F? Is there a left and a right property in nature? How do genes carry hereditary traits? What are the causes of prostitution? There are many kinds of problems in science. This is just what one would expect from the complexity of man and nature. The result of this complexity is that any scientific problem must be the result of selection from all the data that the world presents to us. This also means that no one, in dealing with a problem, can select "all the facts." When defining a problem, scientists do so in terms of a limited aspect of reality they know about.

It is said that the most important part of scientific inquiry is proper formulation of the problem. In the history of science, great advances have occurred when men have formulated old problems in new ways for better solutions. But we do not know exactly how to choose problems that are useful in science. This is one of the least understood aspects of scientific inquiry. We do know, however, that not any problem will do for science. For instance, "Is the moon made of green cheese?" is not the kind of problem that most scientists would regard as well stated or particularly useful. The development of science has, however, given us some guidelines for the characteristics and selection of scientific problems.

One common way that problems originate and are formulated is through our perception of a specific difficulty. We may notice that we have a difficult time getting to and from work and begin to formulate the transportation problem. We may notice the contradictions between the work of two scientists, which poses a problem for us. We may notice the differences between what we see and what we believe, and that poses a problem. Or we may notice prices going up and wonder why; that, too, poses a problem.

The sensing of a difficulty may also come when we want to do something and find that we are not able to do so. It may come when we are unable to identify an object or a situation in which we are interested. A sense of difficulty may arise when we want to understand a person but cannot, as in a case of a parent with his teenage child. Or sense of a difficulty may come when we face unexpected events, such as the depression that began in the late 1920s.

Scientific problems also have much to do with scientists themselves. One of the most crucial requirements of a scientist's relationship to his problem is that he becomes very much interested in the problem. The records of science are full, unfortunately, of problems set by investigators who were not deeply involved in those problems. A strict definition of interest in a problem is hard to set down. But we can say that the best scientific work seems to have behind it a passion that illuminates the work for the scientist.

What a Scientific Problem Should Be

Because there are many situations that give rise to the sense of difficulty and the resultant problem formulation, it is very difficult to isolate the central characteristics of a good problem. In fact, there are not many adequate definitions of what a problem is in science. We do not have to go into the deeper philosophical aspects of this question here, however, and can usefully proceed by concentrating on problems considered as questions. Science has given us useful guides about the natures of the questions we should ask. Knowing these guides, we cannot go far astray in considering how to formulate problems in science.

The ideal characteristic of a scientific problem is that it be important. A scientific problem can be important for several reasons. It can be important because its solution would be useful. For example, if we knew what caused juvenile delinquency, we might be able to do something to prevent it. A scientific problem can be important because it links together knowledge that was formerly thought to be unrelated. Studies with computers have suggested to us ideas about how our brains might operate. Studies of various cultures have suggested that the social environment may be more important for certain things than inherited characteristics. Or a problem can be important because it fills in gaps in our knowledge. One of these gaps is the uncertain relationship of the political process and power structure in our cities to the decline of our central cities.

The assessment of the importance of a problem is still very much an individual matter in science, because we do not yet have well-specified rules for problem formulation. Scientists usually work on problems they regard as important. Most scientists are perfectly content to let any other scientist investigate areas that seem important to him. There is a great democracy in science on this as on other points. Each man is free to go his own way as long as his goal is truth and he follows the general procedures of science. The wide variety of problems upon which scientists work, as different as the men themselves, guarantees that almost all important problems will be worked on by someone. It is obvious that science is pushing forward in all directions.

Once an interesting and important problem has been selected, there are several other definite characteristics of a scientific problem formulation. A problem must be precisely stated in order to allow selection of facts for dealing with it. For example, the question you ask your friend when you see him—"How are you?"—is not a scientific question. Your friend does not know whether to tell you how he feels about his school, his parents, his girl friend, or his car. The problem in science must be stated in such a way that someone could give us an answer to it, and so precisely that the selection of the facts to answer it is reasonably clear.

Another characteristic of a problem in science is that it is unambiguously answerable, which is to say that a problem cannot be stated in such a way that any number of answers will satisfy it. For example, the question "Have you stopped beating your wife?" does not permit an unambiguous answer, for if you answer "yes," it implies you have been beating your wife, while if you answer "no," it implies you are still beating your wife. Thus you could not determine from that question whether the man never beats his wife. "Do children watch too much television?" is an ambiguous question on several counts. Children of what age? How much is too much? What kind of shows?

Another characteristic of a scientific problem is that any response to the problem must be verifiable by others. By this we mean that any qualified scientist who asks the same question will get the same answer. Thus, "Is your headache worse today?" is not a scientific question. Only the person who has the headache can answer and others could not verify it. On the other hand, the question "Do first-born children show greater tendencies to conform to group pressures than their siblings?" can be answered by any scientist who is willing to do the work to answer it.

Other Characteristics of a Scientific Problem

A problem must also be formulated so that the data collection can be done objectively. By objectively we mean that data are available for scientific study without regard to any specific personal characteristics of the scientist.

Another important characteristic of a scientific problem is that it must be answerable by scientific inquiry and data either actually or potentially available. Questions such as "What would happen if everyone had a million dollars?" do not fit into the scheme of scientific inquiry at this time. There is no way that we could do scientific research on this question. This is not to deny that speculative questions are important, because they often are. For example, "Can nations exist in the modern world without war?" is clearly important for all mankind but, because it cannot be framed in such a way that empirical research can answer it, it cannot be considered a well-formulated scientific question.

A scientific problem must also contain measures and definitions about the variables of the problem. If these are not explicitly given, then it fails the criteria of being a scientific problem on two counts. First, without measures and definitions others cannot test the results. Second, science cannot allow definitions and measures to be personal only to one scientist. Measures and definitions must be objective so that any scientist who uses them with regard to the same problem will get the same answer.

Problem formulation is the beginning of scientific inquiry. Not all important questions can be dealt with scientifically. Every scientist is limited in this difficult phase of science inquiry by the concepts, data, experiences, values, and ideas available to him about his subject. This limiting helps explain why science cannot solve all our problems. However, it can solve many of them.

When the problem is well formulated, the outcome of this

formulation is usually called a hypothesis. A hypothesis is a proposition or statement. It is a testable assertion about the relationships being investigated which has consequences that we can deduce from it. Therefore, the next step in scientific inquiry is a testing of the hypothesis, either directly or by testing the consequences we have deduced from it. For example, consider the hypothesis "poverty causes juvenile delinquency." We could, after properly defining poverty and juvenile delinquency, deduce that if the hypothesis were true, children raised in poverty would become juvenile delinquents. We could then test the hypothesis by observing whether all poor children did become juvenile delinquents. In fact, all poor children do not become juvenile delinquents, but if knowing this were not enough to cause us to reject the hypothesis, we could examine all juvenile delinquents to see if they came from a background of poverty. And, of course, this is not true either. Thus a social scientist could deal with a hypothesis like the one we have suggested and would find that he would have to reject it.

OBSERVATION AND DESCRIPTION

Classification, the naming and ordering of characteristics, is an essential part of how scientists observe and describe. Until a nomenclature—the system of names that describes certain characteristics of plants and animals—was developed in the eighteenth century, modern biology was unable to proceed systematically. Until certain properties of the atoms were named and classified at the end of the nineteenth century, physicists and chemists were not able to develop the periodic table that has been such a powerful organizing device of modern science.

The social scientist particularly faces many difficulties in classification because in many essential respects his subject matter, man and society, has already been named and classified in common sense and common language. Unfortunately this will usually not do for scientific purposes. For example, on the question of race, common perception, common sense, and common language have named the black American on the basis of his color and have classified him in the eyes of law, education, and almost every measurable index of American life as inferior to whites. When social scientists began to study the matter more closely, they found that the simple classifications made by American society led to further difficult racial problems and were not at all suitable for science. The social scientists' classification of race is therefore quite different from that of everyday usage.

Because men think mostly in terms of language, all of science has had to develop specialized language to observe and describe the broader range of things that scientific techniques allow them to perceive. It is a characteristic of the frontiers of science that new names are required for new things or new combinations of old things.

No part of the system of science is independent of any other part. Thus either during the period in which the problem is being formulated or after a hypothesis has been proposed, but in any event as a preliminary to collecting data, scientific procedure requires certain intermediate steps. These intermediate steps are in the nature of a double check. One such step is making certain that the problem exists. This means being sure that each part of the problem is defined and the inquiry is limited in such a way as to allow the selection of data.

Another intermediate step is to think about the possible methods of dealing with the hypothesis. This means attempting to formulate the hypothesis in alternative ways and comparing the time, cost, labor, and efficiency of various methods that might be employed in dealing with it. Facts mean nothing by themselves. Before beginning to observe and describe, it is important to consider what to look for and how any facts might fit into the hypothesis. Science provides the plan and structure for inquiry, and the foundations of inquiry must be carefully laid if the scientist is to obtain useful results.

The next step in the scientific system of inquiry is to review what others have done in the past. An important characteristic of scientific knowledge is that it is cumulative; that is, each part of knowledge builds upon past knowledge. When a scientist begins his investigation of a problem, the first step he takes after he has formulated it is to review the literature. This involves a detailed search of all past publications dealing with the hypothesis to be investigated. The literature review tells the scientist what others have done, and it prevents wasteful duplication. Part of the scientific process requires duplication in order that one investigator can verify or confirm what other investigators have done. However, once there is a consensus that things can be done—for example, that rockets can be made to fly to the moon—then there is no need to re-investigate that particular question unless new ways of obtaining the knowledge are involved. Therefore by wasteful or needless duplication we mean duplicating the search for knowledge that has already been established without adding anything new.

A review of the literature often suggests to a scientist the best avenues of approach to his hypothesis. How to design, study, and organize his data are obviously crucial questions. By examining what other scientists have done, he may get very useful ideas about how he should proceed. Sometimes it is possible to see gaps or wrong ways of doing things that should be avoided. Sometimes, luckily, he thinks of new ways of doing things as he reads what others have done. A review of the literature can also suggest where data, models, methods, or scientific instrumentation useful in dealing with the problem can be found. Sometimes reviewing the literature gives the scientist ideas he has not had or new insight into his hypothesis.

The vast proliferation of knowledge in the social sciences sometimes makes literature reviews very difficult. There may be hundreds of bibliographical entries for a particular subject. But every scientist must attempt such a review, and there are many useful aids always available to help, such as bibliographies, abstracting services, and the indispensable well-trained librarian. Chapter 5 of this book shows how you might begin a literature review for a hypothesis in social science. Perhaps we will not have to wait long until our libraries are on computer tapes. Then this part of scientific inquiry will be much less demanding and time consuming than it is at present.

It is at the stage of a literature review that the important problem arises of note-taking and indexing the information that a scientist obtains from his reading. A few people with exceptional memories sometimes can rely solely on memory to retain what they have read, but the vast majority of scientists develop a system of recording the knowledge in which they are interested. Scientists have devised many systems for keeping track of the larger bodies of knowledge with which they deal. However it is done, an essential part of this stage of inquiry which will be useful in other stages as well is the development of an adequate note-taking and indexing system.

Perception Influences Interpretation

Every advanced discussion of the scientific method warns that facts cannot be understood by themselves, but only in the context of some other system of knowledge. From the beginning of time men have seen the stars, but what they saw was very different from what modern astronomers see. They saw animals or perhaps heroes from their mythology. The modern astronomer sees organized galaxies and systems. The same thing is true about almost every aspect of our social life. Men have always seen the different skin colors of other men, but this did not result in racial discrimination. Although men have long watched bees gathering nectar, it is only recently that they have seen how the bees communicate where the nectar is to other bees. We do not perceive without interpreting. The scientist must begin his work of observation by understanding this and then decide what he should look for that can be called scientific.

In the light of his hypothesis, the scientist must first decide what behavior or thing is to be observed or described, and of course recorded, in order to be able to obtain the information he requires. And this means that he must also decide under what conditions his observations are to be made. Just as the conditions of temperature and pressure are very important when you are ready to evaluate the reactions of gases in physical science, in social science the scientist who is interested in the influence of the groups on the individual would have to carefully specify the conditions under which he would want to study. Not only must he then decide what he has to observe and under what conditions, but, to summarize, he must also understand how these are related to his hypothesis. He has still another responsibility in his observation. If the scientist wishes to be accurate, he must attempt to quantify or measure with some kind of standard units so that he can make comparisons. He must be careful to standardize or somehow design his observations so that others can verify them. In other words, he must perform his work in a way that allows other scientists to confirm or duplicate the findings.

Technology Helps Observation

Different sciences use different techniques of observation. For example, in astronomy most observation is done with the aid of instruments, such as telescopes, spectrographs, various photographic apparatus, and many types of radio equipment. In psychological observation the instruments include such things as IQ tests and verbal responses to pictures. In general, a scientist uses whatever instrumentation he feels will aid him in the investigation of his hypothesis. He will be careful, however, to notice that sense perception is transitory and unreliable: what is simply seen or heard can only be remembered, accurately or otherwise. Therefore, a picture or a tape recording is a much better record, and one which can be examined and re-examined. In addition, our senses do not themselves detect large ranges of all phenomena, either social or physical. For example, we can only hear from about 15 cycles to 20,000 cycles, but sound is generated from almost zero to very high frequencies. And the last reason for using instrumentation of various kinds is that our senses are limited and despite the large number of combinations that these senses allow, they do not allow us even to sense a large number of variables that occur in any complex situation. For instance, suppose you are in a crowd. You will only know what is going on immediately around you, while the man with a telescope watching from afar can see not only you, but also what is going on in the crowd.

MEASUREMENT

Almost all scientific methods require measurement. Measurement means comparing objects and assigning numbers to them according to rules. Although there are at least six different sets of rules, social scientists are concerned mainly with comparisons of two kinds, ordinal and cardinal. Ordinal comparisons deal with putting things in order (hence the word "ordinal") in terms of some quality. For example, if your class were to line up by height, tallest first, next tallest second, and so on, you would be comparing heights in an ordinal way. Or if, after an examination, the class grades were listed in order of grade received, one student would be first, another second, and so on. Because ordinal comparisons answer questions like which is first, which is second and so on, or is *A* larger than *B*, is *B* larger than *C*, we do not use counting numbers or a standard when we measure ordinally. Cardinal comparisons use counting numbers. How many pupils are there in a class? These numbers are symbols which abstract out everything but repetition in a group. Cardinal comparisons disregard all incidental characteristics like hair color, height, and IQ, and focus on one (pupil in class). Cardinal comparisons also disregard order (tallest, etc.).

Science uses both ways of comparison and for accuracy adds a third, that of the standard unit. If we wish to compare, for example, brain sizes of animals and men, it would be very inconvenient to have to line up animals and men every time a measurement was to be made. Therefore, a standard measuring system has been decided upon—the metric system—which scientists can use to measure and record for later comparison. Once a unit of measure has been established, cardinal and ordinal comparisons can be made simply. Social scientists usually use the fundamental units of time (second, hour, day, year), length (meter, centimeter), and mass (gram, kilogram) that the physical scientists have standardized. In addition they have devised and adopted their own measures, as, for example, the dollar, used by economists as the basic unit of accounting. But the great differences between the standards of a second and a dollar show how difficult the problem of units of measurement are in social science. By means of atomic clocks and electronic counting devices we can compare any time interval with accuracy of more than a billionth part of a second. But the value of the dollar changes every day, and economists must be content with a statistical manipulation to get a standard dollar for comparison. Of course, just because social scientists do not have their own accurate units of the same kind that physical scientists have does not mean their work suffers. For many purposes, like that of giving grades for some teachers, ordinal measures suffice. For other purposes, like that of the U.S. Bureau of the Census, cardinal measures will do. And less accurate standards like the dollar suffice for still other purposes. Meanwhile scientists continue their efforts to develop units to measure important things like intelligence and social interaction.

Explanation

Once the scientist has observed, described, and recorded the data he thinks relevant to his problem, he faces one of the most important problems of his enterprise, that of explanation. As we have seen, the variety of man and nature has led to a wide variety of scientific problems. This in turn has required the development of different kinds of techniques for observation and description. And you can guess that different kinds of problems with different kinds of observation, description, and methods for gathering data will lead to different kinds of explanations acceptable in the system of science.

Explanations in science answer the question "why." There are four different varieties of explanations used in science— deductive, probabilistic, genetic, and functional. Each type of explanation answers the question "why" for different kinds of questions.

Deductive Explanation. A deductive explanation consists of a series of statements in which the particular conclusion follows the initial postulate or axiom. The classic example is the following: All men are mortal. Socrates is a man. Therefore, Socrates is mortal. The fact that Socrates is mortal is a direct consequence of his being a man. Thus the answer to the question "Why is Socrates mortal?" in this mode of explanation is that he is a man. A scientist, if he accepts the fact that all men are mortal, then might establish the fact that Socrates is a man. He could then deduce that Socrates is mortal. The scientist would never rest with this, however, and would attempt to develop some test to see if, in fact, Socrates was a mortal. Deductive explanations, powerful though they are in certain kinds of science, can be notoriously misleading because they deal with only a few qualities of the phenomenon. More than that, the relations of logic are not necessarily the relationships of man. No scientist accepts a deductive argument without first verifying the premises—e.g., that all men are, in fact, mortal—before testing whether Socrates is in fact a man and finally making a separate test to see if Socrates is in fact mortal.

Deductive explanations answer the question "why" by abstracting certain qualities and clearly defining the relationships of these qualities. In this book, we shall use economics as an example of deductive arguments in social science. Economists have used deductive arguments to answer such questions as: Why is there unemployment? Why do prices rise and decrease with changes in the money supply? Why are some people richer than others? Model-building is also a way of abstracting certain qualities from all the phenomena available, and many models in science use deduction. Economics furnishes us with especially rich examples of this process.

Probabilistic Explanation. There is a kind of question in science which cannot be answered as definitely as the deductive mode allows. This kind of question can only be answered with words like "probably," "almost certainly," or "within a range of 5%," and the answer is thus called a probabilistic explanation. The type occurs when we deal with large numbers of people, or with individuals and their actions when we do not know every factor that conditions their actions. For example, if we ask the question "Why was President Kennedy assassinated?" we might answer, "Probably because the slayer was demented." If we ask, for instance, why higher income families spend money on education, we can only give answers within a range of probability. Political science frequently uses this mode of explanation.

Genetic Explanation.   The genetic explanation answers "why" in terms of what went before. For example, if we want to explain why a child has hair of a certain color, the genetic mode of explanation would be in terms of hereditary factors and the child's parents. Psychologists use a genetic mode of explanation frequently. Why do men act as they do? A result of what happened in their childhood would be a good answer. Why do men see things differently? Why do men see colors? Why do men see? This kind of question can be answered within the genetic mode of explanation by attempting to examine what happened before or earlier. It is for this reason that the genetic mode of explanation is sometimes called the historical mode of explanation.

Functional Explanation.   Another kind of explanation frequently encountered in science, the functional explanation, gives answers to the question "why" by examining the place that the particular subject under discussion occupies in the system to which the unit belongs. Thus when we ask why school children often are made to pledge allegiance to the flag, the functional explanation would be that this is supposed to make them more patriotic, and being more patriotic will perpetuate, in some way, the country and its ideals. Anthropological studies often use the functional mode of explanation. Why are societies different? Why are there different ways of being human? These questions can often be answered in terms of a man's role in different societies.

No one kind of explanation can answer all the questions that science asks. And it is for this reason that scientists utilize different modes of explanation for different problems. Sometimes the scientific quest stops short of completing all the parts of the system we have developed. A relatively simple problem with good observations may be explained simply and the hypothesis either confirmed or denied.

Kinds of Prediction

Most scientists would not be satisfied unless the hypothesis was confirmed in such a way that it allows prediction and control. As you might now expect, the variety of science results in different ways of predicting and controlling that are related to different types of problems and explanation.

Law.   One of the oldest kinds of predictions that some scientists seek is that of law. "Law" in social science means some basic and fundamental regularity that applies to man's nature. In physical science, the laws of gravity are frequently cited as an example of this kind of prediction. In social science there are persons who think they have discovered laws that regulate capitalism and communism. Laws in this sense are supposed to regulate people and things without regard to their will. Although physical and biological science seek for such laws, social scientists have, in the main, given up the search for laws of this nature. The "laws" that most social scientists seek are those that predict according to the following modes.

Projection.   Another kind of prediction is that based on extrapolation, or projections. This type of prediction typically examines the past, and makes statements about the future in the terms of the past. In social science, at least, projecting the past—that is, predicting the future on the basis of the past—is typically more successful for a short period of time in the future than for a long one. Predictions in this mode often involve probabilities.

Structure.   Prediction can also be based on the structure of the thing or institution or person being affected. Every man who is making a career of the armed services can be expected to be promoted from private to corporal to sergeant because the structure of the army is such that this is the way that most promotions occur.

Institution.   Related to structural predictions are those based on institutional methods of operation. A great American social scientist, Ruth Benedict, at the time of World War II, was requested by the War Department to study the Japanese. She did not know Japanese and had never been to Japan, but by closely studying Japanese institutions, she was able to predict very accurately how the Japanese would behave when they were defeated and what the army would have to do to control Japanese behavior in the way the army desired.

Problem.   Another kind of prediction is that based on the problems that man or society will face. If India, with a population of over half a billion people already, cannot increase her food supply, it is not unreasonable to expect that the overriding problem she will face will be that of food shortages. Thus in certain cases it is possible to predict on the basis of a problem that will dominate all others. You could imagine that America, in an atomic war, would deal with almost every social problem in terms of the overriding problem of the war.

Stage.   Yet another mode of prediction is in terms of stages for development in sequence. In biology this is the common kind of prediction, and a very accurate one. Seeds properly nourished will grow in well-defined sequences. Sometimes it holds true for human beings, as in the development of infants as they learn to walk and talk. Some social scientists have even attempted to apply this type of prediction to whole societies, maintaining, for example, that a developing society must begin with a heavy industry if it is to become richer or, as some historians have suggested pointedly, societies rise and then decline.

Utopia. The last important mode of prediction in science is utopian. In this kind of prediction, scientists imagine what might be in terms of what we know at the present. They then predict what could be on the basis of this theoretical construction. Scientists had imagined trips into space long before they were actually able to make such trips. The moons of Jupiter were predicted in terms of what ought to be before there were telescopes powerful enough to see them. And from numerous examples of social science might be cited the improvements in education, which came about because man imagined well before it was possible that everyone might be able to go to high school.

Reporting Results of Scientific Inquiry

Another aspect, the last, of the system of science for any given piece of work is the reporting of the results. After a scientist has finished his work on a topic, or a phase of that topic, he will want to communicate that information to others if it is to have any value for himself and others interested in the same field. He makes his results public.

Results can be reported in a variety of ways—most commonly in a scientific journal. Other ways are in a book or in a monograph—a report longer than the usual scientific article but normally shorter than the usual book and more technical. Still other ways are personal correspondence, talks at conferences, or reports to organizations or universities. Each discipline has developed ways more or less specialized to the discipline for such reporting. And often the journal for which the report is written or the organization to whom the report is directed will have its own requirements about style, form, and material to be covered. Whatever the details, science insists on several minimum characteristics: absolute honesty, clear and intelligible presentation, enough detail so others can judge the work, and acknowledgments.

The requirement of honesty is overriding and complete. No statement that is known to be false or misleading is allowed. The standards of honesty are far greater than even those of a court. These standards are imposed and enforced by the scientists themselves. There have been extreme cases in the history of science where men who have directed research, upon finding out that workers under them falsified data, committed suicide. Once a scientist is known to have made false or misleading statements, other scientists find it very hard to trust him or his work. In one case in social science an author submitted to a journal as his own a translation of another's work. When the editors of the journal found this out, they ran a notice with the page edged in black—like a death notice—explaining what had happened. In the last decade, a man awarded a Ph.D. was found to have falsified references in his dissertation, and the university took back his degree.

Clear and intelligible presentation is required in order that others may understand what is being reported. Enough detail is required so that scholars who wish may judge or replicate the work if they desire.

Acknowledgments are required for two reasons. One is simple courtesy to others whose ideas are being used. More importantly, however, acknowledgments and references allow any reader of the report who wishes to place the work in the body of knowledge—in the history of science—quickly and easily. The ability to do this makes other research easier by facilitating systematic thinking.

Science is public for yet another reason. Social science requires many scientists for its growth—more than do the other sciences. The reason for this is that many events in social science are not reproducible and occur only once or rarely. Science long ago learned the value of many observers making individual observations independent of each other and then sharing them.

WHAT SCIENTISTS BELIEVE

Although the goal of science is not given by science alone but is determined by all of man's experience, there are some things that anyone must believe to use the system of science. These beliefs are not fixed for all time; they have changed and can be expected to change more. But all scientists, working on any subject, share certain beliefs now.

Objective Reality

Scientists believe that things outside of themselves exist. These can be: people; events—for example, a war; states of being—the joy of a happy marriage; processes—the electrolytic decomposition of H_2O; or objects.

This belief about objective reality is required in order that science may be about something besides the individual scientist and what exists in his brain. The alternative to the belief in reality outside of us is that everything exists in our heads. The belief in reality is based on experience, as we all realize when we bump our toe. The work of scientists testifies to the fact that they think they are dealing with some reality other than that which might exist only in their minds.

The word "objective" means that *reality is, in principle, knowable by others.* Scientific knowledge is not a personal possession, but only exists by consensus—others must agree. In order that others may agree, they must be able to perceive the reality in similar ways. Belief in objective reality does not mean that science requires shared assumptions about its nature. The question "Is there life on Mars?" requires shared assumptions about the fact that both life and Mars exist, not about the forms of life or other such details. If we ask about the role of dreams in personal development, we must admit that dreams exist.

Not everything that exists can be well defined or measured in the present state of science. Life cannot yet be created in the laboratory—perhaps it never shall. Those things called feelings or values or emotions are subjective in our present state of knowledge. By subjective, we mean that there are feelings, states, or knowledge unique to the individual in the sense they cannot be well defined or measured for others to study— for example, pain. The scientist, however, says that a subject, once known and defined, even if not defined well, can be studied scientifically. This is also true of subjective data. Think about pain. Men have long felt it. Doctors from before the time of the Greeks were concerned with it, although it has always been a subjective state known only to the individual. The definition of pain is vague and the measurement is crude, but it is a subject about which we are now beginning to understand more and more due to science.

The point is that scientists conceptually separate the subject from the data or what is known about the subject. Admittedly in the social sciences there is much to be studied that is poorly defined, where our knowledge is subjective, and where the data are inadequate. This situation, having occurred in the beginnings of every science, only reflects the youth of social science. As it develops, data that were subjective become objective. Therefore, despite the primitive condition of our knowledge about certain subjects, there is no reason to exclude them from science.

Time

All scientists believe that time exists. They have a sense of past, present, and future. Somehow this fundamental concept, although the subject of much study, has proved very difficult to define accurately. The physical scientists have well-developed methods for measuring it very accurately. For them, the flight of time's arrow is irreversible, unidirectional, and occurring at the same rate for all persons and things. Biological and social scientists have generally accepted the time concepts of physical science, although it is not at all certain that these concepts of physical science need to be the same for their many different subjects. Scientists believe in time mainly because they could not imagine working without it. Despite the lack of conceptual clarity, all of them believe that it exists in one form or another.

Space

Space is a concept like time. All scientists believe it exists and that everything exists in it. As with time, we can measure space very accurately in terms of physical properties. And again, as with time, although most scientists could not define it except in terms of comparative measurement, they accept the existence of the concept because science would be inconceivable without it.

Symbols and Reality

The scientist is obviously not part of the reality that exists outside himself. The blue sky he perceives does not include him. All of his data and experience are made up of responses to his environment. The scientist, as a scientist, exists apart from his subject. To communicate his ideas to other scientists, he must invent symbols which represent objective reality. These are usually language or mathematics. It is the symbols that are communicable to other scientists, not the reality. It is the symbols in terms of which scientists think, not the reality. It is the symbols the brain manipulates, not the reality. Because he believes in an objective reality and knows that he must work with symbols or other representations of reality, the scientist believes that definite relationships exist between these symbols and the reality. If scientists did not accept the possibility of these relationships, they could not believe that their symbolic manipulation could result in knowledge.

The symbols of modern physics are found in mathematics; mathematical manipulations closely represent certain aspects of reality. You only have to think of the accuracy of mathematical predictions of missiles shot to the moon. Almost every usage of the spoken or written language shows that the language symbols represent reality more or less closely. The history of science is full of examples where the symbolic relationships and the symbols themselves had to be invented to represent the reality being studied. When in the seventeenth century Newton and Leibnitz wanted to represent certain kinds of motion but found they could not use the existing mathematical symbols and relationships, they invented calculus, which proved to be a very accurate way of representing certain kinds of events in the real world. Probably social science as it develops will invent more symbols and symbolic relationships that represent social reality.

Purpose

Scientists must believe in the possibility that purpose or will can direct action. Every scientist exercises his own will in his work. If purpose or will did not direct human actions, then what might do so? Chance? Science would then become the study of statistics. Divine will? Science would then be the study of the holy books. By purpose or will, of course, we mean *human* purpose or will exercised on *human* actions. Biologists do not believe that purpose or will determines the growth of a tree. Astronomers do not believe that purpose or will determines the path of a planet in space. But all scientists— social, physical, and biological—believe that purpose or will can determine at least part of their own and other human beings' actions.

Reason

An article of faith of the scientist is that he and all men can sooner or later be free of the obstacles to reasonable action. He hopes that progress will not be blocked by selfish interests, ingrained beliefs, distorted emotions, and other habits and feelings that now restrict and distort understanding. He needs this faith to continue his work. He needs to believe that man's reason will improve so that his work will not be misused or destroyed.

The scientist knows that he cannot give scientific reasons for his faith. This faith, like some other questions relating to science, is not yet capable of being dealt with scientifically. Yet the evidence does not contradict some faith in reason. More men, everywhere, are better off than ever before—at least in a physical sense. Science has given us the potential to cope adequately with most of our pressing physical and biological problems. It has neither solved our problems nor shown how to use our power for man's betterment, but it remains a source of hope.

Causality

All scientists believe in some kind of causality, despite disagreements about the exact nature of cause. The core of the shared belief is that relationships between phenomena, although often difficult to establish, do exist, and that by studying them we can know more. For example, the biologist can show connections between malaria and certain viruses. When injected into man these viruses result in, or are the cause of, malaria. The physicist can observe the relationships between falling objects on earth and then use these observations to conclude that gravity is the cause of the attraction of masses. The social scientist will notice that men under certain kinds of stress behave differently from when the stresses were absent, and he might conclude that the stress caused the behavior modifications.

As long ago as the time of the ancient Greeks men distinguished different kinds of causal relationships. The study is far from complete, but whenever a scientist studies relationships between two or more phenomena he can in the broadest sense be said to be examining some aspect of causality. Put another way, the social scientist believes that certain things cause other things. Usually the cause comes before the event or result. Without this belief, most statements of relationships and indeed most studies would lack meaning in the real world.

It should be made clear that this is a minimum list of beliefs for the scientist. Most of them hold more beliefs. Some might state their beliefs differently, but since science is a system, their beliefs would also be systematic.

DIVISIONS OF SCIENCE

Science can be divided in many ways, each of which is useful for certain purposes. The subject matter of the physical sciences is inanimate objects—things without life. The physical sciences include such sciences as chemistry and physics. The second great division of science is biological. The biological sciences study all living organisms and the processes of life, and include the sciences of zoology and botany. The third division of science is social science. *The subject of the social sciences is man in both his individual and social life.* Included among the social sciences are history, sociology, geography, economics, political science, psychology, and anthropology.

Each of these subjects emphasizes one aspect of the study of man.

All the sciences share the goal of science. They all use the system of scientific inquiry. But because their subjects are different, they use the various parts of the system of scientific inquiry in different mixtures. For example, physical sciences experiment whenever possible. They have no moral or value problem about breaking a chemical down or splitting an atom. But biologists must be more careful about their experimentation; for example, they must not needlessly inflict pain on animals. No ethical social scientist would experiment on people in any way that would harm them. Thus in the matter of experimentation we see that the subject matter of each science requires a different approach, and this, of course, means different methods too.

But a variety of methods are important sometimes for another reason. Different methods are required for each of the different steps or parts of the system of science. The methods of history are very important in problem formulation. History asks the question "What happened in the past?" The historical method is important in formulating problems in at least two senses—one, to allow us to raise questions, for we can only raise questions at present out of our experience in the past, and two, what have others done about the problems we are now facing?

So far as observation, description, and recording are concerned, the difference between the cyclotron, which investigates the inside of atoms, and an IQ test, which investigates parts of the inside working of your brain, are enough to show the variety in methods of observation and description that are required because of the difference in subjects.

The four modes of explanation do not differ because of differences in subject matter. Probably the physical sciences use the deductive model more than the other parts of science, although probability models are increasingly important in all fields. The genetic model is widely used in the biological sciences. The social sciences use all four different modes of explanation.

So far as prediction and control are concerned, the physical sciences search for laws more often than do the social sciences. The other modes of prediction are more widely used in social science since the search for laws has been virtually abandoned.

This sketch of the system of science covers only its bare outlines. Each of the special branches of science has developed its own adaptation of this system. Social science is one part of the body of science and it is to how social science is related to science that we now turn.

Chapter 3

The Relations of Social Science to Science

SUBJECT AND METHOD FORMULATION IN THE SOCIAL SCIENCES

Just as scientists share a common belief system, they have agreed that the system of science should be flexible enough so that any subject can be studied. Thus from each part of the system of science the scientist will pick those scientific methods most appropriate to his problem. Because social science is concerned with man and society, the scientist has had to adapt many of the procedures of science to the special characteristics of his subject matter, just as each of the natural and physical scientists have had to do. And of course social scientists have developed many new methods of their own.

Values

For all scientists, and especially for social scientists, one of the few restrictions on choice of topic is that relating to value propositions, many of which cannot be studied scientifically. A value proposition is one that involves the idea of "good," "bad," "should," "ought," or similar terms. Questions like "Is peace good?" or "Is integrated education a good thing?" or "Should we eliminate poverty?" must be answered in terms of an ethical, moral, or value system that is not given by science. Criteria for what is good or bad are drawn from outside the realm of science, as is the goal.

Social scientists have attempted to separate value assumptions from the central problem. In certain cases the separation can be relatively complete. For example, assuming that integrated education is good, we could proceed to study the problem of how to bring it about. The value connotation is that integrated education is good. The way to achieve it would be studied. But when the separation of the values from the problem cannot be complete, then social scientists attempt to understand the impact of the value issues on the methods and the problem at each stage of inquiry. In effect, every meaningful issue in social science has direct or indirect value connotations. For this reason later chapters discuss values in more detail. At this point we note that the value question affects the science of society much more widely than it does the physical and biological sciences.

Duplication

Another adaptation that social scientists have made in the methods of problem formulation is related to the issue of replication, or duplication of the experimental situation. For the older sciences, problems could be formulated usefully only if the experiment could be replicated by others. Astronomy was one of the first of the physical sciences to find that the idea of formulating a problem in terms of its duplicability was impossible. But astronomers did not have to struggle with this problem very long before they discovered that the motions of the heavens obeyed laws that could be represented mathematically. Since this is the case, if an astronomer knows the motion and position of the heavenly bodies at one time, he can, with great precision, calculate their motions and positions both backward and forward in time and space. Thus he does not need to design his problems for replication. He can check to see if he was right, and others could check on him, by making his calculations and then looking into the historical records to see if, in fact, he had put the planets or stars where they actually were when some earlier astronomer observed them. The examples of astronomy, meteorology, earthquake research, and many other physical sciences show that all problems in science do not have to be formulated in such a way as to be able to be duplicated or repeated, and that science can study single events.

In the case of the social scientist, however, the problem of the single event is not so easily resolved as with the physical or biological sciences. If we ask why Henry VIII had so many wives and treated them the way he did, or why the Russian Revolution broke out when it did, we are dealing with single events that were the result of, or caused by, many complex factors. Moreover, there is no known way for us to falsify or confirm the explanations after the event has passed. It would be foolish to rule out, as some recommend, the scientific study of single events simply because we cannot formulate problems about them in terms of being able to disprove any explanation. Single events are often of great importance in man's social and individual history. The answer that social science has developed for the problem of single events is simply to insist that the other requirements of the scientific system be met when single events are studied. There is no doubt that this is a "softer" kind of science, even more so than astronomy. To exclude any problem in which the single event is involved from the scientific system would, however, result in making most of the study of man and society impossible. It is not on faith that social scientists accept this kind of approach. In every other part of science, physical and biological, no subject requires that *all* the other parts of the system of science be used to study it. It so happens that for social science that part of the system of science which includes duplication is one that is sometimes dropped.

Literature Review

So far as the review of the literature is concerned, social science has had to make few adaptations of the general process. A problem that does arise in making a literature review is that, due to its youth, the language and definitions of social science are far less precise, reflecting a less well-developed conceptual framework than the other sciences. This means that typically the social scientist must review more literature using his ingenuity and historical knowledge of the development of his subject to try to find all that is relevant. Indexes, summaries, and abstracts are also much less developed for social science, and the researcher looking for specific information must generally check out many more entries and headings, including those that sometimes seem only peripherally relevant.

Common-sense Problems

Another modification that social science often requires in the initial formulation is that it usually cannot accept definitions as formulated by common sense or tradition. The reason for certain severe problems in social science is precisely that there have been attempts to use common sense. It is not always necessary to discard common sense in the other sciences. For example, if a breeder of dogs wishes to develop a strain of house pets and finds an animal that is very vicious, he will not breed it. Or in physical science if a piece of apparatus is not working, common sense often suffices to repair it. This is not true of social mechanisms.

It is sometimes said that the results from research are no better than the methods by which they are obtained. This is not quite so. It is entirely possible that we could know something to be true without the necessity for elaborate research methods. For example, common sense and a simple and unsophisticated observation tell us that in our society most people choose mates who are not related to them. Many other kinds of knowledge that happen to be true easily come to mind. The value of methods is justified not necessarily by the truth or falsity of the result, but by its validity and reliability. Scientific methods give us reliable results that other people can confirm, results that we can depend upon; and this is the reason for their power.

OBSERVATION AND DESCRIPTION

Accurate observation and description are essential to the social sciences, just as in all other branches of science. All observation and description begins with human perception of something. An event, a symbol, a thing, a process, a person must be seen, felt, or somehow detected by a human observer. But long ago scientists learned that their sense perceptions alone were not to be trusted. There are many reasons for this. One is that what we perceive is a function of our training, culture, education, feeling state, and other variables. For example, what do you hear when you hear Chinese music? To Westerners trained to listen to our kind of music it seems almost like noise. Can you trust your eyes, when you know that optical illusions exist? This of course is not to say that your senses can never be trusted, but human perception has been found relatively inadequate in science, and methods had to be developed so that what humans perceive is defined, understood, and accurate. The range of what we perceive is limited. Our visual memory cannot be made to last as long as a photograph. We can see only a small fraction of the spectrum of electromagnetic radiation. One solution to the problems of the limits of human perception is instruments. The most commonly used devices of this type in social science are those for measuring time, such as clocks and calendars. Understanding that the range and variability of perceptual observations may be very great, scientists are cautious about their own and others' perceptions.

Pilot Studies

Whether or not names and proper classifications exist that are adequate for the problem, scientists may undertake a pilot study or preliminary observation of the subject in which they are interested. These important pilot studies, which may consist only of observations, enrich and focus the literature review. Pilot studies are a way of economizing a scientist's time and money. If the initial explorations do not suggest confirmation of the hypothesis, the typical scientist will revise it at this stage, where relatively little expenditure has been made, rather than get disappointing results much later. The pilot study may also suggest different kinds of observational methods and new classifications at an early stage of the inquiry.

Collection of Data

In the actual collection of data the social scientist often differs from the physical scientist. The social scientist investigates phenomena of which he is himself a part, actually or potentially. No other science faces this difficulty, and as a result social scientists have had to develop novel methods. Among the many methods that social science has contributed to science in the area of observation and description, three will be mentioned here to illustrate the special nature of the problem.

Participant Observer. In the first of these methods, a participant observer directly observes and participates in the phenomena he is studying. Take, as an example, a sociologist studying the life cycle of a family in a country that is not his own. He will learn the language and actually live with the foreign family, taking the role of a person in that culture of his age. This kind of investigation involves redefinition of the roles of the sociologist. At first he is a newcomer, then, per-haps, he is provisionally accepted. If he is lucky, after a while he is completely accepted. Then as his research comes to an end, people treat him differently once more, knowing he will soon leave. This kind of method is obviously sharply different from observations by a biologist or a chemist.

Interviewing.   Another kind of method that social scientists use widely in observing is the interview. This involves discus-sion with the person being studied. Sometimes it means simply that the subjects answer a questionnaire. Sometimes the inter-view involves many discussions over a long period of time. These are called depth interviews. Social scientists have de-veloped highly refined methods of interviewing. Once again, however, the difference between social science methods and physical science methods appear. Even the biologist's pet dog is not available for interviews.

Samples and Surveys.   A third method deals extensively with samples and surveys. Because human beings are all different and are constantly changing, social scientists are sometimes unable to generalize reliably from examining carefully only one person or one society. This is in contrast to the chemist, who, if he has a molecule of salt, can generalize quite accu-rately about all other molecules of salt. In biology, also, one can generalize with great reliability from one member of the species. But in biology when a subject, an animal for example, is free to behave, then the scientist may generalize only about this particular behavior in terms of more than one animal. For human beings, whose range of behavior is very large indeed, social scientists have had to develop highly refined methods of surveying and sampling in order to be sure about their gen-eralizations. For example, political scientists have worked out techniques that not only allow accurate prediction of the out-come of elections months before they are actually held, but they can often allow us to know who will win before the polls are closed, as the example of television network computers on election days has shown.

EXPLANATION AND EXPERIMENT

The purpose of an experiment in science is to inform us about relationships between two or more phenomena under study. The four modes of scientific explanation—deductive, probabilistic, genetic, functional—therefore can use the information obtained from experiments. But while experiment has proved a very powerful tool in the physical and biological sciences, it has rarely been possible to use it in social science without modification.

What is an experiment? An experiment is a process providing information about relationships between two or more phenomena. Social scientists define those aspects of the phenomena they wish to observe as variables.

Statistical Experiments

One kind of experiment—statistical—could be designed to answer the question "What is the relationship between the number of tosses of a coin and the number of times heads will appear?" The two variables are the number of tosses and the number of times heads appeared. The experiment would then consist of tossing the coin and recording both the number of tosses and the number of heads. One variable, the number of tosses, would be twice the number of heads, which would be the other variable if the coin were tossed enough times. This kind of experiment emphasizes numerical or statistical relationships between variables. Sometimes it does not even need to be performed when enough is known about the two variables. Thus we could calculate the odds that heads would appear without actually having to toss a coin.

Gedanken Experiments

Gedanken experiments (*Gedanken* means "thought" in German) are widely used in all the sciences. These are experiments in which only the mind is used to predict the outcome of relationships between variables. Being able to calculate the odds in tossing coins without even doing it exemplifies a *Gedanken* experiment. Another simple example is predicting the outcome of throws of dice without throwing them. Similarly social science has developed experimental techniques which do not require the manipulation of human beings in order to get results of the same scientific validity as experiments. Some of these methods are explained later in the section on simulation.

Controlled Experiments

To most people an experiment means a laboratory or controlled experiment. This kind of experiment has been responsible for much of our physical and biological science knowledge. It is also a basic model for many modifications of experiments made in the social sciences. Let us imagine that we wish to investigate the hypothesis "aspirin gets rid of headache." First, "aspirin" must be defined. A relatively simple and clear chemical formula will suffice. Then we must define what getting rid of a headache means, and what a headache is, which is a more difficult question. The example was chosen to illustrate how simple things are in physical and biological science compared with social science. Assume, however, that we can define the terms "aspirin" and "headache," and the presence or absence of a headache. One way to proceed at this point would be to give aspirin to everybody in the world with a headache at a given time and then see whether they got rid of their headaches. This kind of experiment in which every subject in the world can be tested is usually impossible in science. But even if such a project were possible, there is a basic flaw in the procedure. It is possible that everyone may have gotten rid of their headaches without aspirin, and the scientist might have been led to the erroneous conclusion that the aspirin was somehow related to getting rid of the headaches. Therefore, the experiment must allow for the possibility that headaches subside without aspirin. The experiment, to prove our hypothesis, must rule out other ways of curing headaches.

To solve the problem of not being able to experiment on everybody or everything, scientists have devised a sampling procedure. They experiment with *some* of the people with headaches. These people are selected at random. This means every person with a given characteristic (a headache) has an equal chance of being chosen for the sample. Once a sample is determined, science divides it into two groups in such a way that there is no reason to expect that aspirin will influence one group any more than the other. One group is designated as the experimental group and the other as the control group, but without the groups being aware of which is which. The next step is to measure the headaches in each group. This is the "before" step in science and is necessary for two reasons. One is to be sure the subjects upon which we are experimenting are the same. The other is to have a base line for comparison so that the results gotten "after" the experiment can be compared with something. In the next step of the experiment, aspirin is given in precisely measured doses over precise periods of time. But it is not given to both groups. The control group receives a little white pill that looks like aspirin but has no effect of any kind, although the control group is *told* that it is aspirin. At some precise time after the aspirin has been taken we measure each person in each group for headaches. The difference between the two groups after the experiment is what counts. This difference would measure some of the effects of aspirin upon headaches. Undoubtedly we would find that aspirin played some role in getting rid of headaches, but it is certain that the hypothesis that aspirin gets rid of headaches would not be confirmed.

Let us now restate the classical model of a laboratory or controlled experiment described above in more abstract terms so that you can see how it can be applied to many situations. The fundamental design of the controlled experiment can be expressed as having four parts or cells. Two of these are the measurements made before the experiment, and two of these are the measurements made after the experiment. Two of the four cells are those measurements on the control group, and the other two cells are the measurements on the experimental group. Many variations of this basic pattern can be used.

Ex Post Facto Experiments

Still another kind of experiment is the natural or *ex post facto* experiment. In this experiment the scientist investigates what happened after some event without his having had any deliberate control over it. For example, scientists must study earthquakes after they happen. This situation is often true in social science, where ethics of social scientists do not permit them to experiment on human beings. Some people believed for a very long time that continual intermarriage of close relatives, such as first cousins marrying each other for a hundred years, would result in some form of physical or mental deterioration of the offspring. No social scientist would force marriages or could experiment in any controlled way to find out. However, they were able to disprove the hypothesis about intermarriage with the analysis in the twentieth century of the descendants of the men who mutinied on the H.M.S. *Bounty.* These men and their wives had lived undetected on the South Pacific island of Pitcairn with only close relatives to marry for over a hundred years and had suffered no obvious physical or mental deterioration.

Proof

Experiments can never really *prove* anything. In fact scientists now rarely use the word "proof" in connection with their scientific work, and there is only one occasion for using the word in modern science. It has a very definite meaning in logic and mathematics, where it refers to a series of statements characterized by the fact that each statement follows by the rules of logic from the ones that come before it in the series, or where every statement is true because the terms in them are *defined* as true. In other words, proof for the scientist is a logical or mathematical characteristic. Furthermore, scientists avoid the use of the word "proof" about their work because it implies a degree of certainty that every scientist knows does not exist.

The exceptional case in which a scientist uses the word "proof" is related to the mathematical definition of "proof." When the scientist is virtually certain that every aspect of the actual phenomena reacts exactly as do the symbols with which he represents it, then, if he can prove the relationships between the symbols, he can be said to have proved the relationships between the phenomena. On the other hand, much experimental and other scientific work is devoted to disproving, and scientists do often use that word. For instance, if you were to allege that the rooster's crowing brought the sun up, then killing the rooster could disprove your hypothesis.

The kind of explanation a scientist seeks will help to determine his research design and experimental procedures. It is also true that any given research design and experimental procedure will also influence, if not directly determine, the kind of explanation a scientist will get about his subject. But in this as in so many other matters, science is open-minded. If the methods are sound and the results empirically testable, it does not matter which way the progress has been made. The history of science has seen advances from many directions.

THE RESULTS OF SOCIAL SCIENCE

The system of scientific inquiry can be justified by its resulting in prediction and control. Within the system of science, the consequences of progress in each part of it will vary from those of the entire system. This is also true of the consequences of progress in each part of the system of social science. As we know and use more social science as a whole, the prospects grow for a richer, more self-fulfilling life of peace and love. As we make progress within each part of the system, better uses for the system of science become apparent. For example, better description can mean better explanations. With these we can predict and control more accurately, because we can then have better problem formulation. Political scientists can and do predict events with errors of less than one percent, as you know from watching television on the nights of presidential elections. Economists can and do predict the next year's gross national product with average errors of less than five percent. And social scientists from other disciplines can also predict certain things they study, even though they cannot always control them.

Prediction and Control

Prediction and control are part of the scientific system of inquiry. Neither is absolutely essential to it although both are considered highly desirable. Astronomy and meteorology are both sciences that can predict but not control. Astronomy can predict many of the phenomena it studies with a high degree of accuracy. But it cannot control. Meteorology seems to be able to predict much less successfully than astronomy but apparently is beginning to be able to control some of the weather. As in the physical sciences, so it is with the social sciences.

And in all the three branches of science there are cases of being able to control through trial and error or the use of mechanisms whose workings are not understood without being able to predict. For example, plant and animal breeders have control of the qualities of some plants and animals without being able to predict in the sense that they know that if they do *A, B* will result. They do it through a process of trial and error. This is often the case in social science, too, where attempts to control something like racial tension often have unpredictable long-term results but it is possible to control a situation for at least a short time. The central characteristics, then, of prediction and control are the same for all of science, but social science requires certain modifications to fit its subjects.

If prediction simply meant being able to tell what would happen before it happened, it would have little interest for the social scientist. Correct predictions have been attributed to guess, luck, chance, the word of God, and many other things. This is not what the scientist means by prediction. He means the understanding of, or the theory of, and accurate knowledge about the process of change upon which the prediction is based. The scientist would expect a specification of the conditions under which the change would occur and description or control of the key factors in the process. And, lastly, scientific predictions are almost always given in terms of an estimate of the probability that the change will occur or, if not that, a statement of the probable next steps involved in the change.

But with human beings these conditions are extremely hard to fulfill. One reason is that if you make up a prediction about a person and he knows it, he can contravene it by an act of will. Many social scientists will therefore refrain from making predictions about individuals, preferring to restrict themselves to groups. Groups are rarely so well organized that even if they knew about the prediction themselves they could or would change.

Up to the present, social science has suffered more from too few efforts to predict and far too few efforts to control than from too many efforts. It is a myth that social science knowledge will bring about some kind of "1984" situation. Discussions of prediction and control in social science are bound up with value problems, a subject that will be developed in the next chapter. At this point we need to stress that control is a goal of the scientific system, for the ability to predict and control is one of the sure signs that we have reliable scientific knowledge. What men do with this knowledge is a separate question.

Order and the System

When some people study science they mistakenly get the impression that scientific knowledge or research is developed by using the system of science in a series of steps. This is not at all the case. There is no necessary order in which the system of science must be used. It often happens, for example, that scientists formulate problems as the result of observation and description, sometimes while they are working on other problems, sometimes because of curiosity or mere introspection. Problems can be formulated as a result of work in any part of the system of science. Once they are formulated, however, other parts of the system of science can be used to give the most reliable knowledge.

Often great scientific advances are made simply because a problem is restated in more manageable form, sometimes as a result of observations someone else can use, sometimes when a new theory is formulated. Which of the parts of the system of science and which of the methods a scientist will use depends on the subject and the knowledge in the field.

Nor does the system of science require that each step be completed. Scientists use the system of science only to the extent they think necessary. For example, life insurance companies have for some time been able to predict average life expectancies in America very accurately, without the benefit of elaborate scientific investigation or even much theory, simply by using certain refined statistical techniques. The fact that they can predict average life expectancies does not mean that they can control them.

Social Versus Other Science

If it is true that social science is a part of science, why then do social scientists not use all the methods of science? And why is social science not as advanced as the other sciences? Physical scientists, philosophers, and even some social scientists who have speculated about these very pertinent questions have sometimes come up with bizarre answers. There have been physical scientists and philosophers who have even doubted the possible existence of social science. There have been social scientists who, not knowing much philosophy or much about physical science, have, on the other hand, thought they were so different that they hardly considered social science a part of science.

It is easy to see one reason for the confusion. Social science deals with the most complex subject—man. Every person in the world is different from every other person. Much more refined methods have to be used to discover both similarities and differences than is the case, for example, with gas molecules or earthworms. In addition to the problems of complexity, social reality is to some extent composed of the meanings that individuals and groups give to their feelings, actions, and situations. Thus the subjects are aware of themselves, which is quite a different situation from that found in the physical or biological sciences. But the methods of physical and biological sciences were generally elaborated before those of the social sciences. These methods, unless adapted, cannot take account of either the complexity of the situations or the consciousness of the subject in social science. Man's consciousness and his complexity are not reasons enough to exclude social science from science.

Since the term "natural sciences" is sometimes used to designate the physical and biological sciences, some wit once suggested that all other sciences ought to be called "unnatural sciences" in contrast. It is true that some old methods of science must be refined, adapted, discarded, and many used in different combinations, and that some entirely new methods must be invented because of complexity and consciousness in social science. But today hardly anyone thinks that social science is impossible. Fortunately two centuries of development have provided a sound basis for the growth of social science. The adaptation of older scientific methods and the development of new ones for social science are important if it is to continue its growth. Complexity and consciousness have required adaptation and development for each part of the system of science. This growth has enriched the entire science system.

Chapter 4

Modern Social Science

VALUES IN SOCIAL SCIENCE

The central distinction between the work of the
social scientist and the work of physical and biological scientists is the much greater extent to which
values permeate the work of the social scientist.
Notice carefully that we have said "much greater
extent"; we are talking about a difference of degree,
not of kind. Value considerations are significant factors in the work of any scientist, but they are often
present in more important ways for the social scientist.

What Are Values?

The term "value" in social science stands for what people think or feel that they need or desire. "Value" is a concept that covers many kinds of human activity. One usage by social scientists relates the feelings and thoughts of people to objects. Americans, it may be said, value their cars highly. The social scientist observes that they spend much of their income and their time on cars and talk frequently about them compared to other objects. This usage of "value" stresses preferences.

Another usage of the term denotes the standards according to which a person, group, or society decides how they should choose or judge events and things. Americans, at the level of the federal government, value spending on military preparation more highly than spending on social welfare. Our society shares this value, and it serves to guide and organize much of our economic activity through the effects of decisions such as those on taxes and the draft.

Whichever usage is emphasized, the relationship of thoughts and feelings to objects or the standards for judgment, like "good" and "bad" or "should" and "ought" or "better or worse," are involved. Values both characterize and appraise; thus "value" is comparative or relative. A value judgment always compares one thing or state of affairs with another. In the defense spending example above, Americans justify their choice not in terms of hating the poor or being content to neglect their country's schools and hospitals, but with reference to another value—freedom—that ranks above those involved in the defense versus welfare spending choice. Large amounts of defense spending are supposed to preserve this freedom. The values associated with freedom rank higher than those associated with spending on domestic welfare programs.

The question of whether defense spending increases our freedom while trouble mounts in the central cities and the air and water become more polluted directs our attention to another aspect of values—namely that their implementation may or may not have the results that are initially desired. The obvious importance of value in both the individuals and groups the social scientist studies and in the work of the social scientist, as a scientist, has led to the development of methods for dealing with it in each part of the scientific system.

The system of science is directed by goals drawn from outside itself. The physical and biological sciences have found little reason to be concerned with value questions, even though they were assumed or implicit in much scientific work. As the social sciences developed, it was discovered that men were deeply concerned with values that affected every part of their life. The system of science required modification to include some consideration of values for each part.

The Influence of Values

Why does one physicist study the problems of gravity and another the problems of light? Why does one biologist study sea animals and another butterflies? The answer is that each scientist selects problems that seem important to him. A social scientist selects the problems that he studies for the same reasons. The sciences are all the same in this respect. The judgments of the scientist are derived from the values he holds. These values determine what is interesting and important to him.

The social scientist, being part of a culture, shares its values. As a result he is likely to select and formulate his problems so that they do not conflict with the values of the culture, even though better choices and formulations of problems might be possible if he were not so culture-bound. The result is that unpopular subjects or points of view are less likely to be deeply studied scientifically. One example of this problem is the long period of American history when racist attitudes permeated the value structure and very little attention was given to the problems of the black by the social scientist.

A second practical difficulty associated with values arises when the social scientist attempts to formulate problems which are themselves value problems. Take the case of the social scientist studying behavioral changes in a Nazi concentration camp. As he observes, describes, and records these activities, he will, if he is a good social scientist, have to describe these activities with value-loaded terms like "cruelty," "sadism," and "torture." These are quite properly descriptive terms, but in addition they also express values such as disapproval. Social scientists often have to insert their own values into their observations and descriptions.

In practice social scientists hold different or conflicting values. The disagreements they have about value questions may be the cause of further disagreement over factual issues. But this situation is not a serious obstacle. Science has built-in error-detection and error-correction mechanisms. Thus the error due to a social scientist's work that is strongly colored by values is certain to be corrected ultimately. We all live in the short run, however, and the knowledge that science will correct itself at some indefinite future date does not console many social scientists, especially those who believe that without more adequate social science humanity itself may be threatened. For this reason they have developed several recommendations to handle conflicting value judgments.

Separate Facts From Values

One point that must be kept in mind about values is the necessity of separating "facts" from "values." The two are often confused because a single word or phrase might have both factual and value meanings. Consider the phrase "law and order." Clearly our society regards law and order highly. But now consider what it means, for example, for many of the "disorders" connected with civil rights in the 1960s. In studying what has happened, political scientists now, and historians in the future, will have to distinguish between the value of "law and order" and the fact of whether or not "order" is always "law." When we have order, is it not possible that the law might be violated in the process of establishing that order? What if the "disorder" broke no law in the first place?

Most social scientists will try to distinguish between facts and values. Once the values of a problem have been isolated, then biases based on these values can be studied and conflicts about them minimized. When it is impossible to distinguish between facts and values, scientific discussion becomes extremely difficult and often impossible.

One way social scientists have attempted to minimize the effects of their values on their work is by stating them as completely as possible. This approach does not assume that scientists will agree on their values once they are stated or that the system of science can reconcile differences. What it does is to separate ends from means, a very common distinction in the social sciences. To take an example from economics, if Americans want a free-enterprise society, they will have to take measures to ensure competition. Economists debating such an issue would first state their preference or values with regard to a free-enterprise society. Having done this, they can then determine what the proper means to achieve the end might be.

Values are attached to both means and ends, but when they can be clearly labeled the system of scientific inquiry can be brought to bear with few distortions. These values, in other words, can be neutralized and accounted for because they are explicit. In many social science problems it is not possible to be so explicit about values associated with ends and means. When this is the case the social scientist must do the best he can and rely on the long-run power of science to develop more truth about these complicated matters.

Another kind of value conflict arises when an observer from one society studies another. Imagine a situation in which an anthropologist is studying cannibals, or a social worker is studying a delinquent group in which a murder is being planned. In this case the conflict of values is not between scientists but rather between two sets of the scientist's own values. In both of these cases the scientist should act first as a human being and a man and, if he can, stop the cannibalism or murder. When he does this, however, he should be fully conscious of the fact that he is departing from his role as a scientist.

Value commitments also enter into what are considered facts. Practical difficulties begin with perception. There is evidence that strongly held values act as a filter to what one perceives. To the extent that this happens the social scientist will not even be able to see the facts. However, this is a practical difficulty of less importance than some others, because not all social scientists are likely to hold values so strongly that they will all filter their perceptions in the same way. Error of this kind may be relatively easy to overcome.

Value Problems Common to All Sciences

There is no doubt that the society in which a scientist is raised, his education, the time in which he works, his viewpoints—in short, his position in history—influence his science. Students of the sociology of knowledge have pointed out that every analysis of social phenomena reflects some special social viewpoint and includes the values at one point in time and space. The social scientist must consider to which extent his special situation influences his work. Most scholars agree that although there is undoubtedly some influence of period and place, it is not unavoidable in every case. For instance, the language of mathematics seems to escape many of the constraints of time, place, and values. So do many other logical propositions. "Two men can usually do more work than one" does not seem to be the kind of statement seriously influenced by value judgments related to position in time and space. The value problems that do exist must be seen as practical ones, however, that exist for every science but which will become fewer as the social sciences grow and techniques are developed to overcome them.

THE CONSTRAINTS OF INQUIRY

It should be clear that social science cannot use just any methods in the conduct of its inquiry. There are four major constraints which direct a social scientist in his work.

Scientific Assent

The entire structure of science is held together by the cement of voluntary consent. Everyone who enters the field of science makes a kind of implicit agreement that everything he does shall be open to criticism by others. Discussion and conflict for many years have led to a consensus about what should go on within the bounds of science. Since scientists make no appeal to outsiders and accept no support from any outside agent, they reserve to themselves the right to make all judgments. The consensus of the scientific community, therefore, is very important in determining work in science.

The very minor drawback is that sometimes consensus impedes bold and creative scientists who wish to strike out beyond its bounds. Scientists know that by restricting actions to an agreed-upon area of consent they run a small risk compared with other possibilities, considering that few men are able to break new ground outside the bounds of present knowledge. If there were significantly fewer restraints, the effort of the majority of those who work beyond the constraints of science would be wasted. In the long run, the rare loss from constraint has more than been made up by the vast gains that come from restricting scientific work to the bounds of scientific consent.

Tradition

A different sort of constraint upon scientific activity and upon the methods à social scientist can use is the force of tradition. This force, unfortunately, operates in science in much the same fashion that it does in the rest of society. While sometimes the forces of tradition stabilize society, they also may frequently hold it back. It has not been demonstrated that the scientific system of inquiry needs any stabilizing force of this nature. That scientific inquiry is held back by a tradition like that of the university departmental organization is abundantly clear. It took decades for American universities to recognize social scientists and to appoint professors to chairs. Today the force of tradition in university science defines success in such a way that many significant problems are not worked upon, effort is spent on trivial or insignificant problems, and most unhappily, as a result, sometimes students are discouraged from becoming social scientists.

Support

Social scientists must eat and manage to survive in our society. It is quite natural that social scientists should, to some extent, be guided in their work by sources of support that they can get. The undesirable side of this constraint is that support is often available from special interest groups—foundations, corporations, and the like—for research of little value except to the supporter, while important projects go unaided. If it were always given to important and significant work no one would have any complaint. However, the scandals of the 1960s which revealed that large universities were working on government contracts that involved social scientists and were directed toward unscholarly, if not unethical, ends are examples of misdirected support for science and scientists.

In no country has the tradition of supporting large amounts of unbiased social science research become established. This has been a major factor in the relatively slow growth of social science and undoubtedly will continue to impede its general progress. We can expect, in the future as in the past, that those studies which receive support will progress much more rapidly than those which do not.

Uses

One of the justifications for social science is its uses. Many social scientists enter the field because they see much that is obviously wrong with society and desire to reform it, or at least influence it. But social science, like any science, requires that its findings be tested in use. Since this is true, just as it is in any science, a constraint upon its development is that its results are likely to be tested, at present, only in areas important and favorable to the dominant power groups. Thus, much that social science has discovered that could possibly better conditions in our inner cities has gone untested because economic and political groups that benefit from these conditions can prevent this kind of testing. Physical and biological sciences have been aided more generously in using their knowledge than social science, partly because progress in these fields does not often directly affect existing social and power relationships. It is quite possible that unless our society uses social science much more in the future, it will not be able to develop in the way that most Americans seem to wish.

DISCIPLINES—ANOTHER WAY OF DIRECTING SCIENTIFIC INQUIRY

Another influence on the direction of scientific inquiry comes from the organization and structure imposed on the work and training of social scientists by virtue of the organization of scientific disciplines.

What Is a Discipline?

The body of science is made up of knowledge, hypotheses, concepts, and methods. Most sciences organize the knowledge, hypotheses, concepts, and methods around a subject— animal life, the earth, motion, matter and energy, and so on. Parts of science, so organized, are called disciplines.

Scientific knowledge advances as the organizational scheme of the discipline is brought to bear on the problems presented by the subject matter. Successful dealing with problems testifies to the usefulness of the discipline, while failures in dealing with problems bring the error-correcting mechanisms of science into operation and sometimes result in the formation of a new discipline.

Disciplines of Social Science

Every list of the disciplines of social science includes history, sociology, geography, economics, political science, psychology, and anthropology. In each of these fields of study, the majority of scholars use scientific methods. Each has its own subject matter, its own part of the study of man. History studies man's past; sociology studies man in his social or group relationships. Geography locates man in earthly space and studies spatial relationships. Political science deals with governments, power, and authority; economics concentrates on the daily business of living, income, and wealth. Psychology studies the individual, emphasizing the mind; anthropology focuses on the ways of life of mankind.

Other disciplines are often included in social science because the complexity of man provides a rich subject matter. Often included in addition are the fields of planning, education, social work, and law. Planning studies man's ways of adjusting his present goals to the future; education studies how he learns; social work studies how to help groups and persons with difficulties; and law deals with the formal ways power controls individuals and groups. These disciplines can be classified as a part of social science because their subject is man and because they often use some of the methods of science. But scientific methods suitable to their special problems have not yet been well enough developed to allow us to rely upon them. Men in a civilized society must rule themselves with the best law they can develop, with or without the aid of science; men must plan for the future even if they cannot use the methods of science at every stage. The young must be taught, preferably with the knowledge science can give, but without it when necessary. And we must aid the underprivileged and try to plan for the future whether or not a complete scientific system exists to aid us. The subject of each of these four disciplines of social science is an urgent and necessary part of man's life to which the methods of science do not yet fully apply.

Behavioral Science

In many fields of the social sciences there are scientists who refer to themselves as "behavioral scientists" or "behaviorists." These terms, however, have no generally accepted definition; there are almost as many ideas about what the "behavioral sciences" are as there are behavioral scientists. But there are some uses of the terms with which almost everyone would agree. Behavioral scientists emphasize the study of behavior, that is, actions that are observable by others. Behaviorally oriented political scientists prefer to call politicians "actors" and count roll-call votes rather than analyze which social forces or frame of mind caused a politician to vote as he did. A behaviorally oriented psychologist might prefer to study how drugs make patients act rather than their childhood experiences or their unconscious mind.

It might be said, then, that behavioral science is a different way of combining parts of the disciplines and methods of social science, so that a much heavier emphasis is placed on measuring exactly what human beings do in certain situations. Thus social scientists from any discipline could call themselves behavioral scientists, but in practice those who most commonly do so are psychologists, social psychologists, and political scientists.

SCIENCE AND ITS USES

It is important to distinguish between science and the uses of science. The man in the street who blames the loss of his job on automation, the woman whose baby is deformed because she took the wrong pill during her pregnancy, the lover of peace impressed by the destructive power of hydrogen weapons, all are sometimes prone to mix up the knowledge that science has given us with how that knowledge is used. Albert Einstein, who was instrumental at an early stage in the development of the first atomic bomb, did not wish to see it dropped on people. Automation is an outcome of science that can free man from labor, but, because for most people labor means income, automation can have adverse effects. Drugs give great benefits to humans but they should not be used before being properly tested, no matter what the profits to the drug companies are.

The knowledge that science gives us carries great power. Physical and biological knowledge can kill and destroy or preserve and make life easier. Social science knowledge, too, can be used for good or for bad. For example, it can be used either for manipulating people with certain kinds of advertising and other propaganda or for their great benefit, as the progress in education shows.

The control and use of scientific knowledge is one of the

great issues of our time. Unfortunately, the powerful system of science has not yet been brought to bear on this issue. Perhaps it never can be. But no scientist can work without some concern for what will be the uses of the knowledge he develops.

Knowing and using are clearly two different things. Thus social scientists find no serious problem raised by the superficial argument that if we know about man and predict and control him, he will somehow become a kind of robot. If the history of science is any example, the same processes that generate the knowledge which some fear might make him a robot also generate the knowledge that has made him freer and with the potential to become freer yet.

The Usefulness of Social Science

If the uses of science are already many, its potential uses are many more. From the point of view of science itself, social science presents a guide or perspective or viewpoint that men can use to comprehend their world. Using social science, men can understand things that were incomprehensible before.

And, of course, social science is useful, just as are the physical and biological sciences, for the making of inventions. These inventions include ways of treating mental illness, educating our children, keeping the peace, and selecting people for various positions. Another use of social science can be understood if we would imagine what modern life would be like without it. We could not begin to understand the economic, social, political, and other forces that determine our destiny. We would not be aware of the kinds of changes that are possible, or their costs.

The light that social science casts on our society reveals that it forms some of our values too. Social science indicates that race does not create personality or "bad" habits simply because of inheritance. Now only those who choose to remain ignorant can hold racism high on their value scale. Thus another use of social science is to form some values and reform others. Nor are social values alone affected. Many of the great social scientists consciously attempted to model their social and individual lives upon the highest scientific ideals. This never was easy, but as more men learned about social science they made the attempt, to the advantage of the rest of the world.

Social Scientists and Society

Robert Redfield, a great American anthropologist, once said, "To every partisan, a social scientist is a potential enemy. It is the nature of the social scientist to doubt, to test, to criticize, to reject an unproven view that is popular or powerful. But a partisan is one who has adopted a view, and now is concerned only with making it prevail, by force if necessary. To be an honest and truly scientific social scientist, is to stand for free inquiry and humility before the facts in the face of partisan and power politics." Sometimes, when they hear their various professors of social science discuss problems, students come to the false conclusion that social scientists are either trouble-makers or pessimists about our society. Some congressmen have recently showed their inability to distinguish social workers from social scientists and socialists. But the quotation from Redfield indicates what the job of a social scientist is and why he must adopt the viewpoint he does. The social scientist has no vested interest except that of the truth. He can be neither a victim of the partisan nor a partisan himself. When he sees problems he is bound to speak out about them. Of course, like any man, he can be wrong in his conclusions, but this does not mean that his motives should be questioned or he should be silenced.

The Role of Social Science

At several points in this introduction to science we have mentioned the scientist's own position in his society. We have emphasized the value problems that social science faces because of its subject. A discussion of the relationship of society to social science would be incomplete if we left the impression that all social sciences have resolved the issues involved in the same way, because they have not. Two opposite conditions exist. On the one hand there is a group of social scientists who insist on "hard" data. These scientists try to avoid dealing with social policy problems. When they have to deal with values, they attempt to measure their distribution, their intensity, their frequency, and their influence for the individual or group under study. Values studied in this fashion can be treated quantitatively, objectively, and generally in a scientific way that avoids some of the value complications. These scientists attempt to make their work value-free.

At the other extreme are a group of scientists called "soft." In their work they try to focus on what they consider the most important problems of society and man. They are often more concerned to introduce rational changes into both man and society. These "soft" scientists try to change environment and character, and to eliminate the conditions which impede our ability to act rationally. The "soft" scientists in their teaching and examples try to encourage everyone to think about our human condition and basic goals. They want to make certain that social science is never used as a mere servant of ruling or influential groups or to manipulate human beings for any purpose that would impair essential human dignity.

Too often these two modes of dealing with value problems and the social scientist's role in society are wrongly presented as conflicting. The history of social science shows that many of the greatest social scientists were very much interested in the reform of their society and the great goals of man. They wanted to do it rationally and based their proposed reforms on objective knowledge. The same is true today. The system of science does not require that one be "hard" or "soft" in the sense that being one excludes the other. The rational use of social science for the great goals of man requires scientific knowledge. An engineer cannot build a bridge without the scientific knowledge of physics, nor can a doctor develop a vaccine to help human beings without the scientific knowledge of biology. The only real danger to social science is that it will adopt one stance without adequate attention to the other.

CONCLUSION

The purpose of the first part of this book has been to review some of the central ideas of the scientific system as social scientists understand it. Most students have run into some of these ideas in earlier courses in physical or biological sciences. But few have had the opportunity of seeing that the very same scientific system works for social science. The fact that man has a conscious will and can direct his actions and that many different factors operate on him at the same time with different degrees of intensity make the study of social science more difficult than many parts of the physical or biological sciences.

In Chapter 1 we were reminded that the goal of science is truth-seeking. Truth can be sought for its uses, out of curiosity, or simply for its own sake. The methods of science are the rules of procedure that scientists follow in this pursuit. These rules cover how scientists view the world, how they manipulate the symbols in terms of which the world is represented, and how these symbols are related to the world. The methods of science do not directly tell us where we want to go, but rather, after we have decided where we want to go, they tell us how to get there in the best manner.

In Chapter 2 we found that scientists recognize many aspects of truth but focus on one, that part of truth which can be systematic, logical, and objective. We observed that science is a system of inquiry that contains within itself the mechanisms for the detection and correction of error. Each of the great parts of this system—problem formulation, observation and description, explanation, and prediction and control—are related to one another so that errors made in one part will inevitably show up in another part, if not in the same one.

Chapter 2 also explained how different subjects require different methods for dealing with them. Each of the four parts of the scientific system of inquiry have sets of methods developed for dealing with different subjects. Also depending upon the subject, problems must be formulated somewhat differently. And the subject also determines how we observe and describe and experiment. Differences in subject matter have led to different ways of explaining and predicting. The great divisions of science are also related to their subjects, whether physical, biological, or social. The subject matter determines to a large extent which of the methods will be used in any part of the scientific system.

Scientists have a belief system. They must believe in objective reality, time, space, the possibility of definite relationships between symbols and reality, the possibility of measure or comparison, and purpose. They must have faith in reason and believe in determinism of one kind or another. This belief system is a minimum requirement for entrance into the group of scientists and accounts for the fact that not everybody can be one—for not everybody shares these beliefs. And of course, even if they did share these beliefs, certain skills, training, and knowledge of methods would be required before they could practice science.

Chapter 3 discusses many of the ways social scientists possess to adapt the older system of science to a more complex and difficult subject matter—man and society. It explains some of the problems of common sense knowledge and how social scientists deal with problems of gathering data.

Experiment, an important method of inquiry, is explained in an attempt to show how social science is truly a part of the overall system of science.

Chapter 4 has discussed the practical problems arising from the widespread influence of values. Once more we have seen that the subject matter of social science requires different ways of handling value issues, but that all the sciences have similar problems. The methods of the social scientist can neutralize value biases.

It was necessary to review the system of science, emphasizing the way that social science has adapted the system of science, before we could come to the study of the methods of social science themselves. Unless you have some idea of what an automobile is, the study of the automobile engine would not make much sense. In a way, the methods of science are the engine of science whereby it can produce reliable knowledge.

Part 2

Methods and Disciplines
of Social Science

This part of the book introduces you to the main
social science disciplines and to some of the most
important methods used in social science. Many of
the major methods of social science are illustrated
in the context of the major disciplines of social
science. It should be kept in mind however that all
the disciplines use all the methods at some times
and that none uses all the methods for any one
problem. The choice of methods depends on the
problem.

Chapter 5

History—
Methods for Beginning
Scientific Study

PROBLEMS IN SCIENCE AND HISTORY

A problem in social science may be of many different kinds. It might involve the determination of a fact: How many people live in China? What do Americans eat? Or it might involve a method: How can we determine human emotional responses? Or the problem could be about an explanation: Why do the poor not vote as often as the rich? Or a theory: What are the determinants of family size? The variety of problems in science means that it is impossible for one set of methods to solve them all.

But some methods are common to all of science. These common methods stem from the fact that what we are and what we know are determined to a large extent by our history. Every social scientist, therefore, must be a historian of sorts.

Problems and Facts

Facts are what science is made of, but facts by themselves are not science. Far more important for scientific inquiry than just determining facts is the selection and arrangement of facts so that they make sense and add to our knowledge. A scientific problem can, therefore, be defined as a question, the answer to which produces knowledge. It can be said, then, that facts make up knowledge, but they are the basis of knowledge, not the knowledge itself.

Accurate facts are a necessary but not a sufficient condition for knowledge. It is their order and relationships which give them meaning. A problem in science is the question which allows us to select and arrange facts so they mean something. Historians early developed many methods of problem formulation later adopted by all scientists. Thus we can use the social science discipline of history to illustrate some of the methods that all scientists use.

What Is History?

Everyone agrees that history is time-oriented, concerned with neither the present nor the future. But this agreement is not enough to define history, for it only excludes two time periods and does not tell us what is included. When we try to understand what the term "history" means, we find that the word has been used in four different senses, some of which overlap. The first is the sense of what happened in the past or any part of the past. When someone says "We can't know history," he uses the word in this sense. He usually means that we can't know everything about any event in the past.

Another sense in which the word "history" has been used is to refer to what we do know about the past from the physical remains that have survived from the past: the bones of early man, the books and inscriptions, the buildings, roads, and so forth. A third sense of "history" refers to the discipline or branch of knowledge that is concerned with mankind's past. When we speak of the "history department," we use the word in that sense. The fourth sense of "history" refers to the knowledge we gain from critical and systematic investigation into the past. These are the main senses in which the modern historian uses the term "history."

History as a Social Science

In the earlier days of social science, people who argued that there was no such thing as social science said that obviously history could not be scientific. We can now say that social science exists and history is a part of it. This is because today science is understood in the broader sense of a truth-seeking system, as explained in this book. Few are prepared to deny that men can seek to know the truth about themselves. If one doubts that men can learn all the truth, it can still be accepted that they can come closer to knowing it, without requiring that they ever know "the truth, the whole truth, and nothing but the truth." The last refuge of those who might deny the possibility of social science or history as a social science is that men never can develop methods to learn more about themselves. But this is demonstrably not so—the very act of writing a history or discussing the problems implies methods for learning about human beings and their past.

Perhaps another reason for the confusion about this issue is that history, like most of the other disciplines, is both a social science and a user of knowledge from the other social sciences. No one thinks it odd that a chemist is both a physical scientist and a user of the methods and knowledge from other physical sciences such as physics. All kinds of relationships between and among sciences are in fact characteristic of the system of scientific inquiry. Relationships between the methods of history and the methods of social science exist therefore on several levels. The different disciplines may use the same methods, but they may have a unique combination of the methods for their own use. The discussions of methods under the disciplines applies to those widely used in that field—in this case, history—and also widely used in the other disciplines.

How is history different from the other social sciences? Not in its subject matter, for that is man, just as it is in the others. Not in its methods, for it uses many of the methods of the other social sciences. But history alone studies the past as its sole time frame of reference. The other social sciences also study the past, but they investigate the present and often try to predict the future as well. Thus the unique characteristic of history as compared with the other social sciences is its emphasis on selected aspects of the past.

Why Study History?

For most people, the main reason to study history is simply that it is interesting. People like to know about mankind's past, which is part of their own. This interest, expressed in history and literature, has almost from the invention of writing been responsible for much of man's knowledge about himself. Another reason many people study history is that they think they can learn from the past. Old-fashioned sayings such as "History repeats itself" are examples of an uncritical acceptance of this idea, and no social scientist would now accept such a view. For the social scientist, history is important not because it will repeat itself but because of what we can learn from it. For example, most college sophomores know more about geometry than the Greek mathematician Euclid did. How did this happen when Euclid was one of the great geniuses in all of man's history? The answer is that Euclid had to discover for himself what others now can learn in much easier ways. Still others could build on Euclid's knowledge and make it grow until now the average college student can easily perform mathematical operations which would have been impossible even for the greatest mathematicians of a few centuries ago. For the social scientist there is no question that the past teaches us, when this is understood in the sense that it has given us objective, reliable, and verifiable knowledge.

Unfortunately, the past is very often interpreted to young people as teaching moral or patriotic or philosophical lessons.

For example, the textbook treatment of the blacks in American history has until very recently been such as to reinforce racial stereotypes. Conversely, the treatment of George Washington in textbooks has usually been one that results in the impression that George Washington was a superhuman model of an American and hardly real. In contrast to accumulating knowledge, writing history to reinforce a predetermined position is not part of science.

HISTORY AND THE SCIENTIFIC ATTITUDE

The true scientific attitude is not bounded by nations or motivated only by self-love. That is why the teaching of history as a discipline of the social sciences must change from the instilling of patriotism in national history courses to teaching world history, as the history of man, with the true heroes being those who tried to cure, to understand, and to stop conflict, oppression, and warfare. The stories of the ruthless men of history—warriors, dictators, kings—fill the pages of history books; but from a scientific point of view these men did not contribute to the highest values we hold in the idea of mankind. The central thrust of the physical and biological sciences has been to make man master of nature, while the central thrust of the social sciences has been to make man the master of his fate.

Problem Formulation

There are few scientists who begin work with problems set for them. Because there are so many kinds of problems, there are also many ways a problem can be stated in science. Sometimes problems are wrongly set. In one case, many early mathematicians spent hours attempting to square the circle, constructing a square with the same area as a given circle using only a straight edge and compass. We now know that this old problem cannot be solved. In the social sciences, like all sciences when young, problems tend to be far less precise at the start. There are not yet convincing or complete rules for problem formulation. Those rules there are have to be understood more as guidelines than as formulas which will guarantee a satisfactory social scientific result. In the cases of a few great historians and social scientists, it sometimes seems that the problem found the man rather than the other way around. However, even when this was the case, a well-formulated problem would have included six characteristics which can be stated as rules:

1. The subject of scientific inquiry must have value. The problem must be such that its solution will add something to our knowledge. A simple but useful test for this rule is to ask what the result will be if the problem is solved. If the answer is that solution of the problem gives us new knowledge, then we can be fairly sure that the problem has scientific value.

2. The problem must be stated clearly. Any scientist with the proper training must be able to understand what is being discussed and exactly what the problem is. All the great works in social science have this characteristic. Adam Smith entitled his great book *An Inquiry into the Nature and Causes of the Wealth of Nations.* The first chapter of Thomas Malthus's book *An Essay on Population* begins with a statement of the subject. Alexis de Tocqueville, in his book *Democracy in America,* presents his subject: "A new science of politics is indispensable to a new world."

These examples draw attention to the fact that the scientific problem need not be stated in the form of a question. Constructing a new science of politics or explaining the causes of population increase need not answer questions, but may mean only observing or fact-gathering. Whatever the problem, a clear and understandable statement of it is required.

3. A scientific problem must be practical, which means that the methods, data, and other resources are available either now or potentially to solve the problem. The classic problem of the Middle Ages, "How many angels can stand on the head of a pin?" is not a scientific problem. There are no instruments and methods that could lead to the solution of that problem.

4. A scientific problem must be related to the existing struc-

ture of scientific knowledge. This means that the outcome of the investigation stimulated by the problem will be such that the knowledge gained can be related to the other knowledge in the field. Put another way, a good problem is integrated with, built upon, and related to the knowledge that others have given us.

5. Whenever possible, the problem should be original. Originality in science is very hard to define, but generally we mean that the solution of the problem will bring out new evidence or a new interpretation of old evidence. We do not necessarily mean that the problem is a brand new one, although this sometimes is the case. It could also be an old problem, originality being found in a new treatment.

6. A last characteristic of a well-formulated scientific problem is its connection to a theoretical or world view; it fits into some intellectual system or theory. For example, the modern development of automation poses many kinds of problems, but leaders in neither the United States nor the Soviet Union have stated them in such a way that solutions would fit their respective economic systems. On the other hand, Congress has passed laws setting up programs to alleviate poverty in the United States that do fit the social and economic structure as they understand it.

To avoid thinking about a problem in too narrow a sense, remember that we are really discussing the subject, and particularly the choice of subjects, of scientific inquiry. The subject of this inquiry can be anything about man. We need to know so much about him that problems of all kinds can be included. The problems can be those of observation, description, interpretation, or many other kinds. The six rules about problems will, if followed, provide a useful guide to understanding what a problem in science is.

THE SEARCH FOR HISTORY

Appendix A of this book is devoted to sources of information available in social science. Here we will sketch the ways you find material. Although this section is written with history in mind, it is generally applicable to all the social sciences. All scientists need to discover what others have done about their problem in the past. The purpose of going back into the record is both to avoid needless duplication of effort and to assure that account is taken of all available scientific knowledge.

The Library and Literature Review

A review of the past writings on the subject being studied usually begins in a library, either one that the social scientist has collected himself or the library of the institution in which he works. Sometimes, if he is so fortunate as to live near one of the great public libraries, like those in New York, Chicago, and Washington, D.C., his search might begin there. The literature review is one of the few scientific methods that are absolutely indispensable in any scientific inquiry. No scientist can work without doing a review of all the material published on his subject.

What is this method? How do you carry it out? You begin with the library. Most colleges and universities give their students a guided tour through the library during freshman orientation or early in the first semester, and this tour generally includes a description of the main parts of the library and how they are used.

As a preliminary to a literature search, the first thing a historian must do is familiarize himself with the library resources readily available. Among the first things he will look for in the library are the card catalog, the reference room, collections of specialized or rare materials, and how periodicals are kept.

The first of these items, the card catalog, is the key to every library. Although most catalogs are arranged by author, title, and subject, they do vary, and it is essential for the researcher to understand fully the catalog's special features to make best use of it. The second thing most researchers want to know about—the reference room—is something that virtually every library has. These collections contain materials so frequently consulted that they should be available at all times—materials such as encyclopedias, bibliographies, dictionaries, and indexes

like the *Readers' Guide to Periodical Literature.* Familiarity
with the reference room can be a great time-saver because the
materials gathered there can quickly guide you to many of
the source materials you might be seeking. Third, because
many libraries do have specialized collections which may be
pertinent to his field, the researcher will want to be able to
make the best use of these collections by knowing their special fields, how they are organized, and if these collections
are cataloged in the main catalog or separately. Very often
there will be librarians particularly acquainted with the specialized collections who can offer personal help and advice
that might not be obtainable elsewhere. Lastly, because much
material in history and the social sciences, and in the physical
and natural sciences also, is to be found in periodicals, it is
essential to know how your library handles them. Most periodicals are in the form of magazines or journals, but there are
also many smaller newsletters and other regularly issued bul-
letins of importance. A large library may receive several thousand separate issues of them at any one time. Most libraries
keep at least the recent periodicals separately. Modern libraries keep much of this material on microfilm, and you will
want to know where this microfilm is located and how to use
the microfilm viewers.

Note-taking

Another essential, although prosaic and unromantic, scientific method is concerned with note-taking. This, too, is universal in science simply because no scientist can remember
every detail of what he reads and thinks about. It is therefore
essential that he keep some record of his own.

Scientific notes are of two main kinds, bibliographical and
content. Bibliographical notes give complete data about a
publication or other source. Content notes describe your own
thoughts or those of other authors. The scientist requires both
kinds. What is acceptable form for bibliographical notes depends to some extent on the discipline. They must all include
information about the author, the title of the work consulted,
the place of publication, the publisher, and the date. Notes

have one absolute requirement: any quotation of another's work must be exactly as it was published.

The key word in any discussion of a note-taking system is "system": the notes must be organized or classified in accordance with some recognizable plan or order. If information put on notes can easily be found and used, it satisfies the requirements of this scientific method.

Some scientists use notebooks for their notes, but most commonly scientists now use cards or half sheets of standard 8-½" x 11" paper. In setting up a note system, account must be taken of handwriting size and the average length of the note. A good rule here is to avoid small cards. The reason for the use of cards or half sheets of standard size paper is that they can easily be filed or arranged in different order. This is another reason why cards at least 4" x 6" in size are generally desirable. They are easier to handle. The exact size chosen is not so important as making sure that all notes are made on that size card or paper only.

The young scientist would do well to give some thought to this, for there are many cases on record where scientists have lost notes or have had to reestablish and redo substantial note files because they did not think about their future requirements.

The procedures of note-taking are important scientific methods. Without adequate notes no scientist could work with more materials than he could carry about in his head.

Verifying Materials

The rule for collecting materials in history, and science in general, is very simple. Collect everything that is of importance on your subject. Of course this is rarely possible, and most scientists modify the rule to read "collect everything that is available that is of importance to the subject." But this modification has an important consequence. If, while collecting his materials, a scientist finds that there is important work to which he does not have access and about which he cannot get records, he is likely to modify his problem or stop work on it entirely. The reason is simple. If the work seems to be of importance, and the scientist cannot know about it, his own work will of necessity be done in partial ignorance and could be wasted effort. Only very rarely will the scientist continue to work when he knows he is missing important information.

Every scientist must, after he has collected his materials, verify or authenticate them to be sure they are what they purport to be. Each discipline has developed techniques to do this. For instance, some of you may know about the famous Piltdown skull that was planted in England to deceive anthropologists about the evolutionary origin of man. It took almost twenty years to prove that the skull was a fake. And in history there are numerous examples of forgeries and other documents which are not what they seem to be. The main scientific methods used to verify documents are three: dating, author identification, and truth tests.

Dating. The date of a document or object must be determined as accurately as possible. The most important reason for this is that incorrect dating can exclude the document or object from the necessity of being considered as evidence or can cast doubt upon its reliability or usefulness. For example, if you read a translation of Aristotle with the words social science in it, you could be very suspicious of the translation, because the term social science was not commonly used until the late 1700s. It is very unlikely that Aristotle would have used any words that came close to modern meanings of social science. If a document is said to have been printed in Europe before the fifteenth century, you might be very suspicious because printing with movable type was unknown then. Or if a document written on paper in pencil was said to have been written before 1500, you might also be very suspicious because pencils were not used in Europe before that time. Most scientists need to know the date of the document in order to determine if it is the most recent material on the subject. It would do a modern social scientist little good to look up the term "behavioral science" in a dictionary that was printed as late as the 1940's, simply because the term was not widely used up to then.

Accurate dating, then, is required in order that we know

when a thing was made or an event occurred. For most modern scientific work, this job is done by the editors of books and journals and publications; nonetheless it is well not to lose sight of the necessity for an accurate determination in time.

Identifying the Author.   Another test for determining if a document reports reliable information is by identifying the author. Experienced scientists learn through their work which authors are likely to be reliable about what subjects. The young scientist who is not certain that the author is indeed an expert would do well to look him up in such reference books as *American Men of Science* or the various directories of the professional associations. Generally speaking, if the author is writing in the field in which he is recognized as an expert, and if, in fact, the author did write the document under discussion, one can trust the facts reported in the document.

Once again modern scientists are spared much labor because the editors of journals, particularly scholarly journals, closely investigate the authors whose works they print. When it comes to popular journals or books, however, it is not uncommon for experts in one field to write in another or even for amateurs to pose as experts. It is a good idea to be cautious of such sources and check their factual information closely. When you are not absolutely certain about a book check the reputation of the author and the work itself. This can be done quickly by reading reviews of the book in scholarly journals.

Testing for Truth.   With regard to his documents, a scientist is the judge, the jury, and the prosecutor all in one. He is interested only in the truth of the facts contained in the documents, and three truth tests have been devised that will tell much. Was the author of the document willing and able to tell the truth? Was the truth accurately reported? Were there independent witnesses to the facts reported in the documents? Generally speaking, a person is able to tell the truth to the extent that he was close to the event in time and space, able to understand what he was reporting, and interested in and attending to the event in question. In other words, the closer to and the more competent a person is about the event, the more likely he is to be reliable. But even if he is reliable, close to the event, and competent to tell the truth, he may not be willing to do so. Need for secrecy, propaganda, patriotism, egotism, ignorance about critical factors, singly or in combination, could make a person unwilling to report accurately about a given event. Generally, then, this rule of scientific method requires that we satisfy ourselves that the author of the document was able and willing to tell the truth.

Once we have satisfied ourselves that the author was able and willing to tell the truth, the next test is whether the event was accurately reported. In the case of the Bible, for instance, even if we assume that the authors of the books of the Old Testament were able and willing to tell the truth, they may have inaccurately reported certain events or, having accurately reported the events, had their report garbled in transmission. The possibilities of inaccuracy must be investigated.

The third truth test asks if there were independent witnesses. In the case of past events that occur only once, say a tidal wave or a revolution, one account is usually thought to be less reliable than several from individual witnesses. Truth is a matter of degree and perspective in many cases and particularly with regard to events in the past. The records of the past are obviously not the same as the unrecoverable fullness of the events.

The hoaxes, forgeries, lies, and simple ignorance that make people write false documents have made all scientists careful about dating, author identification, and truth tests in their documents. The historian, who works more with the past than the scientist, consequently must be more concerned with these tests. Today the documents of scholarly journals and books must pass these tests before they get into print. But many magazines and books are not written with such scientific standards, so all scientists, and particularly those working in the social sciences, must be very careful about the documents upon which they rely for information.

Primary and Secondary Sources

Scientists rely more on primary than secondary sources. A primary source of information is a record. This can be a person, for example, an eyewitness, or a thing, such as a movie film that was taken of the event in question. In other words, a primary source must be contemporary with the event. Primary sources can be of many kinds—documents, coins, bones, stone tools, reports, posters, letters, even works of fiction or songs and poetry. The primary source is the most desirable for direct study of the past. A secondary source of information is the report or interpretation of anyone or anything not present at the event being discussed. The work by a historian about a past event, for example, would be a secondary source about that event.

Secondary sources are of some use, particularly to the young scientist. By reading them he can understand and get the spirit of the times, get leads for his study, and see how others interpret the events. Generally speaking, the longer the time that has elapsed between the event and the secondary source about it, the more reliable the secondary source will be, simply because the accumulation of scholarship tends to add to our knowledge.

External and Internal Criticism

When a document or a record of any kind from the past is examined to see if it is authentic, historians call the process *external criticism.* We have already given the main methods and rules for this above, but to restate and summarize, external criticism asks questions such as: "Is this what it is supposed to be?" "When, where, and why was this written, and by whom?" This kind of criticism only satisfies the scientist about the trustworthiness or authoritativeness of the record. It says nothing about the importance of the record of evidence or its reliability.

Internal criticism asks: "*What does a document mean?*" "Does the record tell us anything besides what it seems to say?" In other words, can we read something between the lines? "What biases might have distorted the vision of the reporter?"

While all science uses the methods of external criticism largely developed by historians, historians borrow heavily from the other social sciences with regard to internal criticism. For example, in one type of analysis—judicial analysis—applied mainly to international laws, national laws, constitutions, and legal proceedings, the methods of the law, that is, legal reasoning, are used to test the documents being considered. Judicial analysis requires a specialized knowledge of law, both present and past, and a legal vocabulary. Another kind of analysis uses insights from psychology and sociology. The works of an author are examined not so much for what he says but for what he betrays about his feelings. Attempts are made to construct certain pictures of his personality from his work. Or in other cases using this analysis, attempts are made to determine the attitude and the opinions of people from the past even where they are not directly contained in the document.

Internal criticism is far more important for history and all the social sciences than for the other parts of science. Problems in the physical and biological sciences often can be formulated clearly without close attention to the past meanings of words and things. The language of the other sciences is more precise. As a result of these and other factors, physical and biological scientists, although they must use caution about the meaning of their records from the past, do not have the problems of precise determination of meanings that face the social scientists.

Change Over Time

Because the subjects of social science have been among the oldest concerns of man, almost every aspect of these subjects and of the problems that man faces have already been embodied in word meanings and common language sayings. The social scientist faces the difficulty of communicating precise knowledge about a subject that has already been much discussed in a language and words that convey many meanings besides those he wishes. The difficulty this imposes on scientific work has been remedied in the physical and biological sciences by the invention of a specialized vocabulary, as any student who has taken a biology or mathematics course already knows. The social scientist has not been completely able to follow this path. As a result, he must pay close attention to word meanings, making his task more difficult.

The rule that must be followed here is that every document and statement from the past must be understood in terms of the meanings given to it in the past. Take, for example, the simple word "family." Today in America most families live in the city. But this was not true fifty or one hundred years ago. Then when the word "family" was used, it referred to a farm family in an agrarian or rural setting. A family like this was very different from a city family of today. And how easy and tempting to assume that family relationships of today are those of the past; such is not the case. Husband and wife relationships, both sexual and occupational, were very different from those now. Children's relationships to their parents and schools were very different. Old folks generally were taken care of by the young folks in close proximity. Then almost every aspect of what the word "family" meant was very different from its meaning now. And so social scientists must follow the rule of determining precisely what the terms from the past meant to the authors who used them.

Some Other Methods

Some social scientists have, for many reasons, adopted inadequate or nonscientific methods, and the discipline of history furnishes us clear warnings about some of these methods. When selecting facts from the past to make judgments about it, you must be careful not to be biased in your choice. It can happen that today's politicians and others who pronounce on social issues make their selections in terms of absolutes—but science does not. Social science does not rest upon absolutes. Even those implied in the scientific system of beliefs are subject to change. The word "cause" should be used carefully. It is almost always misleading, particularly if only one or a first or single cause is implied. Scientific history recognizes very few cases where important events are the result of a single, first, or only cause. The words "proof" and "laws" should also be avoided in history. Scientists reserve the word "proof" for a special or logical case. And no modern historian thinks that history repeats itself in such a fashion as to provide "laws" for the guidance of man.

We have not given all the methods of history. Those we have selected are useful in almost all of the social sciences. Each of the disciplines of science uses a combination of methods appropriate for its subject. History has an arsenal of methods and auxiliary sciences that have helped man to learn and understand much about his past. The methods of numismatics, the study of coins, enable the historian to date certain artifacts, explain what their inscriptions mean, and evaluate economic conditions of the past. The methods of heraldry and genealogy have been important in determining population growth and emigration. The methods of paleography, the study of ancient writing, have enabled historians to decipher writings of entire civilizations that had been previously known only through artifacts. And the list could be extended, as any book on the methods of history would illustrate. These are methods useful mainly to history and only incidentally and secondarily to other scientists. The methods that we have described in this chapter are those that historians and all scientists use.

Finally, historians almost always pay close attention to the literary form and artistic presentation of their results; clear and graceful writing is one of the most prized of the historian's tools. Most other parts of science do not regard writing in this light, as you will see when you begin your reading in scholarly journals. Many scientists assume that the content of their writings is what counts, not the interest, clarity, vocabulary, or sometimes even elementary grammatical usage. As a group, the historians present their work in literary and human terms that other scientists might well copy.

Chapter 6

Sociology—
Observation and Description
in the Study of People

WHAT IS SOCIOLOGY?

Sociology is one of the disciplines of social science. As you know by now, these disciplines, although each very distinctive, also are closely related to each other by their central concern—man. In defining a discipline of social science, therefore, one seeks not for rigid boundary lines but rather for distinctive characteristics. At their boundaries and often for a significant distance toward their centers, the social sciences overlap and share common concerns. One useful way to understand sociology is by knowing its background.

The Background of Sociology

Auguste Comte, a French philosopher of the nineteenth century, coined the term "sociology" as part of his work in proposing a reclassification and rearrangement of science. His life's work was directed toward a scientific reconstruction of society, to which his sociology was fundamental. Comte felt that the facts of human existence—social facts—were more important than philosophical speculation about these facts, and he felt that the use of method in investigating these facts would show that society and social phenomena were subject to general laws. Thus knowledge could be obtained by the four methods of observation, experiment, comparison, and historical research.

Herbert Spencer, a nineteenth-century Englishman, published in 1877 a work entitled *Principles of Sociology*, heavily influenced by Charles Darwin's theory of evolution, where he tried to develop basic laws for all reality of which the laws of sociology were but one part. Spencer differed from Comte in that Comte tried to define the relationships between man and society in terms of social organization, cooperation, association, and status, while Spencer thought about man and society more in terms of competition and a rather extreme version of individualism. Spencer's ideas about evolution led him to think that society should not interfere with what men do, that competition will produce the best results for man and society. Comte was a social reformer, while Spencer was an individualist.

One of the first Europeans whose work was to influence sociology in this country was Emile Durkheim, whose work at the turn of the last century was deeply concerned with the problems of method. He insisted that a social fact (such as suicide rates, which formed the basis of one of his greatest studies) should be studied objectively and carefully, with a view toward duplication, and he thought about these social facts and social institutions in terms of their relationship to human behavior.

Another important figure for American sociology was the

German scholar Max Weber, who in the first two decades of this century made valuable contributions to the sociology of religion, to general economic history, and to methodology. He studied methodology from a point of view he called *verstehen*, which in German means "understanding." He thought plausible explanations of social phenomena could be arrived at through comprehension of social events. He was also much concerned with the problems of values in social science and attempted with his method to analyze specific social institutions.

Today the sociologist studies man in society, and much attention usually is paid to the elementary or primary units of social life: the family, ethnic and class groups, urban, suburban, and rural communities, population, associations and organizations, the relationship of an individual's personality to his group and culture, and individual behavior and social acts in social relationships. Also studied are basic social institutions, such as the family and other kinship relationships and economic relationships. For example, how does an assembly-line worker look at his job, relate to his fellow workers, feel about his family? Religious institutions are important, and sociologists have studied questions such as how being a Catholic affects fertility rates or voting behavior. All of the institutions that make up the web around an individual's life are studied—recreational, welfare, educational, political, legal, and scientific.

SOME ELEMENTS OF SOCIOLOGY

Sociologists have been in the forefront in using observation and description as part of social science. This chapter discusses the methods sociologists have developed, useful in all of the social sciences, for social description and observation. Other disciplines of the social sciences, as well, have contributed to the methods of observation and description that are now common to social science. However, sociologists did much of the fundamental work and, as is true of all of science, they used whatever methods were useful, no matter from what discipline or part of science these methods came.

Observation and Description

Observation and description are important to the scientific system of inquiry, both by themselves and as bases for the other parts of the system. Scientists must keep in mind that their observations and descriptions, to be useful, must be communicated to others.

Observation, correctly, is a matter of identification and classification. As an observer the social scientist must concentrate on well-specified and very particular situations, processes, and events. He works with living people, sometimes, as you will see, on the outside looking in, but sometimes as a participant in the groups which he observes. He attempts to establish true statements about particular events. As a social scientist, he will go beyond this to explain, control, and predict as he develops a theory. The first step of any scientist is to establish true statements about the reality he is studying—and this requires observation and description.

So far in this section we have referred to one facet of the process of observation and description, namely the event that has happened. But there is another facet that is at least as important, and that is the question of how the event is known. Think for a moment of what you know about physical science. Suppose it is reported that the temperature at which ice turns into water is 32°F. That is a simple report which happens to be true. Why do we accept it as true? We do so because scientists who have studied the matter know exactly the way in which the truth of the statement was established. They know what water is, what ice is, and all about sensitive thermometers for measuring temperatures. No science can grow only on the basis of statements, even those that happen to be true. Observation is not enough unless it is also known how the observation was made. No scientist trusts a test that cannot be duplicated. The second facet of scientific observation and description emphasizes not the event itself, but the methods used in the observation which in turn will be the basis of the subsequent description. It also directs attention to the role of the observer—a role of great importance in the

..ial sciences, which do not use instrumentation to the same ..tent as the physical and biological sciences.

Every good description must include, if it is to be of any use, an additional discussion of the way the observations were made, so that the experiment can be duplicated or evaluated. Fortunately the literature of social science is full of descriptions by social scientists of the way they made their observations. Such descriptions are not only interesting to laymen; they are absolutely essential to other scientists so they, in turn, can evaluate the original observations.

Every definition, every term, every name used in a report of an observation only makes sense with reference to a class of other terms, names, and definitions. This is inherent in the very structure of our thought and language. The problem for the social scientist as an observer is not to let these other classes or categories obscure the uniqueness of his observation, while at the same time he must use language which makes order out of the vast number of facts surrounding the event. In using existing classifications, terms, and definitions, social scientists must keep in mind that however useful they might be for certain problems, for many others they will not be suitable. Classifications, terms, and definitions are themselves objects of investigation and inquiry.

Ethical Problems of Observation and Description

Social facts are made by individuals, each of whom lives in his own world of personal problems, values, and other constraints. Very often the facts a social scientist wants could be embarrassing or harmful to the person or group providing these facts. A special ethical problem is thereby raised for the social scientist. He must not, in his role as a social scientist, say or do anything that is harmful to the people or groups he is studying. But what might you say of a case of a secret group devoted to harming society? The scientist would be justified in publicizing personal information in order to bring discredit upon the society? The answer is no. As a social scientist he has the right and duty to observe, describe, and report every fact that he thinks is relevant to his problem, but he is under an obligation as a scientist not to disclose any information he may discover that is not relevant to his scientific purposes. There are three rules that social scientists follow with regard to the ethical problems of observation and reporting.

Don't Violate Confidences. The basic reason for this rule is that a social scientist as a decent human being would never violate a confidence under any conditions. And there are practical reasons too. Violations of confidential information will almost always be found out and that source of information dried up. Social science investigators are very scrupulous about this rule. This is why you find books and studies labeled *Elmtown's Youth* or *Yankee City* or *Plainville, U.S.A.* Social scientists usually change the names of the persons and places they study. They take great pains to prevent identification of their subjects even by those familiar with the subjects. They are careful never to describe any marked peculiarity of the person or place being investigated in such a way that identification would be possible.

But, you may object, does this not conflict with the requirement that others be able to check upon the scientist's findings? The answer is yes—sometimes. In almost every case where this problem has arisen the social scientists who did the original study have allowed other qualified observers to know the identity of the place or group studied. This serves the purposes of science. In other cases, such as studies like the Kinsey Reports on the sexual behavior of Americans, no useful purpose would be served by releasing the personal identities of those whose sexual behavior was reported upon. The reason for the qualified "yes" is that it has sometimes happened that the confidences are of such a nature that the original observer simply cannot violate them. Then social science loses; others cannot check upon the work, which is therefore rendered less valuable. However, social scientists are willing to take the chance of a very occasional loss in advancing their science rather than harm their integrity as scientists and human beings.

Don't Hurt People.   Never use anything to the disadvantage of a person or group. This rule is closely akin to the one given above, but it covers explicitly the fact that social scientists never use their information to harm others.

Do unto Others.   Do unto others as you would have them do unto you. When ethical problems arise that are not covered by the previous two rules, social scientists fall back upon a third more general rule. This rule is not as useful for the simple reason that only very infrequently is a social scientist as debased as the soldier who neither asks nor gives quarter. In other words, some social scientists expect themselves to be badly treated and may also treat others badly. For most people, however, this rule will pretty well cover any cases that the first two do not.

Observation and Description and Other Methods

Science is built upon facts, which in social science are about people. The methods by which we obtain these facts determine to a large extent just how reliable and useful they are. If proper methods are used in observation, chances are much better that science can develop as a result. The untrained observer can make very little sense of what he sees or otherwise perceives. A layman, for example, may not be able to diagnose a pain in his side as appendicitis. This example illustrates that an untrained observer, even though he be directly affected and on the spot, may often not know what to look for, or he may not be able to make the proper connections and deductions about what he is observing. The example also illustrates that we must combine the methods of observation and description with other methods, in this case explanation, to acquire real knowledge.

GATHERING DATA FROM HUMAN BEINGS

A social fact is a way of human behavior, and a statement about it can take many forms. By thinking of social facts as specifics the social scientist puts himself in a frame of mind which enables him to group the phenomena, define the characteristics, and isolate appropriate characteristics for further study. He is then able to achieve a high degree of objectivity and detachment.

The three basic steps in actually gathering social facts are planning, performing, and reporting. Each of these processes has methods developed by social scientists.

Planning

A plan is a series of related statements about what the social scientist expects to do in the future. The first set of statements must be about purposes or goals. We shall illustrate each method of gathering social facts by means of one example. Let us assume that we are interested in gathering some of the facts necessary to provide the members of a trade union with a clinic that will serve their mental health needs. Rule one in beginning to search for social facts is to define the objectives. At the beginning of an inquiry this sometimes cannot be done precisely, but a start must be made. Given the purpose of our example, certain facts are immediately required. How many people are there in the trade union? What are their ages and sex? Will their dependents be covered? We also have to know the incidence of mental illness expected to be in a group such as this in order to determine the size of the clinic necessary. And we have to know the attitudes of the workers towards such a clinic. Will they use it? What does the union mean to them with regard to mental health? Would they, for instance, not want the union to know if they or their dependents had mental health problems? Very often objectives can be defined in terms of answers to questions.

The next step is to be sure that none of the desired facts are already available. Perhaps the union members are already covered by a health plan which, although omitting mental health care, lists the age, sex, and number of dependents of the workers to be covered. Perhaps others have made studies on workers' attitudes toward mental health. For each of the questions as defined by the objectives a thorough search of the literature, as described in the section on literature review in the chapter on historical method, is necessary. In addition, specific records of various kinds with regard to the person or group being studied must be carefully examined. Very often much time and effort can be saved by careful planning. As the social scientist defines his objectives and reviews the literature, he learns more about what is relevant to his plan and can then further refine his objectives.

A social scientist carefully redefines his objectives as he learns more about what he needs to know, but he must also consider what he does not need to know. Suppose he found that for some reason the union kept exact records of the height of all its members. The social scientist would ask himself how relevant this would be to planning a mental health clinic. Probably the relevance of this set of facts would be so slight as to not make it worth recording. On the other hand he may discover, as he reviews the literature, that the racial composition of the union members is of great importance potentially because different racial and ethnic groups have different attitudes toward the treatment of mental illness. If this is the case, the social scientist would then add that item to his list of what he needs to know.

Once he has a fairly precise statement of research aims and objectives, he probably will also have to consider his general theoretical orientation or approach. In this case it would mean thinking about mental illness and the way it could be treated. With these things well in mind, the next step involved is thinking about the practical preparations.

What Must Be Considered?

Budget.   One of the most important practical considerations in planning to get social facts is financial. How much money is available? From whom? Lack of funds is the great constraint that holds back social science research. A multitude of other practical decisions depends upon the finances available. How large will the staff be? Can we afford the fifty dollars or so it might take to interview each individual member of the union, or do we only have the fifty cents it will require to mail them a questionnaire? But what if we only have the fifty cents per member and many of them cannot read or write? Then what do we do? It almost never happens that social scientists have a blank check and unlimited time in which to find the facts they need to know. Therefore, at the planning stage, and as a great aid in making practical preparations, a detailed budget should be worked out. Not every cent of the available funds should be budgeted, for it almost always happens that something unforeseen arises, or costs go up, which increases the amount of money needed in some part of the operation. Therefore some funds should be left aside to meet such contingencies.

Another widely used method in making practical preparations is to draw up a timetable along with the budget. On the timetable, or as supplements to it, are listed what each staff member will be doing at what time while the project is going on. The timetable should also include what results are expected when. And, of course, arrangements must be made for staff space and for the use of equipment—perhaps typewriters, mimeograph machines, and, increasingly, computer time (although we usually cannot use a computer unless we have a programmer).

Sample Selection. Another important step in early planning is to decide exactly with what group we intend to deal. The term sociologists use to include all the people in the group about which they wish to obtain information is the *population.* An individual within the population is called a *subject.* The group of people that will be selected out of the population for actual study is called the *sample.* Planning must specify the population very precisely. In our example it might be all the paid-up union members as of a given date. Generally constraints of time and money do not allow a one hundred percent sample to be investigated. Fortunately it often happens that this is not necessary. The size of the sample that requires investigation is a function of the size of the population and the accuracy of the knowledge that is required. Assume for the moment that one doctor can take care of the mental health problems of two hundred people. If the clinic had one doctor and the union had only one hundred people then we would only have to make sure that the members of this union were not more than twice as sick as the rest of the people in the country. On the other hand, if the union had ten thousand people and only two percent of them were ill, one doctor would be busy full-time. As you study more statistics you will find very precise ways of measuring the confidence with which you can accept the results and of determining sample sizes while at the same time getting results as reliable as you want them. The point to keep in mind now is that decisions about the population must be made early in the planning process.

Role of the Social Scientist.   Assume for the moment that all the members of the union are black. Would it be likely that white investigators could get truthful responses? Or would black investigators be better? Would all males talk freely to young females about their mental health problems? The role of the social scientist in gathering data is crucial. If the social scientist does not establish rapport, some kind of link or ties that enables free communication between those whom he is observing and himself, he is not likely to learn much. One of the first things the social scientist will have to do is to "learn the language." Sometimes, as when studying Puerto Ricans, he will actually have to learn a new language. Almost every group has its own list of special words and meanings which, if the social scientist is to understand that group, he must learn.

Another important thing that will have to be planned for is the status of the observer. By status we refer to the position that a person occupies in a group. For example, if the social scientist were introduced to the union workers by the boss he might risk not being accepted by the workers at all. If, on the other hand, he were introduced to the workers at a union meeting he might have a better chance of effectively communicating with the workers. No matter how he is introduced, however, any newcomer to a group is identified as just that, a newcomer, an outsider, a stranger. Attitudes expressed to such a person, especially on a topic as touchy as mental health, are likely to be quite different from those expressed to a member of the group that is already well accepted. Planning must also consider how the status relationships between the population and the scientist might be altered if that is necessary to get the desired information. One technique for obtaining social facts is that called *participant-observer*. When this method is used the social scientist who is the observer actually joins the group and participates in it. In the case of our example it might mean that a social scientist would join the union and take a job for a period of time working right along with the union members. If this is not possible and the social scientist must act as an observer from outside the group, he must take great care to understand what effect he thinks his presence has on the activities of the group. Planning then must consider the role of the observer, what it is likely to be at the beginning, how it will be likely to affect the data he gathers, and how to change the rules if necessary.

How Data Are Gathered

The next step in the planning process relates to how the data will be gathered. Some might come from the literature review. The census may contain information about the members of the union and many of their characteristics. Or perhaps the union members all live close together. Then, by using information obtained from census tracts, much could be learned about the population simply by writing to Washington, D.C., and paying the Bureau of the Census to gather the desired information. Most commonly, however, schedules, interviews, and tests are required to get the facts needed.

Schedules.   A schedule is simply a listing of related information. Think of a plane schedule. Assume you have the schedule for one airline and want to go from Los Angeles to New York. The schedule gives you the times the airplanes arrive and depart from both of those places. Thus, knowing where you want to go and approximately when, you can, by looking at the schedule, find out your times of departure and arrival. In our example, a schedule that would be useful would be a listing of all the names of the union members and their sex and age—related information about our subject. An experienced researcher uses every bit of knowledge he has. For example, sometimes a simple listing of names can tell a social scientist much. Let us assume that the place is Pittsburgh and the list of names is almost all Polish. The social scientist might guess that the religion of most of the people was Roman Catholic. Knowing this he might be able to deduce or get other hunches about their attitudes.

The information for some schedules might be easy to obtain from existing records. If the proposed clinic, however, is to treat not only the workers but also their dependents, we will need an additional schedule giving the number of these preferably by age and sex, because the incidence of mental illness and its type varies with age and sex. This might be much harder to obtain from union records and might involve the preparation of a questionnaire to be filled out by all union members. The design of proper questionnaires is itself an important task. They should be designed so that the results are easy to tally and, if the computer is to be used, so that the key-punch operator can punch the cards that feed the computer directly from the returned questionnaire rather than having to fill out an intermediate form.

Pilot Runs.   Another rule for preparing schedules and questionnaires is that it is best to prepare pilot runs. By a pilot run we mean working with just a few subjects. The proposed questionnaire should be tested on a small number of what are assumed to be typical subjects. Then the analysis is carried out just the way it will be later. Almost always the pilot run indicates ways of improving questionnaires and schedules. The most common problems are language ambiguities and questions that are confusing. A good questionnaire should be as simple and as brief as possible to get the information desired. Each question should be worded so that it can be interpreted in one way only.

The pilot run may also disclose that you are asking people about things they do not understand. For instance, suppose a questionnaire in our example asked the workers "what is the incidence of schizophrenia in your family?" The pilot run would certainly show that very few workers understood the question, and perhaps that even those who did understand would be unwilling to answer honestly.

Questionnaires and Tests. Sociologists often use the words "questionnaire" and "tests" almost interchangeably. Usually the word "test" is reserved for some instrument given to a subject which forces him to make a choice; and the pattern of choices he makes will then reveal something about him that was not apparent before or could not be obtained simply by asking him, as for example various tests of attitudes. The term "questionnaire" is most often used with regard to an instrument to which the subject responds by giving answers over a broader range than a test allows. A questionnaire will elicit information of a kind that can be obtained by allowing the subject to answer in a way that is not "right" or "wrong." For example, all the phrases below are commonly used attitude answers on a questionnaire: "strongly agree," "moderately agree," "neutral," "moderately disagree," "strongly disagree." In designing questionnaires and tests, close attention must be paid to how they will be scored, especially if it is desired to quantify the results. Following our example, we may wish to design a questionnaire which inquires into the attitudes of workers toward mental illness, probing to see if they would utilize the services of a doctor when they had mental problems. When social scientists have to deal with sensitive areas they often try to design their questionnaires so that the subject is able to reveal what he really feels without directly telling something that he may be reluctant to talk about. For example, the questionnaire might ask something like this: "How do you think the average member of your union feels about using a mental health clinic?" Very often people will reveal what they think about a subject when asked what others like themselves think.

Interviewing. An interview is a face to face meeting between the social scientist and the person or persons about whom he is gathering data. It is a successful and widely used technique.

If an interview is to be more than a "bull session," a social scientist must follow given rules very closely. Otherwise he will get common sense knowledge that he could get from any member of the group. In every case the social scientist specifies the method he uses so other social scientists can tell whether he is recording simply common sense, "baloney," or information structured well enough to provide more reliable kinds of knowledge. Among the things that must be planned for in interviewing are the methods of selecting those persons to be interviewed, usually by sampling procedures, methods of establishing contact with the subjects and group to be studied, how to identify relevant subjects for an interview, how to build desirable social relationships, how to avoid either blocking or becoming too involved with subjects, and how to check findings and reward informants. Methods have been devised for group and individual interviewing of different kinds. For example, some interviews are question-and-answer; some are nondirective, during which the subject is allowed to speak very freely about almost any subject he wishes; and sometimes interviewers use schedules or outlines of topics about which they wish to learn.

Interviewing is a social process, typically used for obtaining an even wider range of responses from a subject than either a test or a questionnaire can provide. It is particularly valuable when little is known about a subject. The kind of information it produces is broader, richer, and deeper than that obtained by tests. But the very virtues point to its defects. Precisely because it is less structured, precisely because it is modified by common sense interpretations, materials obtained from an interview often lack reliability. In our example, a social scientist would probably use a few interviews before he even began to draw up schedules or tests or questionnaires. He might use them again after the pilot run showed some things that went wrong. And he might use them still later if the results of the questionnaires, tests, and schedules were surprising. Interviews are widely used in dealing with personal problems as well as when new studies are undertaken.

Recording. The planning phase must also consider how the data will be recorded. What methods of note-taking will be used? Should every word be taken down by a tape recorder, or should the interviewer memorize an interview and questionnaire schedule and just jot down little coded notes indicating the answers to them? Should an interviewer write up the interview after he makes it? Most social scientists keep diaries and journals while they are searching after facts. And nowadays there are many ways to use modern recording techniques from "bugs" of various kinds to one-way mirrors or closed-circuit TV or movie equipment. Planning must take into account how the material will be recorded.

Performance

No matter how well planned, social science always involves differences between the planning and the performance. It would be easy if one could just say, "Carry out the plan." But that happy circumstance occurs so rarely that a special set of methods has been added for the performance part of the fact-gathering operation.

One set of records that is almost always required is statements about what the social scientist actually does as he gathers the facts. When he can do exactly what the planning called for, that is fine and rare luck. Because this almost never happens, it is very important to know what the activities and experience of the social scientist are as he adapts to unplanned-for situations. If his adaptation results only in common sense knowledge, that is far less desirable and valuable than if he can face a new situation with well-established methods.

Particularly important here are records of the feelings, emotions, and reactions of the social scientist to the groups, persons, and situations he faces. These records of reactions are needed in order to cope with any possibilities of bias on the part of the observer. Perhaps the social scientist is so upset that he cannot pay attention. Or perhaps he is so opinionated about one viewpoint that he shuts his subjects off when they try to give him another. A good set of records about what the social scientist in the field actually did includes how he conceptualized his own role as well as the role of others. Knowing what role he took—that of a complete participant, that of a participant as an observer, that of an observer as a participant, or simply that of a complete observer—can tell other social scientists much about the usefulness of the information he obtained.

For the rest, doing the research simply means sticking as closely as possible to the plan, and when departures are necessary recording these departures and substituting for them other reliable methods.

Reporting Results

The last stage in fact-gathering is reporting results, the importance of which has already been stressed. The final report, the record of observation and description, should contain at least the following:

1. A general statement of purpose and goals.
2. A specific statement of objectives.
3. By whom and for whom the facts were gathered.
4. When the facts were gathered.
5. The facts themselves, that is the observation and description.
6. Details of how the facts were gathered.
7. Explanation of why the facts were gathered as they were.
8. Statistical details including the size of the population and the sampling procedures used.
9. Descriptions of the staff.
10. Descriptions of how the staff themselves and their findings were checked upon.
11. As appendices or addenda, copies of all the questionnaires, schedules, tests, and the like that were used.
12. The budget.

Obtaining social science facts is demanding, expensive, and time-consuming work. That is probably why we have so few reliable facts in social science. How simple it is to know about physical things by comparison. The United States government has kept track of every barrel of salt herring that has come into Boston for almost two hundred years. But we have unemployment figures for only about thirty years. And the congressmen who authorize expenditures for the Census Bureau will not usually allow any questions that reveal the extent of social problems like racial discrimination. Gathering facts requires that the social scientist get out into the field and work with people. How much easier it is to sit in a library or a university office and pore over other people's reports. Of course armchair analysis and synthesis is necessary. But the foundation of social science is social fact and no man can call himself a social scientist until he has at least attempted scientifically to gather social facts.

Chapter 7

Geography and Methods of Measurement

WHAT IS GEOGRAPHY?

Each of the disciplines of social science is concerned with some fundamental aspect of man's
existence. History studies man in time; geography
studies him in space. Space is fundamental to man.
He occupies it, lives within it, and measurement of
it has always been one of his concerns. Geography
has contributed to modern science in a special way.
One of the earliest social science disciplines to be
concerned with measurement, it developed approaches and methods in measurement that have
been found useful by many of the others.

Five Kinds of Geographical Inquiry

Geography as a discipline of scientific study has been subdivided in many different ways. Geographers do not agree about how this should be done, but much of the unity enjoyed by geographers comes from the study of and emphasis upon five different areas of geographical inquiry.

One of the most frequent questions asked is "What are the relationships between man and his environment?" Nongeographers have speculated that climate determines laziness or hard work. Some people have even thought that proximity to water automatically makes sailors! *Natural or ecological geography,* as it is sometimes called, *emphasizes relationships between man and his physical environment.*

Another area of inquiry that has interested geographers for a long time concerns the arrangement and functioning of the various physical parts of the earth. Why do rivers flow north in the northern half of the northern hemisphere? And why do they flow south in the southern half? What kinds of soils are needed to make a forest of coconut trees rather than oaks? How rapidly is the ocean eroding our shoreline? The focus of *physical geography* is on *how the various features of the earth affect one another.*

Regional geography is of growing importance. To a geographer a region is a concept, a part of the earth identified by selecting certain features that are of interest to him. A region, in other words, is a way of *dividing up the earth according to specific features.*

A fourth kind of geographical inquiry focuses on the question "Why are things arranged as they are?" Chicago, for example, is the transportation hub of the United States. Is there any reason that it should be the center of inland water transportation? Or that every railroad in the country should have a terminal there? That its airport, O'Hare, should be the world's busiest? A *focus on questions about the "why" of spatial arrangement* is called *spatial geography, emphasizing location theory.*

The fifth kind of inquiry is called *political geography.* It investigates questions of *how political systems impose themselves on the earth*. The earth is divided into political units, each having a more or less permanent population. By studying these units, geographers have contributed much to our knowledge, as in studies of trade patterns, languages or dialects, and the ratio of productive agricultural land to total population.

In the course of his career, a professional geographer is likely to work with all five kinds of inquiries or centers of intellectual focus.

What Geographers Study

Another way to understand what geography is about is to examine subjects that interest geographers. Here are some:

> Historical geography.
>
> Geographic study of population.
>
> Settlement geography.
>
> Changes through time—for example, the development of land forms.
>
> Population: its location, density, numbers, occupation, age, sex, structure.
>
> Settlements: the occupation of pioneer areas, patterns, and colonization.
>
> Cities and urban centers: patterns of streets and transportation, role of the city in the economy of the area, the city's growth or decline, size, and land uses.
>
> Resources: their location, development, and combination—for example, iron ore must be able to be combined cheaply with coke and limestone to make steel.
>
> Economics: the processes by which people use geographical resources to make a living, markets, production and distribution.
>
> Recreation: the forms of tourism, park use, climate, fishing, skiing.
>
> Agriculture: soil types, climate-crop distributions, land uses—for example, forests or livestock.
>
> Mining: distribution and development of minerals production.

The above list could be extended. No matter what their topic, geographers seek to relate the forms and patterns of earth's features and men's activities to each other. Thus, if they study manufacturing, they determine its distribution, location, relationships to resources and markets. If they study transportation, they want to know what is moved, how much, and how far.

The study of geography teaches us about the differences and similarities of different parts of our planet. The study of climate, soil, water, plants, and animals is important to geography. Medical geography, which studies the diagnosis, treatment, control, and eradication of disease as part of the complex phenomena of place, is a good example of how physical factors like barometric pressure and radiation combine with biological elements like vegetable or parasitic life to influence our health. No matter what the topic, geographers focus on the place.

Man and Nature

The study of geography involves the study of man and the special and distinctive aspects of his place or how he occupies the earth. It entails a collection of facts about rivers, cities, and exports and imports, and sometimes is taught as though it consisted only of a list of descriptive facts about an area, such as the rain forests of Brazil.

Geographers also try to relate natural conditions—bodies of water, climate, and soils—to the human beings occupying a specific area. Being social scientists, geographers know that these conditions do not determine or dominate social or individual actions, except in extreme instances.

Man and "nature" cannot be sharply separated for geographical purposes. The "natural" environment—animal and vegetable life, soils, and climate—are all subject to modification by man. Man can wear out the soil, kill the bison, pollute the water, dam the rivers, drain the lakes. He can even change the climate to some extent. The focus of geography is on how the forces of "nature" and man interact to create the physical environment that exists at any moment.

By now it should be clear that geographers are not concerned solely with boundaries, coast lines, and other material phenomena. The study of geography emphasizes the way men occupy the earth and how they organize their activities spatially. Geographers assume that our ties to the earth are in some fundamental way related to our behavior. They try to find out about these relationships.

Geographers have developed the map, a special record of measurements obtained by observation, to a high degree of usefulness. It is a tool used by all social scientists, not only geographers. Like any record of data, it stores knowledge which can then be used for many purposes—for suggestions as to further hypotheses and problem formulation, and as the basis for future observation, exploration, prediction, and control.

Now consider what a map is in a broader sense. It is a representation of something else—usually a place. Representations of other real things are called models. For example, a paper airplane is a model of one kind, as is a toy car. So is a blueprint. We can also have a three-dimensional model of an enzyme or chemical. A picture of a dog is a model of another kind. Social scientists do not use "model" to refer to an ideal-type like President Lincoln. For a social scientist a model is a physical or symbolic representation of something else. In the models mentioned above, there were represented an airplane, a car, a country or other place, a chemical, a building, and an animal. In each case, the model was not the complete thing, but instead certain characteristics of it were represented. The paper airplane, for example, has the central characteristics of being able to fly, having wings, but without the engine, wheels, etc. The picture of the dog shows how he looks but not his behavior, weight, etc. When models are used in social science they must be carefully chosen with respect to the characteristics they will represent.

For example, consider *scale*. Almost every model is smaller than the real thing. This is one of the great advantages of any model—that it can be made of the same materials or be different from the real thing, its parts can be selected according to any quality one desires; form, function, process, **number**, etc. All sciences use models because they are convenient ways to represent, think about and manipulate important characteristics of the things being studied. When mathematical relationships hold for the real thing, the resulting system of **equations** is called a mathematical model.

Fundamental to the making and use of such models as maps, indeed to all of science, is measurement, the understanding of which is necessary for every geographer as well as **every** social scientist.

DESCRIPTION BY MEASUREMENT

Measurement is description in terms of numbers. The numbers, in their turn, are related to units. Description can be very specific and precise, or very general, or somewhere in between. Measurement, too, can range from precise to general. All measuring is a process of assigning numbers to things in order to represent certain relationships between them.

What Are Numbers?

The concept of number is primitive and very basic. We all have long had the idea of 1, 2, 3, etc. These are called the counting numbers; the rules of arithmetic tell how they can be added, subtracted, multiplied and divided. For measurement in social science, it suffices to remember two more things about counting numbers. First, there is an equal "space" between consecutive numbers—for example, the distance between 1 and 2 is the same as the distance between 101 and 102. This is called the equal interval quality of numbers. Second, the numbers "begin" at 0 and go up. The place where numbers begin is called the zero point.

The Four Scientific Measurements

Science uses four different kinds of measurements, depending upon the purposes and objects of the measurement. Each of these four different kinds of measurement follows different rules of assigning numbers to things, and they are illustrated below by examples from geography and maps.

Nominal Measurement. In this kind of measurement, the numbers are used only to label things. For example most Americans have social security numbers. The rule for assigning these numbers to people is that every person must receive a different one. Telephone numbers are another example of nominal scales. Every telephone must have a different number. In geography, nominal scales are often used to identify maps of parts of areas or to identify any other characteristic of an area.

The assignment of numbers for the purpose of distinguishing one thing or person from another is a convenient practice that allows us to quickly identify what we are seeking. Without nominal measurement we could hardly tell one player from another at the ball game, even with a program. Nominal measurement is extremely simple as it requires merely that every object or person have a different number. For nominal measurement we must be able to determine equality, the sameness of things. The same things receive the same number, while other things unequal or not the same receive different numbers.

Ordinal measurement. Ordinal measurement requires that every instance of the characteristics being measured be put in order; in other words, we rank them. Comparing things will tell us where to rank them. Suppose we wish to measure loudness as human beings hear it. Comparing Noise A and Noise B, the scientist asks "Which was louder, Noise A or Noise B?" The subject being tested replies, "Noise A." Then the ordinal scale is Noise B—Noise A, going from quieter to louder. A whole series of noises could thus be ranked in order of loudness. In four tests, the results might be Noise C, Noise A, Noise B, Noise D. Economists use ordinal measurements in their determination of the satisfaction individuals get from consuming different things. In geography, ordinal measurements are often used to indicate relative size on maps. One can judge relative sizes with the eye and thus rank or order such things as lengths of rivers, areas, and other characteristics being mapped.

Almost every social science discipline uses rank-ordering or ordinal measurement. In addition to the examples given, sociologists and psychologists often use this kind of measurement when they compare attitudes, values, or emotions.

Interval Measurement.   Intervals refer to the distance between two points. In science an interval scale is constructed by following the rule that the difference between the counting numbers corresponds to differences between characteristics of the object being measured.

A ruler laid across a map of the United States with a scale of 1 inch to 100 miles will show a distance of 100 miles for every inch on the ruler. Interval measurements can be understood in another way, using the thermometer as an example. Each degree corresponds to the same difference in temperature, no matter how low or high, above absolute zero. Notice how different this kind of measurement is from that of simply assigning numbers to baseball players or ranking persons in order of their wealth. Some people mistakenly assume that nominal and ordinal measurements are not "real" measurements.

All of the social sciences use interval measurements whenever time or distance is involved. Interval scales, as the examples here show, do not have a *zero point* (see p. 114). When interval scales can be established, they are very useful because we can be reasonably sure that differences in numbers accurately reflect differences in what is being measured.

Ratio Measurements.   In many ways ratio measurements are the most useful and sophisticated. The rule is that equal ratios must have equal numbers. Thus, ratio measurement requires the same rules as nominal, ordinal, and interval measurement, as well as requiring zero points.

The most fundamental ratio scales are those of the numbers themselves. If scientists know enough about what they are measuring to be sure that they correspond closely to the counting numbers, then a ratio scale is possible. However, even in physics there are few qualities that have all the characteristics of numbers. Length, mass, and electrical resistance are examples. In social science certain human physical characteristics have the characteristics of numbers. When these are to be measured, social scientists can use a ratio scale.

Geography can use ratio scales in all distance measurements. It is possible to project the earth in many different ways, for many purposes. Other social sciences which use ratio scales are economics, when price is discussed, and sociology, when population is measured. Ratio measurements lend themselves to very sophisticated mathematical treatment because they follow all the arithmetic rules. The other kinds of measurement do not follow all these rules.

Zero Points—The Basis of Ratio Measurements. How would you locate two points on a ball? You could measure the distance between them, but this knowledge would not be enough to find the points again or to help you tell someone else where they could be found. In order to describe their position, it would be necessary to start from some fixed point, so that only the two points are defined by measurement.

Long ago geometers divided the circle up into 360 parts, or degrees, as well as a starting or zero point, in order to locate points on a circle. Once the number of degrees and the starting point were agreed upon, any point in the circle could be located easily. The problem of locating a point on the earth had always vexed men trying to return to their homes. It became urgent when men began to sail long distances out of sight of land. Finally they agreed that having one zero point rather than many would simplify locating places. It had long ago been agreed that one direction would be called north, the others south, east, and west, and eventually the town of Greenwich, England, was chosen as the zero point. All measurements in an east-west direction were to be made from there, with all north-south ones from the equator. Thus the measurement in longitude or degrees from Greenwich and in latitude or degrees from the equator would allow the exact locating of any place on earth.

Zero points are set arbitrarily, usually in accordance with the characteristics of the object being measured whenever possible. In some cases there is a "natural" zero point, as in a scale to measure light perception where zero would be no light. In most cases in social science, however, there is no natural zero point. How could one find a zero point in I.Q. measurements, attitude scales, or measures of satisfaction?

Scale

One of the important concepts used in science is that of scale. The scale on a map tells you the relationship between distances on the map and real distances. For example, one inch per mile on the map scale means one inch on the map represents one mile on the earth. To broaden the idea of scale from the map type, we see that some sense of scale is necessary in social science. When we use a model, we must know how the real thing is related to our model. The concept of scale as a measured relationship between one thing and another is important in many social science propositions. For example, the things that may be true of the child will not hold for the man; what is true for the individual may not hold for the nation. In fact, one of the most widespread errors in thinking about subjects in this field is failure to consider problems of scale or relative size.

Sometimes we hear statesmen say, "Every free nation ought to determine its own destiny and have a voice in world affairs." The speaker has shown his lack of knowledge in social science. The great differences in size among the more than a hundred independent nations make it impossible for such a situation to come about. Ten of these nations have populations of less than a million, about the size of Milwaukee or Indianapolis. Imagine the results if every group of a million people wanted to be free and independent. There would be over three thousand free nations in the world!

We also hear it said, "What is good for General Motors is good for the country," a statement which ignores the differences in size of the company and the country, not to mention differences in role and operations. One of the rules of science is that every proposition must be evaluated in terms of the scale for which it is intended to serve. The fact that Newton's laws of gravity did not seem to hold for the forces among the atoms was one reason Einstein was led to his work. In the social sciences, different relationships between sizes, qualities, and orders of importance among social phenomena make it necessary that scale factors always be known and considered.

Orders of Magnitude

An order of magnitude is a measurement of differences in which one element is ten times larger or smaller than another. Thus, the population of the United States (over 200 million) is about two (20 times = 2 x 10) orders of magnitude larger than that of Illinois (about 10 million).

Orders of magnitude are of great importance to the social scientist because generalizations about human interactions often depend upon the relative size of the groups. The same generalizations about a two-person group, a boy and a girl for example, will not hold for a group of an order of magnitude larger—for example twenty boys and girls. And as the order of magnitude increases, from 2 to 20 to 200 to 2,000, different generalizations will be required.

Comprehension of orders of magnitude aids perspective. For example, the fact that the United States has spent more than five percent of its gross national product on "defense" may seem a small matter to affluent senators and university students. However, when it is considered that this represents the entire amount that the bottom one-fifth of the human race receives as income, perhaps we can see more clearly the waste involved. Or, put another way, what we spend each year on "defense" is more than all the people in forty countries have to live on. No matter which use is of greatest moment, scientific notation and orders of magnitude have become very important tools of the social scientist.

The Region—How Concepts Are Related to Measurement

The object of measurement is determined by the problem involved. If the object of measurement is right, results are helpful; if not, the measurements may be for nothing. Almost every social science uses the idea of region: economics in studies of international trade, sociology in studies of population and cities, political science in administrative regions, and anthropology in relating regions to blood types, language, and other characteristics. The idea of region is an important one, and it is an area in which measurement is important.

Man's activities are limited by the characteristics of the earth at his place on it. He cannot swim or ski or fish in a desert nor raise corn in the ocean. Notice, however, that we have not said the region determines his actions. The characteristics of our planet do not force man to behave in any special way; they only limit his choices.

The idea or concept of a region is what philosophers call a concept of relation, meaning that two or more specific ideas are related in a special way. For a region, the earth's space and certain other characteristics are related. You may remember from your earlier geography courses that you studied treeless, grassy regions such as the Argentine pampas. In this case, the pampas' climate and soil are the region's physical characteristics, to which the cultural characteristics, large ranches, gauchos, and beef production, are related.

For the political scientist, the United States is divided into administrative regions of many kinds, the states being one such division, each of which has special characteristics of interest. For the sociologist, the United States contains many metropolitan regions, where big cities contain certain patterns of life and affect those nearby.

A region, then, is some part of the earth's surface that is distinguished from the other parts by the presence of certain physical properties, such as soil or climate or patterns of life. The two ideas of a region are the earth and man's use of it. No single characteristic of a region—such as climate or location—is sufficient to describe it. A region always refers to two or more characteristics of a defined space as they stand in relationship to each other during a specified time. With changes in man, his societies, and his relationships to the earth, regions will change. For example, consider the political region called "the American colonies" in 1770. Twenty years later a new set of administrative regions called the "United States" was created. Other changes come about in the earth itself. Continents move, the ocean erodes the shoreline, and man remakes the face of the earth. Thus, new regions are constantly being defined and old ones discarded, their changing definitions dependent upon man's purposes.

The social scientist will develop and name regions according to his own problems. Is the geographer interested in the effects of certain kinds of transportation? He may define regions served by one kind of transportation and study what has happened to resource movements. Is the anthropologist concerned with human interaction? He may define regions based on blood-types and study the relationships of languages. Is the political scientist interested in power? He may define regions where feudalism existed and study the role of the lord. Is the sociologist studying man in society? He may define very small regions based on the way houses are built and study the way the neighbors behave toward each other.

Study of the examples above suggests the immense number of regions possible, as long as the region has a defined space and defined characteristics. With infinite ways to divide the earth and a large, if not infinite, number of characteristics both physical and social, there is no practical limit to the number possible. It is important to remember the purposes of science—a very large number of possibilities become the basis for expanding knowledge, since there will be some among them that lead to more certain knowledge.

MEASUREMENT—A FUNDAMENTAL METHOD OF SCIENCE

You have learned that there are four kinds of measurement that all scientists use and that measurement means relating numbers to things. And you have learned that the way the numbers are assigned to things depends upon the kind of measurement desired. Scientific and other knowledge comes about through relating sets of ideas or things to each other. This is done very often through measurement. Scientists must know how to assign numbers correctly and also must pay close attention to accuracy. It would do little good to know the earth's measurement at its diameter if the number were a result of inaccurate measurement.

Repeatability and Precision

The concept of accurate measurement rests upon repeatability and precision. Repeatability means that the same number will result from measuring the same thing with the same methods under constant conditions. Precision means that any errors in the measurement of the phenomena are known.

In principle, the idea of repeatability is simple. Assume that we wish to measure the number of parents any child has. The scientist decides to use counting numbers. Recall that this already means he has chosen a ratio scale, implying equality of the thing being measured, equality of intervals and ratios, rank order, and zero points. Then he defines parents, calling them the biological fathers and mothers. Given the definition, the methods and the measurement, the test, regardless of the performer, will always yield the number two. Despite the simplicity of this idea, practical difficulties may arise in many cases. For example, in measuring the earth's diameter, the scientist will begin by deciding to use counting numbers and a ratio scale. He must then choose the units to be represented by these numbers. In our first example, the choice was easy as either an adult male or female was a unit corresponding to a number. In this case let us assume the unit is to be the mile.

The exact length of a mile must be precisely determined, then the exact place chosen where the measurement will be made, since the diameter differs in different places. He must also decide whether to make the calculations based on the shadow cast on the moon during the eclipse or to use other methods such as the old Greek way of using the angles of the sun's rays at different points on the earth at the same time. Or he might calculate it from the photographs made by orbiting satellites or from the variations in the pull of gravity of the satellites. These and the other possible ways will all give slightly different results.

Our point here is that for the measurements to be repeated,

the definitions and methods must be specified precisely and it must be understood that even then if many complex variables are involved, repeatability can be difficult. Using another example, this time from social science, assume we want to measure the reading level of third grade children. The scientist must first decide on his measurement scale. It might be only an ordinal scale to rank students according to relative reading ability; or he might decide on an interval scale to determine how much better one student can read than another, which would be a more difficult process. He must then define what reading means, whether word recognition, reading speed, or comprehension is involved. Which kind of test will measure these different things? If all are to be considered, he may need an additional test.

With the proper tests, scales, and definitions established, there still may not be repeatability of the reading measurements because the subjects themselves may vary as well as the conditions under which the test is given. Differences in the way a person feels will affect the test as will the temperature of the room.

Repeatable measurements, enabling knowledge to be acquired, are the scientific ideal. Those which are not repeatable present challenges for the future. For the present scientists work with the knowledge of their errors because they understand the meaning of precision in measurement.

Central to the concept of accuracy is precision. At any given instant, one and only one number can be assigned to the phenomenon a scientist wishes to measure, despite the fact that the methods of measurement may only come close to telling exactly what that number is. The scientist cannot measure with absolute precision in all cases. Consider again the case of the number of biological parents. In this example the number two measures the number of parents exactly, without error. On the other hand, in measuring the earth's diameter, it is impossible to arrive at an exact number. Any number will be subject to error because of the complexity of the measuring process; the result will be imprecise. However, scientists have learned to specify the limits of the error of their measurements, thereby allowing precision.

One way to specify precision is to state exactly how the measurement is made. When this is done, other scientists can estimate the various possible errors due to the method of measurement and decide for themselves how precise it is. For the nominal kind of measurement, precision means assigning the numbers correctly; one football player should not wear another player's number by mistake.

Precision in measurement means that the rules according to which numbers are assigned are followed exactly as specified. Depending upon the kind of measurement, its precision can be stated as exactly as the scientific problem requires and in the way that corresponds to the kind of measurement being made. For example, in the case of the measurement of the reading of third grade children, assuming that an adequate test for measuring reading were developed which ranked children (note the ordinal scale), precision would mean that possible errors in ranking would be known and specified.

Accuracy

Science has no absolute rules about accuracy. The accuracy required in a measurement depends upon the problem. The major parts of the scientific system of inquiry, problem-formulation, observation and description, explanation, and prediction and control do not require the same amounts of measurement, much less the same accuracy.

Geographers, in attempting to explain differences in meat production between the Argentine and Iowa, have to take into account the fact that in Argentina winters are warm enough to leave the cattle outside, while in Iowa it is so cold in winter they must be kept in barns. In this kind of problem, extremely accurate temperature measurements are not needed, but only simple, approximate, temperature averages accurate to within a few degrees. The problem then sets the degree of accuracy required for measurement.

Many nonscientists make the mistake of thinking that "exact" measurements of some kind are a scientific requirement. This is not and never was the case. In the history of science, Mendel made basic discoveries in biology simply by counting peas of different colors. The ancient Chinese discovered and used the compass by observing that a light, floating magnet seemed always to point in the same direction. Darwin developed his theories of evolution by observing, not exactly measuring, differences. The list could be extended.

Most scientific measurement has been done by the physical and biological scientists on things that do not change or that do not change rapidly. Such measurements are called *static*. In the social sciences most measurements must be made on people or groups that are changing while—and sometimes because—measurements are being made on them. These measurements are called *dynamic*.

Dynamic measurements are usually more difficult. One reason is that repeatability is hard. People or groups, once changed in significant ways, cannot be put back into their original state in order to repeat measurements. If a social scientist wants to make a measurement involving the degree of wakefulness or hunger, he will find that the longer he keeps the subject awake, the more tired the subject gets. Thus he must always contend with change, of however slight a degree. Fortunately there are kinds of problems where constant change is not of great importance. While modern statistics and computers provide powerful tools to assess the importance of various kinds of change, dynamic measurements dealing with people do require very careful attention on the part of every social scientist.

Chapter 8

Economics—
Explanations by Deduction

ECONOMICS AND DEDUCTION

The most important scientific reasoning process is that of inference. You will recall that inference allows us to make statements that are probably true on the basis of observations. The statement that "the sun will come up tomorrow morning" is based on a long series of observations. Although it cannot be proved, the probability of its occurrence is very high. Deductive reasoning, the kind you learn about in mathematics, is concerned with the logical and necessary consequences of statements. Deductive statements are cast in the form "If A and B are true, then C must be true." Science uses a combination of inductive and deductive reasoning. Inductive reasoning keeps us alone, close to observation and the facts. Deductive reasoning makes us pay attention to the logic of our arguments and statements.

One of the most important parts of the scientific system of inquiry is that of explanation, which answers the question "why?" Frequently scientists attempt to answer "why?" deductively. They can only do this when the postulates, or premises—the statements upon which the deductive argument is based—are reasonably well established from the process of inference. When this is the case, the deductive method is often very useful. Lionel Robbins, a great English economist, said, "The propositions of economic theory, like all scientific theory, are obviously deductions from a series of postulates." In this chapter we will discuss deduction as a method of explanation used by economists.

The Subject of Economics

Economics is the social science that is concerned with the things that men want and how they go about acquiring them. Those who are experts in the science are called economists. In the United States most of them belong to the American Economic Association. The study of economics includes natural resources, agriculture, and population as part of the economic basis of any society, as well as labor, the consumer, and the health, education, and welfare of individuals and groups. Economics is also concerned with the way international trade and economic fluctuations affect man's well-being.

If nature supplied men free of charge with all the goods and services they want, economics would not be important. The central economic problem, therefore, revolves about scarcity, the difference between what men want and what they can get or make.

In order to deal with the central economic problem of relatively limited goods and services as opposed to relatively unlimited wants, economists have broken down the problem into four sub-problems. First, every society must decide what will be produced, that is, what goods and services it wants to make. Second, every society must decide how it will produce, in other words, how it will organize production. Third, every society must decide how the things it has produced will be distributed. It must answer the question "who gets what?" Fourth, if the society is to exist over any period of time it must somehow adjust what is consumed to what is produced and have something left over for investment and future growth.

THE HISTORY OF ECONOMIC THOUGHT

Men have always been concerned with these problems, even though they could not analyze them in the ways we do now. It is typical of modern science that it makes ever more refined analyses which may in turn lead to increasing progress. For the past two centuries, men have begun to think about their economic problems in a scientific way, and partly because of this more men live better now than ever before.

Three or four thousand years ago men began to free themselves from having to devote almost their entire lives to the solution of their economic problems. The procurement of food, clothing, and shelter was the central preoccupation for most of mankind's history. During this whole period men learned, with little conscious planning or recording, to use fire, domesticate animals, make wheels, hunt game, and, perhaps most importantly, domesticate plants. Only after they were able to obtain the necessities of life with relative ease, could they devote their energies to scientific curiosity. This ultimately led to the great advances which made our civilization possible.

With freedom from the daily search for food, men developed new answers to the four basic economic problems. These answers took three main shapes. The oldest and most important was that of answering each of the questions according to custom or tradition. Men produced the way their ancestors had produced, distributed the way their ancestors had distributed, and provided for the future the way their ancestors had done. Another way that men dealt with the four basic questions was by means of a controlled society in which the answers were determined by leaders with power. Decisions were made at the top about how to produce, what to produce, and who would get it. A third development for answering the four problems was the price system. A price is an amount of money that buyers pay and sellers receive for a given quantity of goods or services. A price is set on every good and service in the society and people buy and sell in accordance with these prices.

Of course, no one society used only one of the ways of answering the four problems. In almost every case we know of where some use of price occurred, some traditional answers were used and some power was present as well. Today, for example, the Soviet Union uses more power in running its economic system and answering the four problems than does the United States. The United States leans more on the price system to answer these questions. And some few backward or traditional societies still use custom to answer the four basic questions. The power of government obviously plays an important role in the United States' economic system, just as in the Soviet Union prices are also utilized. Societies of necessity have always ordered their economic affairs and found solutions to the four basic questions.

Economics and Early Writings

Many of the earliest writings that we know, even those of religion, discuss economics. For example, the book of Deuteronomy in the Old Testament says, "You shall not lend upon interest to your brother, interest on money, interest on victuals, interest on anything that is lent on interest." Another verse in Deuteronomy covers pay. "You shall not oppress a hired servant who is poor and needy, whether he is of your brethren or one of the sojourners who are in your land within your towns; you shall give him his hire on the day he earns it."

The ancient Hindu writings also cover matters of interest and buying and selling. In the religious works of the ancient Jews and Hindus are found regulations about weights and measures, labor, agriculture, and other economic matters.

Plato and Aristotle both discussed economic matters from a social point of view. They talked about inheritance, population, early versions of communism, the role of money and interest, and many other economic subjects. Their thought, however, was not systematic or well-organized enough for others to build a social science upon. This was characteristic of most thinking about economic matters until the eighteenth century when an intellectual revolution laid the foundations of modern social thought. On the Continent, the physiocrats, a group of French economists, and in England, Adam Smith and the utilitarians felt that they had discovered sound and effective methods for dealing with economic problems. They laid the foundation for modern economics in their writings. By the latter half of the 1800s the books which established classical economics had been written. Classical economics used the price system to provide answers to the four basic economic problems. The early economists' special contribution was that they had, by a brilliant series of logical steps, developed a logical or deductive apparatus of great predictive power and persuasion to show why the price system worked the way it did.

Other Schools, Other Systems

The so-called classical school was, however, not left unchallenged. By the middle 1800s Karl Marx had developed his work. He also used deduction and his work was systematic and logical. Of course it differed in many of its premises from the classical system. But the important thing for the development of economics as a science was that by the middle of the 1800s everyone who hoped to contribute to economics had to think in terms of fitting his contribution into a logical system. And the Marxist system was not the only challenger to the classical system of economics. In Germany another group of scholars interpreted economic matters more historically and with more attention to the role of the state than had the classical system. But the German scholars, too, had to pay close attention to their methods. By the turn of the nineteenth century three great streams of economic thought had been developed in their main outline. The classical system relied upon price mechanisms for seeking answers to its problems. The Marxist system stressed the social aspects of control in its answers. And the historical or institutional school looked more toward history and social institutions.

It is typical of the social sciences that different schools of thought exist at the same time. It is also typical that one or more of them will be more widely accepted than the others. In Europe during the nineteenth century the classical tradition dominated economic thought; it continues to be dominant in America today.

In the 1930s, however, another great English economist, John Maynard Keynes, developed innovations that have resulted in the neoclassical system ("neo" means new, "classical" means old and well-established) that most of you will study when you take economics courses. The Marxist system, too, has grown and developed, but in a different manner. No great writer like Keynes has recently appeared on the Marxist scene. Rather, the adaptations of the Marxist system seem to be made on a more pragmatic basis. That is to say, the changes in the Marxist scheme of thought seem to follow from practical pressures rather than intellectual or logical developments.

THE STRUCTURE OF ECONOMIC CONCEPTS

Today most economists accept the idea that economic concepts are related to one another so that they form a system of thought reflecting the working of our economic system, although everyone does not agree on exactly how this system works in every detail.

Economists approach economic concepts by focusing on the central economic problem of scarcity, the conflict between what men desire or want and the quantity of goods and services available. Because there are many ways to resolve this conflict, individuals and societies face the problem of choice. The choices or solutions to the central economic problem are influenced by the economic goals of the individuals and societies and the economic resources available to them. In America, for instance, five economic goals are important: freedom, growth, stability, security, and justice. Economic freedom is the freedom to choose a job and to spend or save one's income as one wishes. Economic growth generally means continuing increases in the levels of living for most Americans. Economic stability implies that there is no fast drop of jobs or incomes and no rapid change in prices, as, for example, there would be in rapid inflation. Economic security guarantees that most people in the society have their basic economic needs met whether or not they are able to work. And economic justice dictates that we keep inequalities of opportunity to the lowest possible level.

Economic resources are what the society utilizes to create goods and services. There are four main resources: land, labor, capital, and organization. Land means the animal, vegetable, and mineral wealth of the soil. Labor means all the mental and physical effort of men. Capital refers to all the goods used to produce other goods or services—for example, railroads or barbers' clippers. And organization means putting the above three together as is done by planners, managers, and those who take business risks.

When these goals and resources are utilized through a political process to make choices, they are influenced by technology. Technology refers to the uses of science. Our society, with its economic institutions like markets for exchange, specialization, the division of labor, money, transportation, and communication networks, combined with political decision-making and technology, builds and runs our economic system.

What Is Deductive Explanation?

For almost two thousand years the rules of reasoning in science relied on deduction, as developed by Aristotle and Euclid. By the eighteenth century, however, man had to come to see that deduction—reasoning from the general to the particular—could not be the only way science would advance because logical reasoning had no necessary connection with the facts. Thus men developed more serviceable techniques of inductive reasoning. Logical reasoning is necessary in attempting to work with and test hypotheses. Very often we must deduce consequences, that is, try to decide what a statement means, before we test it. Then the test can be meaningful to us by confirming our deduction or denying it. Great scientists have always used deduction. For example, Newton knew that Kepler had stated some of the laws of planetary motion, but he also knew that things fell toward the center of the earth. He wondered about this and deduced his laws of gravity. Here, in slightly modernized language, is what Newton wrote: "And the same year I began to think of gravity extending to the moon, and after having found out how to estimate the force with which a globe revolving within a sphere pressed the surface of the sphere, from Kepler's rule of periodic times of the planets, being in a sesquialterate proportion of their distances from the center of their orbs, I deduced that the forces which keep the planets in their orbs must be reciprocally as the squares of their distances from the centers about which they revolve." Although science primarily uses induction, deduction has always been important.

If you ever study logic, you will learn there are different forms of deduction but that all deductive arguments or syllogisms have three propositions or statements. One type starts with a statement of the form, "All A's are B." For example, "All men are mortal." The second statement is of the form, "All or some C's are A." For example, "Socrates is a man." The third statement follows from the first two and is of the form, "Therefore all C's are B." For example, "Socrates is mortal."

Another kind of deduction from among many we could choose is negative. Although it too contains three statements, in this case the first statement is of the form, "No A is B." For example, 'No one who can control himself is necessarily vicious." The second statement is of the form, "All C's are A." For example, "All poor people can control themselves." The third statement is of the form, "Therefore no C is B." For example, "Therefore no poor people are necessarily vicious."

Now if we ask, "Why is Socrates mortal?" we can arrive at an explanation. Deductively, it is because Socrates is a man and all men are mortal. With deduction used alone it is proper to speak of proof since no reference is made to observation; only logical processes are involved.

It is important to notice that whenever deductive explanations are used in the social sciences one of the statements must be a truth relative to everything under discussion as, "All men are mortal." This is sometimes called a premise. The initial condition or conditions for the period the statement covers must be described in another statement, or implication, such as, "Socrates is a man."

Why Do Prices Change?

An example of deduction in social science is the answer to the question, "Why do prices change?" The answer is always given in terms of changes in one or more of the initial conditions or premises from which the actual price change may be deduced. However, since scientists insist on precise definitions, it is necessary to define some terms.

> Price—the amount of money a buyer gives to a seller in exchange for a good or service.
>
> Money—the standard of value in terms of which prices are stated. All economic goods and services have a money price. The statement of all prices in terms of a standard measure or unit of value thus allows for comparisons. Prices then become the ratios of the values. For example, four loaves of bread at $.25 a loaf are worth one pair of socks at $1.00 a pair. It is important to note that the standard of value, money, is assumed to remain unchanged—or what is the same thing, that the value of money does not change.
>
> Buyer—the person who obtains the good or service after the payment of money.
>
> Seller—the person who gives a good or service in exchange for money.
>
> Exchange—the act of transferring one good or service for another.
>
> Good or Service—anything that men want that is not free, i.e. that has a price.

Any deductive explanation requires a precise statement of initial conditions so that the phenomena in question can be discussed without confusion. Prices, we emphasized in our earlier discussion, are part of one kind of an economic system. Usually the initial conditions describe the system under discussion. For the price system, the essential concept is that of pure competition.

Pure Competition

Pure competition defines the five conditions under which buyers and sellers operate to make their exchanges.

Small buyers and sellers. Each buyer and seller must be so small in relation to all other buyers and sellers that his purchase or sale cannot influence the price. This condition is frequently satisfied in our economy—millions of farmers sell wheat; no individual sale by any farmer can affect the general price of wheat, no single purchaser of bread can affect the general price by his purchase.

The same good or service. Each unit of the good or service bought or sold must be identical—of exactly the same grade, quality, and quantity. This is necessary so that our analysis need take into account only one factor and so that buyers and sellers need be influenced by price alone, rather than by other variables, such as quality, as well.

Information about prices. Buyers and sellers must have fast and accurate price information in order to make accurate decisions. This information is found on grain and stock exchanges and in the classified advertising sections of newspapers.

Ability to use information about prices. Buyers and sellers must be able to use the information they have. If buyers know of lower prices elsewhere but are unable to buy, their information would be of little use. In our economy organized markets, easy transfer of money, and brokers make it possible for rapid provision and action upon information.

Freedom from pressure or discrimination. Every buyer or seller must be able to buy or sell to anyone without any fear or pressure.

Pure competition is an ideal-type concept and has never existed. Nonetheless, when considering the departures of the system from pure competition, economic analysis can be of much help. When the conditions for pure competition are met only one price can result at any one time. This price is called the equilibrium or market price.

The Concept of Equilibrium

When a system of prices is in stable equilibrium, any departure from the initial state puts into motion forces which restore that state. We do not mean that the system must return to the original position. The concept of equilibrium refers to a balance of forces. Stable equilibrium means that balance is restored after a change—like a boat with a keel which sails upright again after being tipped by a wave. For a system of prices this means that the prices will tend toward a certain dollar amount; any price above or below that amount will set forces in motion which will bring prices back to the first amount.

Time. In economics an analysis always refers to a specified time period, depending upon the product.

Premises. Keep in mind that the purpose of deduction is to explain why something has happened. We have seen that prices are the result of interaction between buyers and sellers. In other words, economists have learned to state their premises about buyers and sellers.

Sellers and the Supply Schedule. Let us imagine a company that is large and has one billion shares of stock outstanding of which no more than ten thousand are held by any one person. At a given moment each holder of shares will have in mind a price at which he would sell these shares. Years of experience have taught economists that, generally the higher the price, the more of any good or service will be offered for sale. Therefore, a schedule for any individual would indicate that as the price rose he would sell more. However, since not all individuals feel the same way about selling, there will be almost as many selling schedules as there are sellers. Despite the differences in the schedule, economists assume that the general rule "the higher the price, the more will be offered for sale" holds. When all the individual selling schedules are combined, the total number of shares of stock that will be offered at any price can be obtained.

It should be clear, however, that we assume that nothing but the price affects the number of shares of stock which will be offered for sale at any given moment.

Buyers and the Demand Schedule.   We can represent the way buyers respond to changes in price the same way we have for sellers—by making a schedule of the total number of shares they will buy at any given price. Just as we add together the schedules of sellers to make the supply curve, so we can add together the amount that each individual will buy at any given price and make a total demand schedule. Demand for economists has a special meaning in that buyers are both willing and able to buy: at a given price they will buy a certain amount.

How Prices Are Determined.   When competition exists, buyers and sellers exchange goods and services for money until the prices of the good or service reflect just the quantity that sellers wish to sell and buyers wish to buy. When these quantities are equal, the equilibrium or market price exists. Let us see how this works. Assume that the price is $5.00 and that buyers will want 300 shares. However, if the price is $5.00, sellers are willing to sell 400 shares. Thus, sellers are willing to sell more shares than buyers are willing to buy. When this occurs, the price gets bid down because sellers are more eager than buyers.

Now let us assume that the price is $4.00. At this price, buyers would like to buy 400 shares but the price is so low that sellers only want to sell 300 shares. Thus, buyers are more eager than sellers at a price of $4.00. What will happen then? If buyers are more eager than sellers, the price will tend to rise.

At what point will the price be decided? At the point where the amount that sellers wish to sell is exactly equal to the amount that buyers wish to buy. If prices are above this point, they will tend to fall down. If prices are below this point, they will tend to rise.

You now have the outline of the way economists think about prices in competition. They assume that buyers and sellers act only on the basis of price changes. The explanation for the tendency to the equilibrium or market price is purely deductive.

Other Things Equal

For every scientific problem we can select only some of the relevant factors in attempting explanation. The premises and initial conditions for deduction must specify very closely the conditions and subjects under discussion. Those factors not specified are assumed *not* to change. This is what is meant by *Ceteris paribus* or other things equal. However, the narrower the specification, the less the range of the explanation. That is, economists know very well that pure competition does not now exist and perhaps never did. For this reason, very few real facts can be explained unless we change some of the initial conditions. Put another way, a scientific explanation must clearly set forth what it is explaining, which factors are relevant to the explanation and which are not.

Our discussion of the premises and initial conditions has shown what we are talking about and what we hold constant. Once we are reasonably sure of our explanation, we can broaden the range of phenomena with which the explanation deals. We can make the explanation more useful by making it more inclusive. To do this, we examine carefully what it is we have held constant and what it is we have assumed in our statement of premises and initial conditions. Then, by carefully tracing the effects of the changes of the premises or initial conditions, we can often modify the whole system of explanation to include many more phenomena.

For example, let us study more closely what we have said about demand. Up to this point, we have assumed that buyers act only on the basis of price; in fact, however, we know that buyers act on the basis of many more factors than price alone. What a buyer will buy will depend on his tastes and preferences, his income, and the prices of related goods. For example, as color television sets are improved, fewer people wish to buy black and white sets; their tastes change. As income rises, standards rise. On the supply side, we have held many things constant—for example, technology. The improvement of technology very often lowers costs and therefore increases the amount that sellers are willing to sell at a given price.

Let us see how the deductive mode of explanation works in some of these cases. Consider why the price of black and white television sets has fallen. Before the advent of color television, a supply and demand curve existed for any given kind of set. But now we shall explain what happens by deduction. Lower demand (A) means lower prices (B)—statement one. Changing tastes for black and white television (C) lower demand (A)—statement two. Therefore, changing tastes for black and white television (C) lower prices (B).

Now, see if you can figure out why the price of steak tends to rise as people become richer. Keep in mind that by an increase in demand we mean that at any given price people will buy more steak, just as by an increase in supply we mean that at any given price people will sell more. And, of course, the opposite is true for a decrease in supply or demand. Thence, increased demand increases prices. Rising incomes increase the demand for steak. Therefore, rising incomes raise the price of steak.

USES OF DEDUCTION IN SOCIAL SCIENCE

Most social sciences and most real problems in the social sciences deal with many different factors or variables. For most of mankind's history these variables were so complicated, or at least appeared to be so complicated, that men were not able to think logically about many of their problems; but as social science has grown it has become apparent that deduction is a very powerful tool. Using deduction we can, after stating our premises and initial conditions, arrange our conclusions and explanations in ways that allow us to determine what is wrong with either our premises or initial conditions.

Being able to test logically helps in constructing better theories, in designing experiments and observations, and in determining precisely where we are right or wrong.

We must never forget that deduction is logical and has nothing to do with the real world. The kind of reasoning that rests on observation of the real world or facts is called induction. Deduction is thus only a tool, part of the scientist's arsenal in his assault on ignorance. It can never be used by itself because it is only a logical method, while science insists that its knowledge be testable in the real world. Although most of the other methods of social science are those of induction, deduction used with induction has furnished mankind with some of its greatest advances.

Economics and the Other Social Sciences

Like all the other divisions of social science, economics relies on the other disciplines for many things. For example, economists take it for granted that man has needs or wants. They leave the study of how these needs or wants are formed to the psychologist. The economists examine what happens as a result of any given group of wants. In another example, economists know that the family is the basic consumption unit in the United States. But they leave the study of the family itself to the sociologists. Land and other natural resources are required for every economic activity, but economists draw on geographers for this kind of knowledge.

In the early days of economics the subject was called political economy. This draws our attention to the fact that all modern societies make economic decisions within a political structure that determines such things as levels of taxation, government spending, and money. Once again, however, economists do not study the political structure that determines the framework within which the economic system operates. That is left to political scientists. Nor do the economists study how society makes its goods or services in the sense of technology —the kinds of factories or computers that are used—and especially the advances that come from improving technology. Economics assumes that technological advance will be studied by other social scientists and accepts whatever technological advance occurs as given and beyond its own specialized problems.

The deductive mode of explanation is widely used. By its use, scientists can tell if their reasoning is sound and where it departs from reality. The deductive method is especially useful whenever experience has shown that the initial conditions and premises of the logical system correspond closely to reality. Then, by logic scientists can unravel very complex problems and develop knowledge. Perhaps some of you have seen a planetarium where the position of hundreds of stars can be shown as they will be thousands of years from now and as they were thousands of years ago. Astronomy uses deduction to calculate the position of the stars. A rocket scientist uses deduction to place our rockets where we want them. Economists, although not as successful as astronomers, have found that the deductive system works very well to explain many aspects of the behavior of prices and other things of interest to economists. The method of straight thinking called deduction is a must for any scientist.

Explanation in science is of several different kinds. But all kinds answer the question "why?" The deductive mode of explanation answers the question "why?" in terms of logical process. Logic alone can tell us nothing about the real world. When deduction is combined with induction, which rests on facts and observations, it is one of the most useful methods of explanation in science.

Chapter 9

Political Science—
Explanations by Intention
and Probability

THE SUBJECT MATTER OF POLITICAL SCIENCE

Political science exists because all men, as they live together, must govern themselves. They must establish ways to reconcile the differences that cannot be resolved through personal effort. Law and the constitution determine the legal framework for resolution. National, state, and local governments involve citizens variously: the legislative, executive, and judicial branches of government play distinctive roles in making, interpreting, and enforcing laws; public opinion is shaped by ideology, manipulated by propaganda, and expressed through political parties; power and its manipulation appear in every relationship among and between men as well as among and between states.

Because power, control, authority, regulation, and influence are so important, and because they pervade so much of our lives, no satisfactory definition of political science has yet been found. But broadly speaking, political science encompasses the way in which members of society cooperate and compete to make the decisions which result in the distribution of those things that society values. Political science observes the practices and behaviors of men in society as they work out associations to deal with political problems and to express their political values and ideologies. A good way to understand the nature of political science is to examine some of the questions involved in the debate over its scope.

The Scope of Political Science

Politics is an important part of political science. Politics occurs when private individuals or formal organizations pursue goals that conflict with the goals of others. Politics is a series of actions, debates, negotiations, cooperation, arguments, discussions, or uses of police or other powers or persuasion by means of which the issue involved is settled. Politics always involves public issues, that is, those which individuals cannot or do not wish to settle privately. It is not a public issue when a young child wishes to go outside without putting on his coat and argues with his mother or when a young man argues with his girl friend about which movie to see on Saturday night. An issue becomes public when more than two people are involved and when power exists to resolve the issue.

When politics focuses mainly on issues or struggles a great deal of what governments do has to be ignored. Political science is partially concerned with cooperation, not only with competition. An example of this can be given from contemporary international relations. What make the headlines are items such as potential and actual conflicts leading to war or the threat of war and the uses and misuses of atomic energy.

Yet at least as important as conflict is the fact that the nations of the world cooperate with each other: they agree to deliver each other's mail, to regulate the number of whales killed to prevent their extermination, to have uniform safety standards for ships and air communication. The list could be greatly extended and is also relevant to many activities on the national, state, and local levels. Most decisions about running the nation's schools are arrived at through cooperation rather than competition. Nonetheless, the decisions are still political.

Almost all political scientists agree that conflicts over public issues fall within the scope of political science. International relations, the world power structure, the balance of power, nationalism, and international law and organization, are well-established areas within the field of political science. Political scientists have been concerning themselves increasingly with deterrents of war and with limited war, as well as with nation-building, socialization, and the establishment and preservation of effective government in other countries. Studies of international scope often emphasize comparisons of the political systems of various countries.

Political science also focuses on government, and especially on government through law. This focus has led to studies of policy in agriculture, water resources, government-business-labor relationships, and such government agencies as the Tennessee Valley Authority. Some of these studies have described the arrangement of an institution as well as the functions and policies of government.

Still another focus that political scientists have found useful is that on process, and particularly on policy-making. Some hold that political science should be a science of policy with emphasis on the processes used to make decisions. From this point of view, political science attempts to identify important persons and associations and the interests they represent. Law and its institutional arrangements, along with the methods and procedures used to resolve issues, are then studied. Finally, an attempt is made to analyze those influences and roles which lead to the result. For example, political scientists have discussed in detail the way in which Congress passes certain kinds of law. A study of this sort would include those people interested in passing a certain law, the congressmen important to the law, the congressional committee structure, and so on.

Political scientists disagree on the extent to which values should be discussed. Some hold that discussion of the possible good and bad consequences of a decision or the reason for the emergence of an issue should be part of a study of this sort. This kind of value judgment, however, is considered by some specialists to be outside the realm of political science.

Political science also emphasizes political systems, an approach viewing political life as a system of behavior: the political system distributes things of value to society through its authority. This system is distinguished from other systems, such as the economic system. By analyzing systems, it is possible to analyze the way in which a political system responds to crisis by changing its structure and hence protecting its processes from dangers posed by forces either inside or outside the system.

Areas of Rapid Advancement in Political Science

Elites.   Those who hold high positions within a society are considered to compose its elite. This especially includes government leaders and those with the greatest control of values. Political scientists have identified elite positions, who occupies them, the way in which the elite is recruited, and its attitudes, from the community to the national and international levels.

Opinions.   An opinion is a belief, a viewpoint, a judgment, or a conviction an individual holds about a certain issue. The opinion can be expressed or unexpressed, important or unimportant, and held for good reason or no reason at all. Political scientists know a great deal about mass or public opinion in many countries.

Voting.   Voting statistics are records of who votes for whom and when. Political scientists accumulate the voting records of legislative bodies and of the voters themselves, as well as the voting records of other groups such as nominating conventions. By carefully studying these records they are now able to predict the outcome of certain elections with a very high degree of accuracy.

Content Analysis.   Content analysis involves the study of campaign speeches and other records in terms of the key ideas that are in the records. Often word counts are used. Political scientists are developing a large store of such analyses.

Statistics.   Much statistical data useful for understanding political issues are being drawn together and published by political scientists. Although these data are often gathered for other purposes—the collection of population figures from a census by government or private organizations—when properly understood and utilized such statistical data can lead to valuable insights into political structure, its processes and changes, under different conditions.

Historical data.   Data from the past are being rediscovered and restructured for new uses. Data from earlier periods allow the construction of time series and the study of them for possible trends. For example, historical data in the form of lists of various kinds—the number of deaths from wars as well as from domestic political violence—are being collected.

Comparative data.   Data are being collected which survey research in other social and behavioral sciences, but which are focused on questions or topics of importance to political science. Both surveys have been made for communications, persuasion, small-group behavior, patterns of decision-making, organizations, and many other fields.

Data Storage and Retrieval.   With the increasing use of computers in political science come data composed of the computer program, statistical routines, and other mathematical and analytical techniques developed for information storage, retrieval, and analysis. It is now possible for political scientists, like other social scientists, to manipulate larger amounts of data than ever before. The data can be studied with ratios, common statistical distributions, correlations, and in other ways previously impossible because of the labor required. Storage, manipulation, and retrieval of data are techniques essential to the growth of political science.

Theory. Political scientists are developing better models and theoretical frameworks of conceptualizations for their work which enable them to reconstruct the discipline. Formerly, models for political science were built to answer such questions as: What is the best form of government? How does one obtain power and manipulate it?

The Broad Concerns of Political Science

As a field of study, political science is widely extended, overlapping to some extent with history and sociology. Politics is encountered in every part of life, wherever people seek to achieve highly valued ends. There is politics in unions, in towns, in schools, and in churches. People play politics in business firms, clubs, and, of course, in political parties. The ubiquity of the subject, coupled with its importance, may make it highly unlikely that neat and tidy boundaries for the discipline are either to be expected or desired.

Political scientists' methods must reflect the diversity of their subject and the differences in the issues, problems, and knowledge they seek to study and gain. The political scientist, like every other social scientist, uses most of the methods of the other social sciences as he develops knowledge about his own science. In this chapter, as in the others, we discuss some, rather than all, methods of political scientists, methods which are also used widely by other social scientists. We must not forget, of course, that political scientists often use the deductive method (explained in Chapter 8), although they have also developed other methods of explanation to a high degree. Two of these, explanation by purpose or intention and explanation by probability, are discussed below.

EXPLANATION BY PURPOSE OR INTENTION

One method of explanation which social scientists use is not used in the physical or biological sciences. This method explains in terms of aims, plans, goals, or intentions. Whenever human beings are studied, the social scientist must take into account the fact that they have wills and can change their future. Think of it this way. On the one hand, deductive reasoning is a process of logic which depends only on the application of certain rules of thinking. At the other end of this continuum is common sense, which depends on no logic at all but which often does satisfy the requirements of clarity in communication. Between these two extremes are several other kinds of explanation which vary in their logical rigor. As a result they must be used very carefully and the limits of their use must be understood.

The Goals of the Individual

Why did the Founding Fathers separate the legislative, executive, and judicial functions in our government? Because they wanted to avoid the centralization of power which they thought was so wrong. They debated, planned, and executed their ideas for the construction of a government of a certain kind as expressed in the Constitution. Why will Uncle Joe vote a straight party ticket? He plans to because he hates the other party. Why did Andrew Jackson veto the act extending the life of the second Bank of the United States? Why did Woodrow Wilson fight to get the Versailles Treaty ratified in the Senate? Why did Lyndon B. Johnson prosecute the Vietnam war the way he did? Why does George drive to work instead of taking public transportation? Social scientists know that whenever human behavior must be explained, either in terms of the individual or in terms of groups, the plans, intentions, and goals of individuals themselves must be taken into account. We call this *explanation by purpose*.

Explanation by purpose is commonly used in two situations. First, a social scientist may ask a person what his purposes or intentions are or were when the purpose of the action the social scientist is attempting to explain is not clear. "Why did you kill your wife?" "Because I was mad at her." In this case, the questioner is attempting to find out something about an individual's purpose with regard to an act he has performed.

Secondly, this kind of explanation is sought when the social scientist is ignorant of the connections between the actions of the group and the goals of the individual. Thus a political scientist might ask someone, "Why did you not vote in the last election?" Which might elicit the answer, "I wanted to express my disapproval of all the candidates I was offered." The respondent's purpose in not voting was thus to express disapproval. Whenever a social scientist attempts to explain human actions in which the actor has a choice—that is, whenever there is any question of goal-directed behavior—purposes, reasons, or intentions must be explored.

Social scientists cannot always be satisfied with the answers they receive about purposes, and, therefore, some regard explanation in terms of explicit intentions or purposes as unimportant. One problem stems from the fact that this kind of explanation assumes that the actor's intentions operated in such a way as to produce the actor's behavior. In many cases this is obviously true. "Why did you turn on the light?" "Because I wanted to see better." "Why do you eat lunch?" "Because I am hungry." These are trivial instances, but notice the assumption behind them—the intentions of the actor operated in such a way that the behavior followed. When this is true, the explanation by intentions or purpose works reasonably well.

A hazard to explanation in terms of intention is that not all of an individual's purposes result in actions. In other words, there is no one-to-one relationship necessary between purposes and actions. Does a man's intention to vote wisely mean he will succeed in doing so?

Another difficulty with explanations of this sort is that an individual's intentions might be unrealizable. In general, social scientists do not consider as goals any ideas about the future which an individual never intends to act upon.

Still another disadvantage to explanation in terms of an individual's goals lies in the fact that it is hard to tell whether behavior is the result of a given goal or the means to some further goal. Does the precinct captain who votes a straight party ticket and gets everyone else to vote the same way do so for the satisfaction he receives or because he hopes to be rewarded with a promotion in the party structure, a better patronage job, or for some other reason?

A last difficulty of this method of explanation is that much behavior is not consciously goal-directed, in the sense of being explainable by conscious or explicit purposes on the part of the actor. Behavior may be unconscious, accidental, automatic, inadvertent, involuntary, or even uncontrolled. If you are suddenly and unexpectedly pushed into the pool, you utter a shout of surprise. It would be hard to explain this shout in terms of purpose or goals.

Many human actions, therefore, are not intentional; they are not the result of a conscious plan or purpose. Whenever this is the case, explanation by purpose will not work. Either the actor has not acted on the basis of any preconceived plan or intention, or if he did, it may have been unconsciously. Probably most individual and social actions are intentional only in the sense that they are not done by mistake, by accident, involuntarily, or because of unconscious motivations. However, neither are they done as the result of any particular thought on the part of an individual. Put another way, many routine mundane actions are neither the outcome of a consciously expressed and explicit goal nor the means of obtaining a consciously expressed and explicit goal. In many cases an actor's intentions or goals may not be relevant to the social scientist's problem.

There are two requirements for explaining actions according to an actor's goals or purposes. The first is that he must have known and been able to express his goal. The second is that he must have thought there was a connection between his goal and his action. When these two limiting conditions are met, this method of explanation is useful.

The Goals of the Group

When a social scientist attempts to explain the behavior of more than one individual, his difficulties are increased because of the difficulty in knowing the goals of the group. For example, in the early 1960s, a presidential commission published a statement of goals for Americans, a papal encyclical set forth the goals of the Roman Catholic Church, and the Twenty-Second Congress of the Communist party of the Soviet Union set forth the goals of the Soviet Union. What do these statements explain in terms of the groups involved? Very often such statements are simply put out to reinforce the faith of the true believer. All of those mentioned above are incomplete in that they do not cover many of the goals of the publishing groups, and they are all inconsistent: some goals conflict with others, while those goals set forth are not ranked in order of importance. In most cases, explanation of the actions of the Vatican or the Communist party or the United States by reference to official goal statements would be very inadequate. Although some social scientists feel that only individuals have purposes or goals, it must be recognized that individuals combine to form various groups which can be said to have goals. Individuals often contribute their ideas to the group of which they are members; within a group, evidence of compromise is always present. However, because in the past, explanation of group behavior in terms of group goals has often been vague or misleading, it is rarely attempted. In the case of the use of purposive explanation with regard to groups, the two conditions that were specified for individual behavior—a previously expressed purpose and a connection between the purpose and the action—do not hold. Purposive explanation when used for groups can only be *ex post facto* (after the fact). Ordinarily, group purpose must be deduced from its action rather than the other way around, for often the group's actions do not follow from its statements of goals. However, in well-specified, coherent, and functioning groups, this method can be used.

In order to understand the way in which one can explain individual behavior in terms of group goals, consider the following examples. Statement A. One of the goals of the United States Congress is to perpetuate existing political party relationships by giving power and prestige in the Congress to faithful party members. Statement B. Congressman X is a faithful party member. Statement C. Congressman X's intention in being a faithful party member is to get the reward of power and prestige that Congress bestows. This method of explanation has a limited usefulness for all the reasons given above, yet when used carefully and with due regard for the limits, it can explain certain kinds of behavior.

Unintended Consequences or Goals

Perceptive observers of the human scene, artists, writers, philosophers, and many social scientists have known for a long time that many human actions have unintended consequences. That is, actions directed toward one goal may or may not achieve that goal, and may result in a situation that was no part of the original plan. A frequently quoted example in social science is that the goal of raising the educational level often has the unintended consequence of raising the suicide rate. Hitler's decision to invade Russia, like Napoleon's, had the unintended consequence of a complete defeat of the invading army. The improvement of automobile transportation in the United States had the unintended consequence of killing and maiming more people than have all America's wars. The social scientist must pay full attention to the unintended consequences of actions, taken by either individuals or by groups, because these are the consequences that often lead to social problems. Whenever it can be shown that there are unfavorable results of actions or situations, explanation in terms of purposes is not likely to be particularly useful except to the extent that it directs attention to the differences between goals and the results of action based on them.

Using Explanations by Purpose

The familiar and important explanations by purpose are often the best we have, frequently furnishing guides which lead us toward further knowledge. However, despite this, they are among the most hazardous of explanations. But without this variety of explanation, social science would not have

gotten as far as it has. There is no question that this explanation is useful, particularly in generating further inquiries. On
the other hand, its misuse and the hazards inherent in its scientific use plague many social scientists who are consequently
brought to distrust it. This distrust is further reinforced by the
fact that the method has no place in the physical or biological
sciences, in which, of course, goals, intentions, dispositions,
aims, or plan are not relevant to the subject of investigation.
Contrastingly, few social scientists are prepared to say that
human beings are entirely without purpose. If this were the
case, it has been argued, science itself might be limited because scientists themselves might not be able self-consciously
to direct their own inquiry. Consequently, this method of
explanation is very successful for certain uses and valueless
for certain others. It can be misused or used brilliantly. Restrictions on its use and careful application of rules are required
for the method's success.

PROBABILISTIC EXPLANATIONS

Probabilistic explanations occur when a social scientist says,
"If a country is attacked, it is likely that it will defend itself."
Or, "If the weather is bad on election day, the number of
people voting will be smaller than would otherwise be expected." Probabilistic explanations use terms of probability,
not certainty, and the degree to which the premises follow is
sometimes called the degree of confidence, and is sometimes
given as a percentage. This is in marked contrast to deductive explanations, where, given the premise, the conclusions
are inevitable. Probabilistic explanations also are in contrast
to explanations by common sense, in which there is no necessary logical connection between any part of the argument except that imposed by the rules of language. In a probabilistic
explanation the central constraints are the rules of mathematics
and probability.

When a political scientist knows the characteristics of a
voter, his age, income, place of residence, religion, and past
voting habits and then says that the probability that this person

will vote Democratic is sixty percent, he means that the information which he has is not enough to tell him exactly how the man will vote but rather that the particular set of characteristics he knows about the voter is enough to enable him to identify the individual as one of a group or class. Knowing that an individual falls into a specific class, the political scientist can then make statements about the individuals within the class and expect to be right about sixty percent of the time.

Determining probability is a process of assigning numbers to a process when the outcome of any individual event is not certainly predictable but can be predicted to a certain extent and with some degree of confidence. Consider a coin-tossing experiment. If the coin and toss are fair ones, the outcome of any individual toss cannot be predicted with certainty, yet we can say that there is a fifty-fifty chance, or one chance in two, that the outcome of any given toss will be a head. Where probabilistic explanations are given, we find numerical values which represent a degree of confidence, such as one chance in two, that one specific outcome will result.

Chance and Deduction

Recall one variety of deductive logic. Statement (1) says that every X is Y. Statement (2) says that all or some of M is X. Therefore, Statement (3) says all or some of M is Y.

One way to think about how a probabilistic explanation works is to change Statement (1). A probabilistitc Statement (1) would be that there is a ninety percent chance that X is Y. The second statement, (2), would be M is X. Statement (3) would therefore be that there is a ninety percent chance that M is Y. Probabilistic explanations, in other words, are not as certain as deductive explanations.

Probabilistic argument is important in the social sciences because of the complexities and uncertainties that surround many of men's actions. Perhaps some day we will be able to be so certain about everything that we can use positive deduction in explaining things, but for the moment many of the problems that social scientists face require explanations that are based on less than certain knowledge. Thus in answer to a question as to why he expects a certain student to succeed in college, the social scientist might explain as follows. He expects the student to succeed but his prediction will only have a probability of ninety percent accuracy. Second, his prediction would not be based on logically rigorous rules but on the fact that the student's characteristics fit the characteristics of most successful students. These characteristics would probably include test scores, motivation measures, and the results of interviews. Taken altogether, this knowledge might lead the social scientist to a cautious statement that he expects the student to succeed.

This is only one way to think about the probabilistic explanation in science, and perhaps the simplest. Students commencing this subject must be warned that there are very significant differences of opinion among mathematicians, logicians, philosophers, and scientists about the nature of the meaning of statistical inference and probabilistic explanation. In this chapter, we are only trying to discuss a few of the more generally accepted ways in which social scientists use probabilistic explanation.

For example, why is the government of country X not very democratic? Governments which are not very democratic seem to exist more frequently in cases in which there is a very small ruling class or elite which does not interact much with the majority of the citizenry. Country X has a small ruling elite which does not interact with the masses. Therefore, it is likely that the government of country X will not be very democratic.

Premises and Circumstance

In a probabilistic explanation, it is not necessary that the premises contain an exact probability statistic such as one-half or sixty percent. Many social scientists would settle for statements using "likely" or "trend" or "probably." State legislators whose margins of election are narrow tend to follow their constituents' lead closely in voting. In another case, people who are very active in political parties *are very likely* to come from groups that put high values on social activities. Of course, most social scientists would prefer exact statistical per-

centages to "trend," "likely," or "probably," but often the
extent of available information simply will not permit it. In
fact, numbers given in some cases cannot be said to mean
much.

It is important to notice the relationship between the premise and the situation to be explained. The premise always
includes, in terms either statistical or probable, a statement
about a group or a situation. Another example may make this
clear. In big cities controlled by powerful political machines,
the machines have favored maintenance of the existing pattern
of racial segregation in order to continue their political control. Proposals for public housing, especially its location, usually have been the subject of widespread disagreement.
Explaining probabilisticly, we will seek to understand why it
took so long to build so little public housing in Chicago. Chicago is a large city which has long been controlled by one
political machine. It therefore fits the general group of cities
described at the beginning of the paragraph, and it is not surprising that studies of public housing in Chicago show that
disputes about the location and size of public housing are long
and bitter. In this example, a statement of probability was
made about a group or situation. An individual situation was
found which shared the same characteristics as that about
which the statement was made. Therefore, the same probability holding for the large group holds for the individual situation, in this case Chicago.

Numbers and Measurement

Social scientists disagree about the usefulness of specific
numbers or ratios, rather than "trend," "likely," or some other
term, as part of a probabilistic explanation. When a number is
used, its use implies an exact measurement. Measurement in
the social sciences must be conducted according to rigidly
specified methods or it is not likely to be of much use. As the
measurements in explanations of probability are usually not
precise, their uses are very limited indeed. When the methods
of measurement are known, the scientist can judge the adequacy of the methods of measurement as well as explanation.

However, we must remember that at least one premise in a probabilistic explanation must be statistical. Example: three out of four first voters select a candidate from the same party supported by their parents. The second premise must be a positive statement, without statistical qualification, relating a specific individual or situation to a statistical generalization. Example: John has just turned twenty-one and is voting for the first time. The conclusion then follows that the probability of John's behavior is the same as that of the class within which John is included. Example: therefore, we can conclude that the chances are three out of four that John will vote Democratic as his parents did. Notice carefully that the probability part of the explanation occurs in one premise, not referring to the individual whose behavior is to be explained. The individuals in the above example must fit the group about which the statistical generalization is made.

The inquisitive mind might now say: All right. You have explained this much, but now how do you explain the generalization itself, namely that seventy-five percent of first voters vote the way their parents do the first time they vote? That statistical generalization is obtained by other methods. We have indicated elsewhere that explanations can be carried out backward indefinitely, although they need only be carried as far as the purpose of the inquiry indicates.

Perhaps by now you have figured out that the truth or validity of a probabilistic explanation depends primarily on the truth or validity of the statistics. If the statistics are not correct, our explanation of John's behavior will not be correct. If, for example, nine out of ten young people vote as do their parents, then we cannot conclude that the chances are three out of four that John would vote the way he did unless we have some other information.

Deductive Statistics

Because the usefulness of probabilistic explanation depends entirely upon the validity and reliability of the statistical generalization upon which the explanation is based, it is important to say a little more about statistical laws. Statistical statements or laws are obtained by following very rigorous methods that you will learn much more about if you ever take statistics courses. Earlier in this book we have given you some idea of what was meant by chance or probability for simple things like coins and dice. Social scientists utilized other very powerful statistical methods to determine probabilities of group behavior. Without giving you exact numbers, here are some of the things that political scientists have discovered. Since 1916, no more than two-thirds of those eligible to vote in an American presidential election have, in fact, voted in any one election. A higher percentage of men than women vote, although since 1920 the percentage of women who voted has been increasing. Wives tend to vote as do their husbands. A higher percentage of urban dwellers vote than do those who live in small towns or the country. The more education a person has, the more likely it is that he will vote. Rich people vote in higher percentages than poor people.

By carefully analyzing voting patterns, political scientists have found out who votes. They have also studied which groups vote for whom. For example, Catholics and Jews have voted Democratic more often than have Protestants. Statistical generalizations, then, are established by carefully following the appropriate scientific methods, but—and the but is important —they are always based on past performance.

Consider the weatherman. Let's say we are interested in determining how often he is right in predicting snow. After defining snow and what successful prediction means, we must then keep a record of all the times he predicted snow and of all the times his predictions were fulfilled. We must also decide if we shall deal with the problem of the times it snowed when he did not predict it. Thus if the weatherman in a five-year period predicted snow a hundred times and it snowed during the next twenty-four hours one hundred times after his prediction, his probability would be one hundred percent. But what if it snowed one hundred times and he only predicted it eighty times? Two kinds of problems arise here. Should we give him a mark of one hundred percent if he predicted snow eighty times and, in fact, it snowed eighty times? What do we do with the twenty times he did not predict the snow? And what if he predicted snow eighty times but it only snowed sixty times after he predicted it and forty times when he did not? Modern statistical methods give us ways to treat this kind of problem.

No matter how we resolve the issues above, the central point remains that whatever the probability finally decided upon, it is always based on past performance, although sometimes the generalizations are so good that we can explain and predict on the basis of them with remarkable accuracy. For example, since 1948, political scientists have been able to predict the outcome of presidential and other elections based on their statistical generalizations with less than an average of a three percent error. And what is more, they can usually tell us the degree of confidence with which they make their predictions. By a degree of confidence, we mean that we know how great any error in our statistics is likely to be in percentage terms.

Generally speaking, the larger the number of observations upon which statistical generalizations are based, the more confidence we can have in the generalizations. What we have been discussing is part of the subject of statistical inference. Inference, you may remember, refers to a general process of obtaining knowledge. Statistical inference refers to the processes by which we use statistics in obtaining knowledge.

The Importance of Probabilistic Explanation

There are two related reasons for social scientists' frequent use of probabilistic explanation and statistical generalizations. First, the subject matter is inherently complex. For the most part, we are not able to identify, single out, or measure each factor or variable that is important to any given problem. We cannot state precisely the exact conditions on which the varieties of human conduct depend. Assume that you were asked to state the reasons people voted in the way they did. Some of the variables you might find important would be: sex, age, race, place of residence, religion, occupation, and education. While all of these factors have been found important in explaining voters' behavior, none of them completely explains it. Thus social scientists have to consider a large number of variables that are in turn related in many complex ways. Statistical or probabilistic methods are one way to do this.

The second reason for the importance of probabilistic explanation is related to the fact that people can choose. Because human beings are often free to choose and have different goals and purposes at different times, social scientists have been able to discover very few invariable regularities in individual or social phenomena. When we add to this the fact that men's actions are also determined to some extent by the way in which they interpret what happens to them, and since all men interpret things somewhat differently, it is very difficult to discover universal generalizations that relate individual and social reactions to well-defined external factors.

Neither of these reasons means that social scientists will never be able to discover laws as universal or as precise as those more common in the physical or biological sciences. They only mean that up to now social scientists have not been able to discover many such laws. Difficult problems have been solved before in science. Imagine how difficult and complex it must have been for a Roman, using Roman numerals, to try to extract a square root. Even to multiply or divide long numbers was very difficult. However, with the relatively simple but very important device of Arabic notation, which we now use, calculation became much easier. At the present state of development of social science, there is no question of the appearance of complexity with regard to many topics. However, this is always the case early in the history of a scientific discipline; there is no reason whatsoever to assume that ways will not be found to deal with this complexity.

From the point of view of science, one of the most appealing things about the probabilistic method of explanation is its firm foundation in fact. The statistical generalization, always a part of probabilistic explanation, is, or at least can be, rooted in the data. The data are not necessarily complete, correct, or properly chosen, but they are public, and the basis on which they are obtained can be known. The method of obtaining the statistical generalizations as well as the generalization itself can be public and, therefore, tested.

The weakness of this kind of explanation, on the other hand, lies in the fact that it does not pass the test of logical rigor as does deductive explanation. There is no logically necessary connection between the fact that John is young and voting for the first time, and the fact that he probably will vote Democratic as in the example above. But all science must pass two tests, those of logic and of the real world. No methods of inference or ways of knowing about the world pass both these tests. Deductive explanation passed the test of logic and reason, of course. But if its premises do not correspond with the real world, then that method of explanation is weak. In a case of probabilistic explanation, we know the degree of correspondence of the premise with the real world. But it is never a certain correspondence in the logical sense. Therefore, this kind of explanation is weaker logically and stronger in terms of its data.

Science, however, need make no unpleasant choice in a case like this. There are different methods of explanation in science, each of which is appropriate in a greater or lesser degree to different kinds of problems. The political scientist has set for himself the task of explaining both individual and group behavior. Like other social scientists who face similar tasks, he has found probabilistic explanation to be a powerful method.

Chapter 10

Psychology—
Explanations by Origins
and Development

DEVELOPMENT OF PSYCHOLOGY

Like every discipline of social science, psychology
can be defined from several points of view—in
terms of subject matter, methods, outlook, or aims,
or in terms of those who practice it. Each approach
to a definition is useful for a different purpose, and
ours here is to give a general idea of the discipline.
We will stress how psychology grew and its most
important schools. The method of explanation described is that called historical or genetic. All the
social sciences use it when the origins and developmental stages of the subject being investigated are
well-known.

Orgins of Psychology

Self-awareness, a distinctively human characteristic, is found in our earliest written records, which show that man was concerned with something he called "mind" or "soul" or "will." We know that early man was concerned with what caused his mind to act the way it did. He felt that some sort of mind, not necessarily his own, not only caused his own actions but also almost everything else. From the earliest times the problems of the mind and causation were related, although not scientifically. By Plato's time, however, men had recognized the separation of mind and body, today called the mind-body dualism. Aristotle, following Plato, made only very limited use of the experimental method in studying people. He thought there were three kinds of soul, which he attempted to understand mainly through introspection. His style of studying psychological questions and his philosophical framework were to last for more than a thousand years.

Three hundred years before Christ, there were debates about free will and the immortality of the human soul. Although Christianity affirmed that the soul was immortal, it allowed several solutions to the problem of free will. In the middle of the thirteenth century, St. Thomas Aquinas distinguished between scientific truth, based upon observation and experiment, and religious truth, based upon the church.

Even in the early 1600s, following the revival of science, problems of the human mind were still primarily religious and philosophical. René Descartes, the great French philosopher and mathematician, thought of reality as having two distinct and separate aspects: one, the physical domain of matter; the other, the non-physical domain of mind. Material things, including physiological processes and mechanisms that occur in the body without being guided by a mind, he thought of as complicated machines. Only the mind could think, reason, know, remember, or exercise a will. Descartes's philosophy began with his famous statement, "Cogito ergo sum." (I think; therefore, I am.) Of course, Descartes knew that part of man's behavior was determined as a result of his mind interacting with his body and other material things. Some of the things he studied were impulses to action, imagination, and sensation. Debate about the nature of the mind continued for almost two hundred years. The English philosopher Thomas Hobbes, for example, thought that man was more of a machine; and, in France, philosopher and physician La Mettrie actually wrote a book called *Man, A Machine.*

Early Psychological Explanations

Men also speculated about where ideas came from. The English philosopher John Locke thought there were no innate ideas; Bishop George Berkeley felt that all ideas were God's gift and that external reality existed only in man's mind. The Dutch philosopher Baruch Spinoza saw mind and body as different aspects of the same thing. By the middle 1750s, David Hume in England had argued that neither God nor the external world gave us our ideas but rather we got them from sensations and associations.

The schools of empiricism, or British empiricism, and rationalism, or German rationalism, had developed by the nineteenth century. The former emphasized sense perception and learning in the development of the mind. John Locke had asserted that the mind of a newly born child was blank and that everything to fill it had to come through the senses. The British empiricists directed their attention, mainly through speculation rather than scientific methods, to the nature of the physiological and mental processes that were important in perceiving, remembering, and learning.

The rationalists, on the other hand, paid much less attention to perception as the main source of knowledge or ideas. They claimed that the mind is able to develop ideas independent of the stimulation provided by the environment, emphasizing that people can decide what they want to perceive. According to the rationalists, an individual thinks about what he wants to hear, smell, see, or taste, and then goes about finding these things. The mind was considered very important, which explains in part the name "rationalists." The German rationalists based much of their thinking on the philosophy of Immanuel

Kant, an eighteenth-century philosopher who had also divided the mind into departments containing the intellect, emotions, and will.

The First Experimental Psychological Laboratory

In the early nineteenth century philosophers had discussed in great detail many important questions relating to psychology. Religious dogma had firmly established its positions. However, neither religion nor philosophy gave satisfactory answers to what happened in the mind, nor did they do enough to explain behavior. Because the scientific method was teaching so much about other subjects, some people began to wonder whether it could not be applied to the study of man and his mind. Experimental methods in physiology had reestablished distinctions that were known to the Romans, for example those between motor and sensory nerves. Nerve fibers which carry messages enabling us to move are different from those enabling us to see and hear. By the middle of the nineteenth century, experimental methods had established that voluntary movement was closely related to the brain, while reflex or involuntary movement was not. Among the many physiological discoveries were those locating the speech center in the brain and identifying the parts of the brain that control seeing and hearing.

It was not until the late 1870s, however, that German psychologist Wilhelm Wundt established a laboratory at the University of Leipzig for psychological research. His laboratory, in which he investigated such things as reaction times, sense perception, association or similarities, and continuity in space and time, was not very much by our standards. But one of his great steps forward was the attempt to establish psychology as a science using scientific methods. The three great influences in the development of his laboratory were philosophical discussions, experimental physiology, and psychophysics.

Science was rapidly growing in the early part of the nineteenth century. Many of the great physical scientists were concerned with how the actual changes in the physical world were related to what men felt or became aware of. That the time was ripe for the use of scientific methods in discussing psychological questions is demonstrated by the fact that American psychologist William James had also set up a laboratory. James's laboratory, for demonstration purposes only, was set up at Harvard shortly before Wundt established his. Like all progress in science, the establishment of Wundt's laboratory did not mean that suddenly psychology became a science. The influences we have discussed show that it was already in the process of becoming one, though developing slowly, even before the installation of Wundt's laboratory.

MODERN "SCHOOLS" OF PSYCHOLOGY

Wundt's laboratory acted as a magnet for young scholars from all over the world. Many of America's most brilliant psychologists studied under him and worked in his laboratory. At the same time, of course, other people were studying psychology scientifically elsewhere. A convenient way to understand different scientific approaches to the study of psychology is by examining the main "schools" of psychology that developed. Any classification of the main trends of a science into schools is bound to be rather arbitrary, so it should not be thought that a person is a member of only one school. Sometimes he may start out as a member of one and change to another. The schools often overlap. We use the term "school" here to refer to a dominant or important set of ideas, approaches, and concerns that unite a group of psychologists. Today there are few psychologists who admit themselves to be members of any given school. The main schools were largely broken up about the time of World War II. They had done their job: each had contributed much in its area of concern, enabling psychologists to use the methods, knowledge, approach, or insights of any school that defined his particular problems.

Structural Psychology

One of Wundt's most brilliant students was an Englishman named Edward Titchner. After he attained his Ph.D. in 1892, Titchner came to the United States, where he influenced a large group of American psychologists. The school that developed under Titchner's influence—*structural psychology*—took its name from its attempt to *learn about mental phenomena by studying feelings, thoughts, and images*, which were thought to be the three most important *elements forming the structure of consciousness.* Structural psychologists attempted to analyze and describe in detail the conscious states that resulted from stimulation of various kinds of physical energy.

The method used was introspection—a careful and elaborate description of conscious experience performed by trained observers. It would not be enough to say, "I feel an electric shock." The sensation would have been described in detail in terms of such qualities as intensity, duration, quality, magnitude, and clearness. Psychology, in this view, was primarily a descriptive science in which causal explanations were found in physiology. It was an early example of the "pure science" attitude that ruled out such subjects as learning, motivation, personality, the abnormal mind, and intelligence—many problems of interest to psychology and pursued by other schools. The structuralists made many important laboratory studies in such fields as perception, imagery, and other physiological bases of behavior.

Functionalism

The functionalists in psychology were more united in opposing the relatively narrow definition and approach of the structuralists than they were on a positive program of their own. Their opposition was based not only on the restricted scope of structuralism but also on the rather narrowly defined methods of introspection and the analysis of very complex states of consciousness into a relatively few sensory elements. Functionalists, such as the American psychologist William James, emphasized the changing and dynamic character of mental activity and sought to find out more about what a mind *does* rather than what it is.

The name *functionalist* was given to those psychologists who were *concerned with the activities or functions of the mind.* They emphasized the processes *by which man continually adjusts to a changing environment* and wanted to discover how thinking or emotions meet the needs of the organism. The structure of the mind was not so important as its function. For them, psychology was mainly the study of interactions between people and their environment, which includes, of course, other people. Often, the more they became concerned with interaction and adaptive behavior, the more they shifted to problems of learning. John Dewey, one of America's greatest psychologists and educators, is generally classified as a functionalist. He concerned himself with questions such as how behavior can be modified. For example, how does the learning of a motor skill, like typewriting, a conscious process in its early stages, become much less conscious as it is learned? Dewey's famous slogan "Learn by doing" was an important influence on education.

Recognition of the fact that complex behavior can be performed without conscious awareness was one basis for the functionalists' opposition to the structuralists. The functionalists attempted to be scientific not through introspection but through objective observation of events and other persons. Thus as they broadened the range of their subject matter, they were able to use children and animals as subjects of observation. The functions of the mind such as perceiving, making decisions, or remembering served the purpose of adjusting an individual to his environment. Their broad definition of psychology and its different methods allowed many new kinds of human problems to be examined. They made great progress in applied psychology—for example, mental testing, learning, and working in factories and studying the effects of noise or light on workers. Because there were no leaders for this approach, there were few boundary lines.

Behaviorism

The school of *behaviorism* emphasized *the direct influences of environment,* such as teaching, *on shaping behavior and* studied *how behavior changes with growth and development.* It also explored the roots of present behavior in past experience. The behaviorists contributed much in the fields of learning, motivation, and perception, and were instrumental in defining psychology, as is commonly done today, as a science of behavior. One aim of the behaviorists was to establish laws relating stimuli and responses so that if the psychologist knew the stimulus he could predict the response or if he knew the response he would know what the stimulus had been.

Two names are most frequently associated with behaviorism: Ivan P. Pavlov and John B. Watson. Pavlov, the distinguished Russian physiologist who won the Nobel Prize in 1904 for his research on digestion, became interested in the reactions shown in behavior when various types of stimulation were applied to a subject. While working with dogs, he noticed that they would salivate not only at the sight of food, but also when they heard people bringing it or opening their cages. He began a series of experiments to see if he could get the dogs to salivate in response to unaccustomed sounds such as a bell ringing; soon he had established such a "conditioned reflex." By means of conditioned reflexes, Pavlov studied learning processes and attempted to discover the physiological processes and mechanisms that control behavior. In his research he did not refer to either the structure or the function of the mind.

The American psychologist John B. Watson arrived at an emphasis on behavior by a different route. He claimed that science demanded observation and measurement of things or events, which for psychology meant behavior as opposed to what the mind is or does. Consequently, he proposed to abandon consciousness, as well as mind, as proper subject matter for experimental psychological research. Watson wanted to gain knowledge about human beings by inferring it from what they actually did, the questions they could answer, the problems they could solve, the jobs they could do, and the language they used. Like Pavlov, he studied animals, which behaved more simply than human beings and could therefore be more readily investigated and understood. Watson defined behavior very broadly and tried to understand the relationships between behavior and physiological process. For him, behavior could be studied in its own right—in learning skills or as indicating mental processes. In accordance with his theory, he had his own subjects writing verbal reports of the steps they reached in solving a problem.

Gestalt Psychology

Gestalt, a German word, has the connotation of the whole or big picture seen all at once. This meaning tells us both the origin and the emphasis of the school of *Gestalt* psychology. The German psychologists who developed the leading idea felt that neither experience nor behavior could be broken down as the other three schools claimed. For them *experience and behavior were things to be seen as a whole*, even if certain relationships between the whole and its parts are discovered.

Gestalt also means "a unit segregated from its surroundings." *Gestalt* psychologists studied experience and behavior in terms of its pattern and how it was organized, emphasizing that the whole is greater than the sum of its parts and arguing that attempts to analyze the parts often destroy the unique qualities of the whole. It was pointed out by one *Gestalt* psychologist, for example, that the other three schools could not account for the illusion of motion when lights go on and off in rapid succession as they do with moving neon signs. Thus, although they disagreed with the structuralists about breaking down subjects for analysis, they did think the method of introspection was useful. They attempted to verify all of their theories by experimental research. Studies of perception and learning in *Gestalt* psychology were from the point of view of problem solving or reasoning rather than the behaviorists' conditioning or habit formation. The *Gestalt* psychologists contributed significantly to personality theory, social psychology, perception, learning, and thinking.

Psychoanalysis

The great name in the history of the psychoanalytic approach to psychology is Sigmund Freud, who as a doctor attempted to cure people who had mental or nervous disorders. Freud's work stands apart from the other schools of psychology because he made no major attempt to use older scientific or laboratory methods to verify his theories. He was concerned with trying to cure people by interacting with them in certain ways and then observing the results. This system led to the scientific method of psychoanalysis, a method still very young and, to some, very controversial, although no one denies its great influence. A major part of Freud's method is "talking out." By listening carefully to what his patients said in their free associations, their unconscious slips, and the ways in which they said things, Freud attempted to discover what in their past had made them ill, what had made their bodies act the way they did.

Freud drew the attention of psychologists to the part of the mind that is unconscious. He thought that adult problems often had their origin in conflicts and frustrations the patient had experienced as a child. He emphasized the dynamics of personality, stressing conflict and motivation, and introduced the importance of sexual factors in human behavior. For Freud, no behavior was irrational in that there must be a cause for it, and he sought these causes in all aspects of man's existence, including his dreams and instincts.

Both in what he found and in the way he went about finding it, Freud developed a revolutionary and controversial approach to psychology. The hypotheses his theories suggest for studies of motivation, abnormal behavior, and personality development are slowly being subjected to scientific verification. As is the case with any pioneer in science, his theories do not always prove to be correct, but the overall scientific fruitfulness of the approach has given Freud an unchallenged high status in the history of psychology. Although many of the usual scientific methods cannot be applied in the case of psychoanalysis, it cannot be stressed too often that the whole approach requires an emphasis on cause and effect, which is one of the hallmarks of science. Thus even irrational behavior is determined by forces which can be understood by a rational man.

PSYCHOLOGY AND GENETIC EXPLANATION

In dealing with such a broad range of problems, psychologists must inevitably use a broad range of methods; and they must be concerned with the overall explanation of a situation as they attempt to cope with immediate problems. One of the most commonly used methods of explanation is the genetic, also frequently used by all other social scientists when they face a situation that is very complex and to which few laws of a deductive type seem to apply or when the broad range of data necessary for the probabilistic explanation is lacking.

Explanation is crucial in the solution of actual problems because we need to know why specific phenomena in a specific situation interact the way they do. There are usually several levels of explanation for complex phenomena, and the genetic level of explanation is that which tells us why and how a phenomenon occurs in terms that we can comprehend. We only seek to know why up to the point where things seem to be understandable to us.

Here is an illustration of levels of explanation. Suppose the question, "Why does our body digest food?" is raised. One answer might be, in order to provide the body with energy so that it can live. That level of explanation will satisfy many people. However, the question might also be raised, "Why does the body continue to try to sustain its life?" This must be explained on another level. There is no end to levels of explanation, and philosophers of science discuss this in terms of infinite regress, when every answer to a question can itself be further questioned. A popular expression of this kind of idea is the old saying, "Every flea has its little fleas."

When Genetic Explanations Are Used

Genetic explanations trace the development of important events that cause a given situation to come into being. Why does a person attempt to commit suicide? A genetic explanation attempts to find out what critical events in the person's past made him behave the way he did. Why do Americans use the British system of weights and measures? A genetic explanation describes the way the British system came to be used in America. Why do children from culturally deprived families learn more slowly than other children? Genetic explanations look for the reasons for the different rates of learning in terms of the child's past.

Social scientists use genetic explanations when they do not have general laws to cover specific phenomena. There is no general law to describe why an individual might want to commit suicide, for example, or how human beings evolved, or why they evolved the way they did. Probabilistic explanations often are not possible whenever unique events must be studied. Much that happens in a person's life happens to him alone. Nor can probabilistic explanations usually be used for unique social events such as the Chinese Revolution.

We have emphasized, and our examples have shown, that genetic explanations are also used whenever complex phenomena are involved. Here we refer to phenomena resulting from many interacting forces, such as those within a society or those contributing to an individual's emotions. Genetic explanations do not make use of every event of the past in order to explain specific phenomena but select happenings from the past relevant to the event under study, rejecting all those not relevant.

But, you might ask, how do you do that? In a genetic explanation events of importance are selected on the basis of assumptions as to what is relevant to the event under study. Studies of learning, for instance, emphasize such factors as vocabulary size, reading skills, adequate eyesight, and motivation. Thus the genetic explanation must always contain assumptions, preferably explicit, about what things cause other things. If, for example, it is said that an adult's fear of height was caused by his fright when as a child he was held over a cliff, one possible implicit assumption could be that things which frightened children continue to frighten them as adults. When the assumptions about causes are made explicit, they can then be tested.

Genetic explanations, then, always contain general assumptions about causes, which may be laws or law-like statements for which evidence is available and which can be tested. Sometimes the assumptions are probabilistic, as when a psychologist attempts to find a reason for an act or when an anthropologist attempts to investigate the way an institution specific to a given culture developed.

However, whether the assumptions are explicit or implicit, whether they are reasonably well established in the form of laws or just probabilities, the fact remains that the premises or assumptions about cause cannot alone provide the necessary and sufficient conditions for the phenomena to be explained. If this were the case, then we would have deductive or probabilistic kinds of explanation.

Explaining and Describing

You will recall that the process of description involves the observation and recording of the features of phenomena which distinguish them from all other phenomena in a way that makes them understandable. Recall, too, that classification puts something into a group with similar characteristics. And, of course, explanation answers the question "why." So explanation is different from description and classification, except in the case of genetic explanation when the description of the origins of certain phenomena also explains how the phenomena came into being. Then "how" and "why" questions are closely related.

Take the simple question, "Why is that an oak tree?" One reasonable answer is because it developed from an acorn. Or to another question, "Why is that baby not running?" The mother might reasonably answer, "He hasn't yet learned to walk." Whenever the developmental stages of specific phenomena are very well known, a description of the origin leading to further development is an adequate genetic explanation for the phenomena.

Although a description of origins is satisfactory when the laws, stages, or sequence of development are well known, this is often not the case. Therefore, it is necessary to examine two other kinds of situations in which genetic explanations are useful, those that refer both to the origins and to the subsequent development of phenomena and those that refer only to the development, growth, or change of phenomena.

All genetic explanations are, of course, time-related. Some writers go so far as to call genetic explanations historical for that reason. Generally speaking, genetic explanations tell what happens or what causes a given thing, event, or process. But precisely because the genetic explanation is time-related, it is always possible to move to an earlier and different level of explanation by moving backward in time. What is the beginning of one event may be the end of a second or the middle of a third.

This reinforces the point made in Chapter 2, that social scientists might use several methods of explanation for any one problem. A case in which genetic explanation might be useful could be the explanation of a black's reaction to a white policeman in one of our large cities. A description of the child's parents as black suffices to explain why the child is black. A genetic explanation of the development of his feelings toward white policemen could easily be made in terms of important episodes from the child's past relating to white policemen.

Sometimes a genetic explanation is used to describe the development of a process, a person, or a situation, without discussing its origins. In a historical process one could start from the beginning and go up to the present, or one could start at the present and go back to the beginning, or, as in the case we are presently discussing, one can simply take a slice out of the middle, between the beginning and the present. One might, for example, look at a person's momentary behavior. "Why are you limping, George?" "Because I sprained my ankle skiing yesterday," George might reply. Why George went skiing, why he had the accident, and indeed many other questions may be interesting, but as this example makes clear, it is entirely possible to get satisfactory answers to the question "why" for part of a process or development without necessarily going back to origins or beginnings in any important sense.

Genetic explanations attempt to pick out major causal factors and always require time sequences. This is not required in deductive and probabilistic explanations, which refer respectively to necessary and uniform connections and to probable connections. In both cases dates are not always required because the connections themselves are independent of time, and what is stressed is the nature of the connections or relationships rather than the times at which they occur.

Genetic explanations, however, direct our attention to cause and effect, answering the question "why" by referring to the causes of specific events and specified processes or stages. They clearly differ from deductive or probabilistic explanations, which deal with specific events only as members of classes of broader events or broader classes. Genetic explanations do not attempt to establish universal laws or broad generalizations. A broad generalization cannot state the historical origin or exact development of any particular phenomena in which people are involved. Neither an individual's nor mankind's history is absolutely predetermined by its origin; development is subject to many of life's chances. In considering causes unique or particular to an event, genetic explanation thus complements the other forms of explanation in social science. Where the developmental stages are well known, it simply describes the origins or both origins and development. Here the origins are usefully thought of as statements of initial conditions and the development as statements of important causal events.

For both probabilistic and genetic explanation, the conclusion is not a logically necessary consequence of premises or assumptions, even when all of these are known and stated. Thus one cannot use a successful genetic or probabilistic explanation as the basis for prediction in the same way one can use a deductive explanation. Generally, genetic and probabilistic explanations mention some, but not all, of the necessary and sufficient conditions for the events they attempt to explain, and the premises are not stated in a logically rigorous way.

The psychologist cannot deal with the whole man any more than the historian can study everything which goes on in a given period of time. Most social scientists must break many of their problems into parts—analyze them. They must then attempt to explain what is important about the parts they have chosen, how they relate to each other, and how one event causes another. The genetic explanation is admirably suited for this kind of task.

Sequence and Continuity

Because genetic explanations have no logical necessity built into them they vary in degree of validity or strength, sometimes in ways that are not easy to measure. If a genetic explanation were to hold always and everywhere, let us see what would be assumed. The departures from these ideal assumptions will then illustrate how the explanation gets weaker. The further the actual explanation is from the requirements for the ideal situation, the weaker the explanation.

The first assumption is that the same sequential process occurs for every person or event. For example, it has been fairly well established that, with individual variations, developmental sequences are about the same for all children. So it can be said that most children make noises before they talk and talk poorly before they talk well.

Another assumption for a very strong genetic explanation is that development is continuous. One stage or situation evolves from another, the earlier influencing the latter. For example, the head grows more rapidly than the rest of the body while the digestive system, the liver and heart, develop relatively slowly in childhood and more rapidly in early adolescence.

A third, often unexpressed, assumption in genetic explanation is that stages of development are correlated. Different parts of a system are related to various developmental stages, as in the observation that there is a set of relationships between patterns of behavior and sexual maturity.

Certain patterns of human development, particularly those of early physical development, have been studied in great detail, making possible the use of genetic explanation. When a mother asks, "Why do my baby's lower teeth come out first?" one could answer that in human beings the lower teeth erupt before the upper, the biting teeth come in before the molars, and the first baby teeth which come in will be the first to be replaced by permanent teeth.

Almost all parts of physical development seem to be subject to orderly trends. Gland development, language development, creativity, size, changes in height, weight, dental arch, motor development, sensory perception, all seem to follow patterns. The exact age at which either a physical or a functional change appears is fairly, although not exactly, predictable.

There also seem to be predictable development patterns of intellectual functions such as memory and reasoning. When such patterns are very well established, genetic explanations often seem too simple. Yet they are important and must be understood. When the mother asks the doctor, "Why can't my six-month-old baby talk yet?" the doctor will explain that the baby is too young to be expected to talk. On the other hand, if the baby is three years old and still cannot talk, the doctor will want to make further tests.

Explaining from origins when developmental sequences are well known is a successful method of answering the question "why." Generally, we can say that if we know the precise origins of the person or event, for instance the baby in the above example, and we also know the pattern of development that babies go through when they grow up, we then can decide where the baby is in the developmental sequence simply by comparing any one baby with the pattern—usually by his age and sex.

Origin and Development

A child's behavior becomes increasingly variable as he grows older, because behavior depends upon learning and is very flexible. When the genetic explanation is used for individual behavior or feelings, the explanation will be weaker the further we are from specific well-known patterns of individual behavioral or mental development and the more the individual has learned.

Below is a rough sketch indicating how classical Freudians have analyzed the development of personality. Given such an analysis, a scientist could isolate the time-span during which a particular problem arose, and by means of genetic explanation could then examine how the usual or "normal" development was interfered with and proceed to try to resolve the problem. This illustrates a specific instance in which the method of genetic explanation is used.

Generally speaking, according to classical psychoanalysis as it was developed by Freud and his early followers, the first year of life can be described as an oral stage, in which pleasure for the infant is derived through the lips and the mouth as in sucking and eating. This is significant for future personality development because the infant, in getting food from others, thus lays the foundation for his dependency needs. The second year is generally characterized as anal, in which pleasure is derived through the retention and expulsion of his feces and through the general exercise of muscular control. Personality traits associated with this stage of life are those of being obstinate or stingy or compulsive if one is "anal retentive." Properly handled, however, bowel training leads to creativity and productivity.

In the third, fourth, and fifth years, the stages are phallic and Oedipal, in which pleasure is derived through genital stimulation and mental preoccupation with the parent of the opposite sex. So far as personality development is concerned, as the child resolves the Oedipal preoccupations he begins to identify more fully with both parents and develops a super ego, or conscience.

From the sixth year until puberty is the latency stage, during which there is temporary repression of sexual interest, pleasure being derived from the external world and knowledge and curiosity substituting for gratifications. According to one group of psychologists, this is an important period for the social development of the child, who is acquiring knowledge and skills which he will later need.

From adolescence on is the genital stage, in which pleasure is derived from sexual relationships with a partner of the opposite sex. During this period, one turns from self-love to the love of others, develops altruistic motives, and is freed from dependence on parents.

Genetic Explanation in Terms of Development Only

The type of genetic explanation last discussed above was concerned with occurrences within a specific time and the processes by which they might be explained, focusing on a slice of time rather than on origins or conclusions. Suppose we ask why people who after a lifetime of blindness acquire sight must learn to see? The genetic explanation in this case would be that at least minimum physical stimulation seems to be required for the development of any of our senses. This in turn can be related to a broader generalization which seems to hold true, namely that contact and stimulation of various kinds—social, mental, and physical—are necessary for normal human development. Notice that this example involves only a period late in a person's life. Notice, too, that there is relatively little reference to the causes for his loss or renewal of sight and that the explanation is only as strong as the more general statements of development upon which it relies.

As we have seen, the genetic explanation requires, in the case of simple development, a series of dated occurrences and the selection of major factors that have caused the occurrences which answer the question "why."

Chapter 11

Anthropology—
Explanations by Functions

WHAT IS ANTHROPOLOGY?

Many anthropologists consider their area of study to be that of man and his works at all times and places. This can hardly be said to be a definition, however, because it is so broad. How then can we understand anthropology? In this chapter we will discuss some of its history and its relations to other social science disciplines. We will see what anthropologists study and describe some of their tools of investigation.

The Five Fields of Anthropology

Anthropology has its roots in three well-established fields of scholarship: the physical, especially the biological, sciences; the humanities, especially social philosophy; and the early social sciences. By the end of the 1800s advances in all of these fields led some men to seek a synthesis of the science of man, and by the middle of the twentieth century anthropology was making a bid to achieve this.

Broadly speaking, anthropology is concerned with five major areas: prehistory (including archaeology and evolution), physical anthropology, linguistics, ethnology, and social and cultural anthropology. The study of prehistory, archaeology, and evolution developed rapidly after Darwin's pathfinding work in the middle of the nineteenth century. His hypotheses about animals led to the investigation of mankind's own origins. Prehistory refers to the very long period before the development of writing. Archaeologists explore the beginnings of culture through their investigations of physical remains from cultures of the past. Evolutionists study the way mankind developed. Some anthropologists have studied the evolution of writing, for example. Another subject of their study is the evolution of a specific tool—such as the plough.

Physical anthropology developed after it was acknowledged that man himself is an animal whose body, structure, and functions can be studied as can those of the lower animals. For many years, and still in much of Europe, the term "anthropology" was regarded as synonymous with "physical anthropology." The first physical anthropological studies were devoted to physical measurements and the classification of man, according to skull sizes, colors of skins, flatness of shin bones, and hair characteristics. Today physical anthropologists study heredity, structural anatomy, and genetic processes as well. Physical anthropology is closely associated with biology; both are concerned with the physical characteristics of man as they are distributed among men around the world. Physical anthropology often attempts to establish relationships between the human body and human behavior such as temperament or personality.

Linguistics, the third of the major divisions of anthropology, has many of its roots in the humanities. It is concerned with the nature, the sounds, the structure, and the syntax of languages. Within linguistics, phonology is concerned with the sound patterns of a language; morphology deals with the way words or other language forms combine to create units of language which, in turn, convey meaning, and syntax deals with the way in which words are combined into phrases or sentences. Historical linguistics, or philology, studies the connections that exist between languages in the same family—for example, Spanish, French, and Italian are all Romance languages, languages derived from Latin—and the way language and language families change through time. Anthropologists study the relationships between languages and cultures.

Ethnology, the fourth division of anthropology, refers to descriptive studies of human societies. In the past, these studies have often been of primitive or so-called non-literate societies but some anthropologists now use the term to cover any descriptive study of human society, although others restrict the use to more historical studies. The historical study, fairly common at the end of the 1800s, was the earliest. It reflects some of the social science roots of anthropology—interest in history and in other cultures.

Social and cultural anthropology, the last of the primary fields of anthropology, is probably the most popular subdivision of anthropology. Some anthropologists distinguish social from cultural anthropology, social anthropology emphasizing the study of social behavior and cultural anthropology focusing on general laws about culture. They would almost all agree, however, that man's social behavior both influences and is influenced by his culture. Social and cultural anthropology is closely related to the study of psychology and sociology.

The subdivisions of anthropology are interrelated. Archaeological studies describe the physical context in which the remains of men are found. Physical anthropologists measure these remains carefully and attempt to determine the point of their physical evolution. Ethnologists will take the findings of both the archaeologists and physical anthropologists as raw material for their historical and theoretical studies. When written records, such as hieroglyphics or cuneiform writing, are part of archaeological discoveries, linguists will study them. And, finally, any theory of social behavior or culture change that social and cultural anthropologists develop must be consistent with the findings of the archaeologists if it is to be valid.

Culture, A Central Concept

By the middle of the 1950s, the term "culture" had come to stand for a central anthropological concept. Although anthropologists have used and defined the term since the 1870s, there are many variations in its meaning. Generally, however, *culture refers to behavior patterns of men at a given time and place that distinguish one group of men from another.* It refers to the total way people behave in a group or community. Sometimes it is condensed to mean their "ways of life." Sometimes "culture" is used by anthropologists to refer to the actual behavior of the group and sometimes to the group's shared model for living. Almost all would agree that the term refers to learned behavior and the conventional meanings that the society attaches to acts or objects.

Anthropologists often speak of particular cultures, such as those of deep rural southern Americans, of the Kiowa Indians, or of the Samoans. They also consider it proper to speak of culture in general and have drawn up lists of elements that are shared by all cultures about which we know anything. All cultures have in common athletic sports, dancing, education, and property rights, among other elements.

Anthropology, scarcely more than a hundred years old and one of the newest disciplines of the social sciences, is firmly established as a social science. In the words of anthropologist Clyde Kluckhohn, "Anthropology holds up a great mirror to man and lets him look at himself in his infinite variety." The first modern department of anthropology was established at Columbia University when Franz Boas was hired in 1896. By now nearly every college and university offers an undergraduate course in anthropology.

Technological Tools

Partly because of its relative newness and partly because of the wide area with which it is concerned, the study of anthropology has seen the development and use of many technological aids—more, perhaps, than any other social science. The archaeologist, of course, has long used spades, trowels, scalpels, and camel's-hair brushes, to carefully dig up whatever remains he might find. But increasingly archaeologists are using new techniques, such as chemical methods to preserve footprints in the soil or to reconstruct objects which have turned to rust but which can now be reduced back to iron. Aerial photography is used to obtain population counts, and X-rays are used on unwrapped Egyptian mummies to determine the state of their teeth. Anthropologists now use ultraviolet light to study faded labels and to distinguish various fibers from one another, recording machines to study linguistics, and drawing and drafting machines to make accurate records. Measurements are made with photography; photogrammatic techniques are used to measure and map the ground from the air. Working with machines and a series of photographs, archaeologists can make three-dimensional reconstructions of people or places. Archaeologists use vacuum techniques with vaporized metal for replicating enameled surfaces on teeth and polarized light to examine skeletal remains in the ground. Motion pictures record the way primitive people make bows and arrows. Still pictures have long been used for scientific records.

While anthropologists are far advanced in their use of the devices of modern science, they are handicapped by lack of money and lack of training. Typically, a single engineer in his senior year will have more technological training and more expensive equipment to practice with than will the entire graduating class of anthropologists at many of the major universities in the country.

ANTHROPOLOGY AND THE OTHER SOCIAL SCIENCES

Like all the social sciences, anthropology is related to the other social sciences and has borrowed heavily from them while contributing to them. Among the social sciences relationships are reciprocal, each needing the other and all contributing together. One of anthropology's distinctive characteristics is its broad viewpoint. One of its major contributions to the other social sciences is to increase the understandings that are achieved by the other more specialized approaches to a subject. For a long time physical anthropology has been developing much statistical data covering many individuals and groups. To determine the interrelationships of these data, how they are correlated, and their significance, anthropologists use techniques of multivariate analysis that have been developed by mathematicians and other social scientists. For all of the social sciences anthropology stresses the idea that people should see themselves and others as objectively as possible, perhaps attempting to do so from the point of view of another person or society. Anthropology also emphasizes understanding people and groups in terms of a system in which each individual and act is thought of as part of a larger culture.

In the field of law, anthropology's emphasis on aspects of culture, including social control, the formation of norms of behavior, and enforcements and sanctions which are as persuasive for other societies as law often is for ours, has opened new areas for contemplation. Political science, too, has benefited from the cross-cultural approach common to anthropology, which has conclusively shown that there are very many ways that men can govern themselves besides our own or those commonly found in the western tradition.

Feedback in the Social Sciences

Anthropology has borrowed from the other disciplines, but it would be foolish to try to decide whether it borrowed or contributed more. This is because the modern social sciences are interrelated in such a way that discoveries and knowledge in one discipline are constantly and rapidly fed back into the other disciplines. Thus sociology was enriched by anthropology when anthropologist Ralph Linton made progress in the theory of status and role.

Economics has recently been concerned with the problem of economic change and development. Economists have turned to the anthropologists for information about such things as exchange rituals, patterns of ownership, and other trade relationships. Psychology has also contributed to and has shared in the benefits received from anthropological study. For example, some anthropologists tried to test for the Freudian system in other cultures, which was a valuable attempt to see the extent to which the theory was valid. However, the results were not conclusive. Anthropology, by testing theories developed in one culture for their applicability to another culture, performs a valuable service to social science. As a result of anthropological findings, some psychological theories have been refined.

Anthropologists use observation as well as interviews, questionnaires, and other data-gathering techniques. Some of these, as, for example, the participant-observer technique, were significantly contributed to by anthropologists, while others were borrowed from the other social sciences, most notably sociology.

ANTHROPOLOGY AND FUNCTIONAL EXPLANATIONS

Anthropologists have found functional explanations to be very successful and consequently have used and developed them to a greater extent than have the other social sciences.

What Are Functional Explanations?

The functional explanations, sometimes called "teleological," explain events or behavior by stating the function or functions that an object, an action, an institution, or a person performs in order to maintain the social system to which the object, action, institution, or person belongs. They also describe what part an object, action, institution, or person plays in bringing about some social goal. For example, the couvade or "male childbed" is a custom observed in many societies. In the couvade, the husband takes the place of his wife who is giving birth and he is the one who is visited, commiserated with, and congratulated. A functional explanation for the couvade would examine the social system in which it occurs. In almost every case, it appears that through this device the father announces to the world at large his responsibility for the child. Once he has done this, he may himself have a particular status or he may locate the baby in a definite set of social relationships. In some cases, the father thinks he is protecting the mother and child by drawing to himself any spiritual, mystical, magical forces that might harm the baby and its mother.

How Functional Explanations Work

Functional explanations answer questions in terms of the way a system works; they direct our attention to interrelationships. Functional explanations may be used in two different ways. First they can be used to explain a particular action, institution, or object which occurs at a given time. For example, anthropologists observing a Kwakiutl man burning up his wealth logically asked, "Why is he destroying all his most precious possessions?" A functional explanation is that by destroying his wealth a Kwakiutl man establishes his power and position in his society. He is doing it in order to gain prestige.

Second, functional explanations can be useful to explain phenomena that are present in all systems or all systems of a certain kind. For instance, it has been observed that all social systems use language. A functional explanation for this is that language enables the members of a social system to communicate with each other. In another example, in every society funeral rites include some way of getting rid of the body and some expressions of grief. Functional explanations for these cultural universals would observe the unsanitary consequences which would follow from not getting rid of the body and would also note that every death creates a mourner.

In functional explanations, however, it is not necessary that the anthropologist explain an event in the same way it is understood by its participants. A *manifest function* is one for which the members of a society can give a reason. If, in the case of the couvade, a father groaning with pain while his wife was giving birth when asked, "Why are you doing that?" replied, "I'm doing it so that the evil spirits won't notice my wife and baby, who are both weak, but will pay attention to me, who is strong," the function, or reason, for his behavior is manifest. Or, more familiarly, the American custom of a new father's giving away cigars is a modified form of the couvade. In this way he announces the birth of his child, recognizes that he is the father, and generally establishes the child in a set social, religious, and economic framework. However, if the American father were asked, "Why are you giving out cigars?" he would probably not know, although he might answer, "Because everybody does." This is an example of a *latent function.* The anthropologist answers a question about the cigar custom in terms of what the anthropologist understands rather than in terms of what the actor can explain. A latent function is one in which an action has a social function of which the actor may be unconscious.

As the example of the cigar-giving father indicates, functional explanations do not require that the action be done with conscious goals in mind. Science explains some things in terms of human purposes and goals, but these cases have been discussed separately and have been described as explanations in terms of purposes. Teleological explanation in the sense in which we are using it refers not to individual purposes but to the purposes or goals of a system or society whether they be consciously pursued or not. Consider the following example. A social scientist observing a young man being inducted into the army asks why. One kind of explanation, a teleological one, answers the question something like this: the army is set up in order to defend the country. But not enough people want to defend the country voluntarily, so some men force others to do so. The explanation is teleological because it refers to an institution, the army, and social goals, those of the nation. The young man's purposes in being inducted may be quite different. They may simply be to avoid the punishment of going to jail or social stigma. One must thus distinguish explanations or kinds of explanations about purposes or goals by discriminating between the purposes or goals being discussed. The central distinction is that between individual goals and social goals.

Functional explanations are not focused on the past as are genetic explanations; nor are they focused on logically necessary conclusions which proceed from postulates as do deductive explanations; nor are they probabilistic or focused on the future as are explanations in terms of purpose. Functional explanations attempt to take a slice of time and to examine the way an act, person, institution, or object fits into the social system existing at that time.

Consider an anthropologist who has observed a society in which a stone axe is very important. He asks himself "why." The axe is useful for cutting wood which, in turn, is used for fuel and for building. Part of the social meaning of the axe is found in simple utilitarian considerations. However, it is also used in dances, in cutting off people's heads, and in war. The privilege of waving an axe at a dance is reserved only for the very brave or for religious leaders; having one's head cut off with an axe is an especially degrading form of punishment; having an axe in war gives one a big advantage over an opponent who does not have one. The point of this example is to stress that functional explanations are concerned with one particular time period, not with the past or the future, or with the way in which the axe came to be, how it took its form, why religious leaders use it, and so on. Functional explanations seek to determine the relationship of the axe to a specific social system at a specific time.

If a functional explanation has any hidden or implicit assumption, it is usually that a society seeks to maintain its status quo—to remain in the future as it is in the present. When change does occur, the implicit assumption often is that a society attempts to bring about change in a fashion consistent with the preservation of the main elements of its social system.

Dysfunction and Social Change

Functional explanations are not often used to explain problems arising from social change, except when forces disruptive to society and its social system have been introduced. In this case, the disrupting forces are examined for their *dysfunctions*, to see their effect upon previous, accepted functions of the society. If the new forces are found to have changed or disturbed accepted patterns of society, then the forces are studied in terms of their dysfunctions.

When missionaries first observed a certain Australian society, they saw that only the men could own stone axes. A stone axe was considered a source of great power in the society because it was used to cut the wood used for fuel and for building. The women, however, did all the cooking, gathered the fuel, and did the building. Nevertheless, women could not own stone axes; they had to borrow them from the men. When the men were angry at the women they would not lend their axes, although the women still had their jobs to do. The result of this arrangement was that the women were virtually slaves to the men and were often grossly abused by them.

The missionaries were shocked by this practice and wrote home to their missionary society for a shipment of metal axes, explaining to the church members at home that they would give these metal axes to the women to free them from a humiliating dependence on the men; perhaps they could make a few converts as well. When the metal axes finally arrived the missionaries did give them to the women and got a mighty surprise. The entire society was disrupted. The women became completely independent. In possession of a much superior axe, they found they did not have to work as hard as before; moreover, they never had to do anything they did not really want to do for the men. The entire social structure of the society split apart. Families were disrupted as women got rid of oppressing husbands. In general, the consequences of the introduction of the metal axe were dysfunctional in that the older functions of the society were seriously disrupted.

What Is Function?

You can think about the function of something by thinking about the role it plays in the system of which it is a part. What is the function of an engine in a car? To provide the power necessary to operate the automobile. What is the function of the heart in the human body? To circulate blood. These simple examples not only illustrate the meaning of function but also describe an important aspect of functional explanations in general. In any complex system, one part is related to the other parts of the system in more ways than one. Thus the function of the automobile's engine is not only to provide power to the wheels but also to generate electricity to run the radio and the air-conditioning system. Precisely because functional explanations are concerned with relationships of parts to wholes, they are not explanations of logical necessity. They are never complete in the sense that they cover every relationship. A functional explanation answers a question in terms of what appear to be the important and relevant relationships—not in terms of *all* relationships.

These simple examples also illustrate another important aspect of functional explanation that is related to the nature of a system. A system exists, in one sense, by itself. In another sense, it exists in relation to the rest of the world. Thus the human body is a self-contained system for many purposes. A doctor can treat a broken arm or the usual case of chicken-pox by considering the system of the body as a whole, existing relatively independent of its environment. Thus a doctor might answer your question, "Why must I have my tonsils removed?" by saying, "Your tonsils are infecting the rest of your body." This functional explanation is made on the assumption that your body is a closed system.

When environmental forces put pressure on the body, a functional explanation must take that into account. Usually many more variables are involved. To find out the complex relationships between the body, as one relatively closed system, and the environment becomes very difficult; then functional explanations become less and less useful. Consider the case of the soldier subjected to the severe environmental stress of combat. He is tired from lack of sleep, has broken out in a rash from not washing, and is hungry from not eating. There is noise all about him. He is in an unfamiliar environment. He is shocked at the sight of his friends being killed and wounded.

He is morally horrified as he kills someone. If we ask the doctor, "Why does this soldier have a stomach-ache?" he can no longer answer simply in terms of the body as a closed system. He must consider all the other variables that we have mentioned and perhaps many more besides.

Functional explanations are therefore most useful when the system is relatively closed, small, and the connections between the parts are reasonably well known. As the system becomes more open, that is as more and more variables have to be introduced, as it becomes larger, and as the parts of the system are related to each other in more and more complex ways, functional explanations become less successful.

Cause in the Context of a System

A functional explanation can be thought of as a kind of causal explanation in that it states how phenomena which are part of a system are causally connected in some important way with the maintenance of the system. For example, a social system always involves two or more people and the interactions between them. More generally, the concept of a system refers to a group of persons or things which function together in some specified way to do something. We have already pointed out that an important assumption of most functional explanations is that the social systems they refer to are self-perpetuating. Functional relations in this context examine the causal relationships between the parts of the system that operate to make it work continuously.

Sometimes this is referred to as a self-perpetuating system. The idea of self-perpetuation is useful in many fields; the human body, for instance, is self-perpetuating. One of the characteristics of the self-perpetuating system is that it maintains at least one of its properties in a stable equilibrium. A central property of the system must always continue in order to maintain the life of the system, even when there is variation in parts of the system. In the human body, life continues despite relatively limited variations in body temperature, food intake, amount of sleep, exposure to light, etc. The continuance of one property despite variations in other parts of a system is called homeostasis. Obviously, the variations that affect the system cannot be too great; for example, life cannot continue if the body temperature drops much below 80° or rises much above 108°.

Homeostasis. Every system that persists has homeostatic mechanisms, or self-regulators which adjust the system to change. This involves the concept of feedback. Consider the common thermostat in your home. It is a homeostatic mechanism, the purpose of which is to maintain temperature in the room within a certain range. Every homeostatic mechanism must first of all have sensors which detect changes in the system. In the case of the thermostat, the sensor is a thermometer which detects and registers changes in the temperature of the room. In addition to the sensor and the register, some mechanism is required to stimulate change in another mechanism. When the room temperature gets too low, the thermometer detects and registers the change and then transmits an electrical signal to the furnace, which turns on to heat the house. The thermometer registers the rise in temperature and when the temperature is as high as desired another electric signal is sent to the furnace, which turns off.

Negative feedback. Self-adjusting systems such as this have the property of negative feedback. This is illustrated by the thermostat's signaling the furnace to turn off. The rise in temperature is fed back into the very mechanism which created the rise in temperature. The increasing heat causes the thermostat to turn off the furnace. The separate parts of this system are related to each other in that changes in one part cause certain changes in the other parts. This is the sense in which we say that functional explanations are causal. Functional explanations are used whenever one part of a system is assumed to be causally related to another.

Now we can put together the relationship between causal relationship and negative feedback and homeostasis. If we assume that a social system is relatively stable, keeping in mind that the parts of the system are related to each other, it becomes apparent that if the system is to be stable the parts of the system must be characterized by negative feedback. Changes in one part of the system will cause changes in another part which in turn will react to restore the system to approximately its original situation.

Here is a simplified example of the way anthropologists use the ideas of equilibrium and negative feedback in functional explanations of the causal kind. First they observe that human societies generally attempt to avoid social disequilibrium. However, they also observe that in many societies conflict between husbands and their wives' relatives often occur. Sometimes these conflicts are so serious they could lead to serious social disruptions. What happens when these conflicts occur? What kind of outlet for this tension exists? Many societies have well-developed "joking relationships," which are customs in which husbands are either allowed to or are required to behave in a disrespectful or insulting way toward their wives' relatives. We can now see how the negative feedback works. When conflicts arise between the husband and his wife's relatives, instead of divorce or wars of one kind or another, the joking relationships release tension and are one way of dissolving the conflict. Conflicts that threaten to disturb the society are avoided and equilibrium is maintained.

Well-founded Evidence and Proper Application

It should be clear from what we have been saying about functional explanations that they will not work if the evidence upon which they are based is not true. If no joking relationship existed, or if there were no tensions between husbands and their wives' relatives, then the explanation for such a situation would be invalid. Another hazard is that the evidence could be misapplied. Perhaps a joking relationship is observed without the causal connections of conflict and social disequilibrium. If functional explanations are to be useful, the causal relationships must be well established and the constant variable must be well defined.

FUNCTIONAL EXPLANATIONS AND LAWS

Functional explanations are not laws. They refer to specific systems at specified times and places and hence are not general or lawlike statements, which are explained below. Sometimes, if what is being explained is widespread or universal, functional explanations can lead to lawlike statements. Three factors are required before a functional explanation can become a lawlike statement: one, a widespread characteristic; two, a well-defined property; and three, a well-defined and well-founded set of causal relationships within the system. These three characteristics do not occur together very often, which is why functional explanations, although very useful and indeed extraordinarily successful tools in certain cases, usually do not lead to laws.

Which Comes First, Lawlike or Functional Statements?

A scientific goal is the establishment of causal laws, or laws which involve a notion of conditions for a state to exist or an event to occur. The conditions specify the relationships that must occur between two or more phenomena.

A well-known law of physics specifies how fast a body is falling or moving when it falls from a given height, or, alternatively, how far a body will fall in a given time. Perhaps you remember that the law is $V = 1/2 \ AT^2$, where V is the velocity of the falling body, A is the constant of the pull of gravity, and T is time. This kind of statement is called a law in science because it precisely specifies the relationships among the variables it covers. All the conditions for knowledge of the phenomena are included. If we know the velocity, we can calculate the time. If we know the time, we can calculate the velocity. Knowing either, we can calculate the height from which gravity has pulled a falling body.

Functional explanations do not provide laws, which require a precise statement of conditions in order to be valid. However, functional explanations often provide some of the conditions with which to understand phenomena. When this happens, a functional explanation can be said to provide a lawlike statement. As the precision of our lawlike statements improves, we come closer to being able to state laws. On the other hand, if we know laws which can be said to govern a phenomenon, we can make functional statements.

What is a lawlike statement? Consider the functional statement, "Two functions of the family are the reproduction of the race and the raising of the young." This is a lawlike statement which enables us to give functional explanations to questions like "Why does every society have some form of family organization?" The answer in functional terms is that the institution of the family provides for the rearing of the young during their long period of dependence. Notice, however, that this is not a law. Families are not essential to child-rearing, as the existence of orphanages shows. Thus, in this case, the functional explanation does not provide all the conditions for the correct understanding of the problem. In other words, young people as they grow up need much more than a family. They also need food, clothing, and love. The initial statement does not provide conditions sufficient to understand the relationship of the family to child-rearing.

A functional statement may describe conditions that are neither necessary nor sufficient, when taken by themselves, to explain a relationship. On the other hand, a lawlike statement provides a necessary condition or a sufficient condition but not both.

In more abstract terms, here is the way a functional statement appears. To say that the function of X (family) is Y (the rearing of children) is to indicate that usually, but not necessarily and always, and not only, X (the family) brings about or helps to bring about Y (grown children). Functional statements therefore give us a less precise basis for prediction than either laws or lawlike statements. But they are still useful as long as their limitations are recognized.

Despite the obvious difference between laws, lawlike statements, and functional statements, there are no grounds either in the history or theory of science to require that any choice be made with respect to the order in which the statements are investigated. All scientists are engaged in the same pursuit, that of gaining reliable knowledge. Whether they begin their studies by pursuing cause, functional statements, or lawlike statements is of little matter. As they approach reliable knowledge, they will find themselves having to ask and answer the same kinds of questions. Therefore, the order in which scientific investigation begins depends upon the bent of the individual scientist and the progress of his work, rather than on any mandate from the methods of science. The history of science testifies to the fact that the establishment of laws can be initiated by looking for them directly, by examining the assumptions of a system and its parts, or by attempting to establish lawlike generalizations. A functional explanation, to be successful, requires comprehension of the way a system works, a definition of the parts of the system, and a description of how the parts are related to each other. When comprehension has progressed to this point, lawlike statements and even laws are often possible.

The Strengths and Uses of Functional Explanations

Not all attempts at functional explanation meet the requirements we have just stated. Many, in fact, are of a much cruder kind since the social scientist lacks the precise knowledge required. Nonetheless, often even this type of explanation is very useful, since it may direct our attention to the concept of social systems. A social scientist often finds functional explanations useful in understanding both the self-perpetuating social system and the way its parts are related to each other.

A functional explanation can be used to summarize a scientist's information about a system and to indicate its causal factors and their importance, and it will also allow the scientist to forego speculations about human motives; he can concentrate on factors which can be more objectively determined. Similarly, the functional explanation eliminates the immediate need for speculation about the way institutions originated or how they change. This is sometimes very important when dealing with very complex situations. When the social scientist is able to set aside, for the moment, problems of motive,

origin, or change, he is able to define his problem more precisely than he would have been able to if he had had to take
these factors into account.

Functional explanations also allow the social scientist to
integrate, although of course only at one level of social system,
all the phenomena of the society which he is studying. Formerly, before the development of the scientific method, attempts to integrate such phenomena were mainly religious or
philosophical. The testimony of man's progress in the last few
hundred years as compared with the millions of years that have
gone before is ample witness to the relative power of the two
types of integration.

Although it may seem paradoxical that one of the weaker
forms of scientific explanation is also one of the most useful,
the paradox ceases to exist when it is considered that the scientific study of man is very young. Therefore, a method of
explanation which enables a social scientist to integrate many
factors, summarize much information, and state the relative
importance of the causal factors present is indeed very useful
in understanding the relationships which might ultimately
lead to laws.

COMBINING PURPOSES AND FUNCTIONS

Sometimes social scientists combine two or more methods
of explanation when they deal with a complex problem. This
is risky when proper procedures are not carried out, but under
certain conditions combinations of methods of explanation
can be useful. Sometimes, of course, they can also lead to confusion. An example from political science will illustrate how
two kinds of explanation—here, explanation by purposes and
functional explanation—can be combined in a way that increases knowledge.

You will recall that explanation in terms of purposes takes
into account the goals that the individuals involved are striving
for and answers questions about society partly in terms of
these goals. Since each person, even though part of a social
system, has his own separate goals, it is often useful to com-

bine the method of explanation in terms of purpose with the method of functional explanation.

Consider the following question. "Why was Harry Truman nominated as candidate for vice-president of the United States at one convention of a political party and for president at another convention?" Generally speaking, any explanation involving an individual within a well-defined system can be investigated using the two methods of explanation. Recall the first question, "Why was Harry Truman nominated first to be vice-president and then to be president by the Democratic party?" Recall that the American Constitution says nothing about parties or about the process of nomination. When our Constitution was set up, no plans were devised for political institutions which would assure responsibility of the government to the people, enable political considerations to control administration, or nominate for president and vice-president. By 1944, however, political parties and other institutions, such as interest groups, were fully developed to fill these functions. The nominating convention for the offices of president and vice-president was, by 1944, a well-established part of the system of party government in the United States.

In other words, part of the answer to the question in functional terms is that the one function of the nominating convention in our political system is to nominate the president and the vice-president. Although this part of the explanation defines a relevant part of the political system, it does not, of course, establish why Harry Truman was nominated. It only sets the framework necessary to understand how this could happen.

Turning now to explanation by purposes, we must look not at Harry Truman's but at Franklin D. Roosevelt's purposes. It is enough to say that Harry Truman in 1944 was an undistinguished senator sponsored by a corrupt but very effective political machine that was part of the national party system, an important part of which was the President's right to choose his vice-presidential candidate. And here the purposes of Franklin Roosevelt were important. He wanted a man who would fit into the system, help him get votes, and generally

be very much in the background. Franklin Roosevelt's purposes were to get elected. In pursuit of this, he chose Harry
Truman as his running mate.

This, of course, is a very abbreviated account, but you can
see that two methods of explanation are being employed together and in combination provide a reasonable explanation.

Unintended Consequences of Purposeful and Functional Explanation

An important characteristic of social institutions is that they
bring about unforeseen consequences as change occurs. This
is also true, on a different level, with human actions. Thus
when Franklin Roosevelt, in the pursuit of his purposes, chose
Harry Truman, he did not expect that Truman would become
president as a result of his own death in office. When Truman
became president, the structure of American party government
virtually guaranteed that he would be nominated for president
at the next nominating convention. Thus the answer to the
second half of the question needs only to take into account
the belief that Truman did want to become president in his
own right. However, the important facts relevant to his nomination are all functional and relate to American party government and the way it works.

This example of the combination of two methods of explanation leads to the observation that other methods can
also often be usefully combined. The example also indicates
that social scientists other than anthropologists use the functional explanation as well.

PREDICTION AND EXPLANATION

Now that you know the major types of explanation, you can
understand that explanatory methods are not all the same and
do not all allow for prediction in the same way. Although prediction can never be certain, it can approach certainty or it
can be a simple guess. If, for example, you turn on the

lights in a dark room you can predict with virtual certainty that the lights will go on. You can make such a prediction because you know the initial conditions important to turning on the light and you know the relationship between pressing the switch and light. What are the initial conditions? The electricity is on; the switch, circuits, and light bulb are all in good working order. What are the relationships? Closing the switch allows the electricity to flow into the light bulb, which in turn heats a filament to such a high temperature that it glows and produces light. In other words, successful prediction requires knowledge of the initial conditions and of relationships. Or, put another way, you must know the necessary and sufficient conditions for the lights to go on. The necessary condition is that electricity flows into an operating light bulb. The sufficient condition in this case is that pressing the switch will allow electricity to do this.

Deduction and Prediction

Not all the methods of explanation are based on enough knowledge to allow prediction with a high degree of competence. Deductive explanation, when the premises hold, allows prediction with the greatest degree of confidence. But even in this case, although the deduction expresses a logically necessary set of relationships, other factors could intervene to destroy the prediction. In the example of the light, a meteor could hit your house at the instant you press the switch and your prediction that light would result would be falsified. However, when no such extraneous factors hold, the deductive method allows prediction with a high degree of accuracy. The probabilistic explanation and the arguments upon which it is based allow predictions with a degree of confidence which is stated in probability terms. A probabilistic explanation in the example of the light switch would be something like, "Whenever the switch is pressed, the light goes on eight out of ten times." For some scientists, probabilistic explanations are most satisfying because they allow a number, a probability factor, to be placed into the predictive framework.

Functional Explanations and Prediction

Functional explanations and explanations in terms of purposes are used less frequently for prediction than either of the other three kinds. When they are so used, they are usually used very cautiously. Since the basis of functional explanation is observation of a specific social system, one usually cannot get the number of observations necessary for estimates of probability. Because of the variety of social systems, most social scientists are very skeptical about statements of logically necessary relationships between the parts of a system which would allow for deductive explanations. It is clear, therefore, that explanations of different kinds, using different methods, will yield predictions of different degrees of confidence.

Part 3

Applications of Social Science—
Prediction and Control

The uses of social science are, to many, its most important aspect. The part of the scientific system of inquiry most relevant to its uses is prediction and control. Some of the ways prediction and control work in social science are discussed in connection with selected problems of three practical social sciences, planning, education, and social work. Other aspects of prediction and control are discussed in connection with related fields of science. In the scientific sense of "control," we refer to the practical application of scientific knowledge and the testing of this knowledge in use—not manipulating people.

Chapter 12

Planning —The Prerequisites
of Urban Renewal

WHO PLANS?

Every scientist is a planner for the simple reason that
he has a goal of his own to try to reach. As our society has grown, it has long been apparent that there
is no guarantee that all individual plans added together will make a livable world. Moreover, many
individual plans conflict. Consequently, the word
"planner" is increasingly used to designate a spe-
cialist in planning for a group.

In this country, business does a great deal of planning. Every large corporation has executives in

charge of teams to plan products, production, marketing, strategy, how to get favorable legislation—in fact, everything affecting business. Cities also employ planners, who, among other things, try to work out highway needs and zoning requirements. Compared to metropolitan government or to business, the states and the federal government do little planning. Most federal planning is measured in terms of expenditures, done largely by the Department of Defense. Since no one can be certain whether a plan will be successful, planning has sometimes not been included as a discipline of social science, and it has even been thought that it should not be studied in universities. However, since it now appears that modern society will not automatically provide a better life, we must, if we want one, plan for it.

Planning applies the findings of all the social sciences in its prediction and control. In this sense, planning is related to social science as engineering is related to physics. An engineer uses his knowledge of physics to build engines or bridges. His special knowledge is in the combination and application of other knowledge to the real world. Similarly, the planner combines and uses special knowledge which the other social sciences teach.

What Is a Plan?

A plan is directed toward rational action. But more than that, its purpose is required to distinguish a plan from all other rational actions. A fruitful way to explore the concept of "plan" is to consider the most important attributes of a plan: (1) A future time-orientation. That is to say, a plan is a series of statements formulated in the present for future execution. (2) A statement about conscious changes in the state of persons (behaviors, feelings) and often, through them, things. Even if a plan calls for or results in no consciously attempted change of state, the idea of "plan" assumes there could be change. For example, you will be in class tomorrow or you won't. One is a change from the other. (3) Goals. A plan is a set of statements that are to promote the achievement of certain goals. Goals and plans are correlative—one cannot be thought of without the other. (4) Some model, image, or description of the process, the future state, and the present reality involved in the changes the plan hopes to bring about should be explicit, but is always at least implicit, in a plan. (5) Action. A plan sets forth what must be done.

It is apparent that the concept of "plan" is complex. Each element—time, change of state, goals, models of state, and process and action—is related to the others.

It is useful to make explicit certain assumptions that the idea of a plan requires. Reviewing these assumptions makes it clear that the act of planning sets limits to the assumptions allowed the planner in much the same way that being a scientist circumscribes his beliefs. These assumptions are:

Cause and Effect.   A plan assumes cause and effect at least to the extent that the actions which the plan calls for will, if the plan is successful, have certain or probable effects. Every action postulated in the present with results in the future is subject to uncertainty. Although planners must assume some cause and effect, they do not always know exactly what effect will result from each cause. If future events were not subject to some determination by previous events, planning would be fruitless.

Objective Reality.   A plan exists only in the mind or as a written or spoken form, but not in the reality the planner hopes to affect. Planners therefore must distinguish between the reality of the symbols and the reality of what the symbols represent. The distinction requires recognition of the existence of reality that the symbols represent. A planner must believe in objective reality for reasons akin to those of the scientists. The scientist must believe in the objective reality of others— without this belief the scientific canons such as those relating to replication, assent, and disproof, to name but a few, would be impossible. Similar arguments can be adduced for the planner's belief in the objective reality of things and events; a belief in the existence of space in which people and things exist is part of a belief in objective reality.

Definite Relationships Between Symbols and Reality.   Because planners must work with words, models, symbols, images and descriptions while they hope to manipulate people and things, they must accept the fact that certain, definite relationships exist between the symbols, people and things. Otherwise, they could not believe that their manipulations of the symbols would result in foreseeable changes.

Time.   Despite well-known philosophical difficulties in defining time, planners accept past, present, and future. Unfortunately, they are also prone to accept the physicists' biases— that time's arrow is irreversible, unidirectional, and constant— which obviously are not all necessary for the idea of "plan." It is possible, for example, that the assumption of different rates of time for different things and processes could be useful.

Measurement or Comparison.   Planners must believe in the possibility of measurement or comparison. If they did not, they would have no way of knowing that differences exist between present, past, and future states and objects. The whole question of measurement in planning is an interesting one. The physical science paradigm which dominates planning assumes that one set of basic units (e.g., meter, second) will suffice for both theory and practice. This usually unexamined assumption has been questioned recently by proposals for the establishment of other units of measurement. However, the theory of planning measurement needs much more work, as the comments on time above suggest.

Purpose.   Planners must believe that purpose or will, not necessarily theirs, can direct action. When this is not the case, a plan becomes something else. If chance alone directs action, planning becomes statistics; if Divine Will directs action, it becomes theology; if unconscious motivations are directing, it becomes psychology.

What Is a Goal?

Now, perhaps it should be clearer why the idea of a plan is discussed before the idea of a goal. Every plan has one general goal: more rational action. But every plan also has specific goals: those that the plan is intended to carry out.

A goal is something or some condition we want which, it is assumed, is in some way worth having. Goals basically involve: (1) A future time-orientation. Goals exist in the past or present for future materialization. This attribute is characteristic of both "plan" and "goal." (2) Visualization, or imagination, or some idea about a future state. (3) The possibility of a change of state. However, concern about a possible change of state also involves the chance that the goal is to keep things the same in the future as in the present. To put it another way, although one could hold as a goal a future condition that is the same as the present condition, the concept "goal" would only make sense if the possibility existed that some other state could come about.

THE SOCIAL SCIENCES AND URBAN RENEWAL

Urban renewal exemplifies some of the ways planners use the methods and findings of social science. The improvement of our cities has been a challenge for most of our lifetimes; it is a challenge that will remain indefinitely. Planners are bringing all their skills to bear on the problem, so far with only limited success. Examination of the way they approach the problem illustrates the many strengths and weaknesses of applied social science.

History—Does it Make the Problem?

Every college student knows that the large cities with which he is familiar have changed during his life. The schools are running down, new highways cut the city apart, the air and the streets get dirtier, neighborhoods change, narrow-minded politicians abound. Most of those who can afford it move to the suburbs where the new shopping centers, bowling alleys, and theaters are found. The city, everyone agrees, is not what it was.

Many scholars, some mayors, a few governors, and even an occasional president noticed these and other changes during the years before World War II. But they were so busy with other things that very little was done to ensure that urban growth would result in a better place to live. When the war came, even less attention was paid to the changing cities. By the 1950s the great cities had changed so much, and were changing so fast, that even the most unperceptive state legislator noticed the changes, which were widely deplored.

History played its part. Memories of green grass, clean air, and uncluttered streets faded. Downtown merchants remembered when their business was primary; they resented their losses to suburban shopping centers. Factories and other businesses moved out. Public transportation seemed slower, more crowded, less safe, and more expensive.

When city planners were called in, their problems were rarely well defined. They were usually told that things were worse now than they had been—and they were asked to do something about them. However, a problem, to be resolved, must first be defined, and for this the history of the city was of little help. Obviously, no planner could try to turn the clock back in order to restore some version of a golden past.

The goals of urban renewal had to be developed from a vision of the future. Here social science could be of some help. While social scientists have goals and social science can give us knowledge of goals, these goals are only implemented through groups—primarily political institutions. Thus the planner had to turn to political science for leads on what goals would be acceptable and for the means which could be used to implement them.

The obstacles to successful urban renewal were numerous: Federal, state, and municipal funds were insufficient for the development of extensive housing projects and intensive renovation of existing housing. Most cities had outmoded zoning laws, and builders could rarely use modern materials, designs, or labor-saving devices. Most of the available private capital was directed towards expanding business and commercial enterprise rather than improving residential conditions. Most American cities are laid out in square blocks, which meant that such new housing as there was had to be built in dull and conforming patterns. The list of problems the planners encountered could be extended. However they defined their problems, they would find massive investments of money, a crowd of social institutions, and many vested interests blocking their proposals.

Defining the Problem

It soon became apparent that improved housing would not be enough to make a better city. Better housing was certainly part of the urban problem, but it was by no means the sole problem. Before urban planners could tackle the job of improving the quality of American cities they found it necessary to call upon specialists from other social science disciplines. They needed the assistance of political scientists to study the adequacy of existing governments and their overlapping authority and to determine what the power structure was and how to implement the planner's goals. They needed the geographer's skill to determine the location and adequacy of major arteries of commerce, to indicate shifts in population, and to help in the location of new public facilities. They needed the sociologist and the accumulated wisdom of his field to create a healthy social environment. They needed the anthropologist because he works with the idea of a whole social system. And, of course, the planners needed the economist to handle the enormous burden of determining cost and resources.

Urban renewal's lack of well-defined goals ensured ineffective programs. It is no wonder that America has not developed urban renewal—and won't unless we decide what we want and are willing to pay for it.

As one considers the difficulties of planning, one wonders how so much good work is done. It is easy to draw up a list of differences between planning and science. Explanation is not fundamental to planning, as it is to science. In planning, the range of variables is greater than a more precise scientific endeavor; consequently, the subject is more complex and less easy to control. Planning allows more goals, which results in more conflict between them. And, finally, planning is less orthodox in approach, each planner having less support from the past.

PLANNING AND PREDICTION

There are three very different ways to think about the future. One is in terms of desire or what could be, another in terms of choice or what might be if, and a third in terms of what will be. Utopia exemplifies the first way, planning the second, and "hard" science the third.

The importance of prediction for the scientist lies in the relationship of prediction to the confirmation of hypotheses and the possibilities of manipulation that confirmed hypotheses give him. The planner must have a very different slant. He must not only be accurate, but also attempt to construct a plan which can be implemented. The knowledge that a "hard" scientist gives us is absolutely dependent on a rigidly circumscribed system of definitions, methods, instrumentation, and language. However, the planner's fundamental job is to transplant or transfer knowledge from one system to the other. The planner, if his work is perfectly executed, must begin where the scientist leaves off in order to visualize the future and attempt to bring it about.

Uses and Misuses of Planning

There are those who associate all planning with compulsion and fear that we will soon reach a situation in which men's free actions will be rigidly circumscribed within a specific pattern of behavior. Spontaneity would be inhibited and freedom limited. But would they? It depends on what is being planned, the goals, and the way the plans are to be carried out. Almost any action can result from planning and almost any goal can be planned for. Plans can, of course, be made for bad goals, but this does not make planning bad. It is also possible that a plan directed toward a praiseworthy goal—for example, the elimination of cancer—could involve immoral methods such as the injection of cancer cells into unwilling healthy people. However, even an incident of this sort would not cast blame upon planning, as such, but only upon this particular plan. The plain fact is that we have no choice but to plan. What we must have are valid goals and methods—justified by the highest values of our civilization. In formulating a plan, one must always remember to ask how many will it help and how much?

Why Planning Is Necessary

The scientific system of inquiry requires planning. Even without using science, planning in a technological world is a necessity. Planning is not the result of any instinct but is rather the rational determination of men to achieve their ends. The fact that in some cases there appears to be ways other than by planning for men to achieve their ends still does not make planning dispensable. So long as men want things or states of affairs that do not presently exist, at least some of them will not wait hopefully but try as rationally as they can to bring it about. In many cases planning appears to be the best way. And given the complexity and interdependence of the world, other men, even those who do not want to plan, will be caught up in the relationships of those who do plan. Ironically, if they only wish to avoid being caught up, they too must plan. We can therefore conclude that planning is a necessity which stems from the fact that when some men plan—and they can be counted on to—other men must.

Planning, A Hope for the Future

Because the great aim of applied social science is the betterment of society, planning toward this goal has long been considered one of the techniques of social science, as in education, law, or social work. Better planning cannot develop without better social science. It is virtually certain, however, that the planning required by past and present industrialized societies will be of a type very different from what future societies will need because of the complex nature of modern industrialized societies. This in turn is due to a number of cultural lags, a large amount of cognitive dissonance, mixed with a large dose of old theory combined with a little new technology. This complexity is also due to the characteristics of political mechanisms, cultural diversity, personality structures, and theoretical outlooks that are all of varying ages and are not developed to work together harmoniously. Many planning problems are caused by discordance within a culture.

The development of a new computer-controlled technology, better education, and modern social science holds forth the prospect that any society which will utilize these things in a planned way can, in relatively short order, bring about faster social change than history has ever seen. The very complexity of modern societies can be reduced through the use of modern science. To bring about desirable changes, assuming a society rich enough to consider them, we need more planning based on a more informative social science.

Chapter 13

Education—Preparing for the New Social Studies

THINKING ABOUT EDUCATION

Men are educated by everything that happens to them. The time they spend in school is only a small part of their lives, but it is during this time that they formally learn what the community, acting through political institutions, thinks young people should know in order to become useful and desirable members. The term "education" is thus used to designate the in-school process by which young people are trained for their future roles in society. Almost all definitions of education relate the development of the young individual to the society in which he lives.

Precise definitions of education have limited usefulness when one thinks about education as a social science. How long should the young be in school? Is chronological age a useful index in determining the length of time an individual should remain in school? Once in school, what should the pupil be taught? Who should pay for the schools? Questions like these are as old as recorded history. Our society, like all others, is constantly forced to make new choices in education as our needs and desires change.

The Vast Educational Establishment

The American educational system is vast, heterogeneous, and complex. As of 1970 more than 60 million Americans out of a population of more than 205 million made education their full-time work: there were approximately 37 million pupils in elementary schools, 15 million in high school, and 8 million in college. The figures will go even higher. There are more Americans in school than there are people in all England, or Italy, or combined in forty-two of the countries in the United Nations. The group called "student" covers every conceivable human difference.

If the single greatest failing of American education is that it does not treat the student as an individual, numbers alone could account for the problem. More than 2.5 million teachers man the classrooms, over a million in elementary schools, almost a million in high school, and more than half a million in colleges. Looking over the teacher's shoulder are more than 100,000 principals and supervisors and over 50,000 other administrators ranging from superintendents of schools and administrative and library staffs, to college and university presidents. In general charge of the whole establishment are over 650,000 state, local, and college board members who allocate the over $55 billion per year it costs to run the schools. In 1970 gross national product, that is the total market value of all the goods and services produced in this country, is approximately $960 billion. Americans spend about six percent of their gross national product on education, which, in recent years is less than they have been spending on defense.

Few generalizations are likely to hold for all American education and still be meaningful. Those that do hold will of necessity be statistical statements.

Some Aims of Education

What are the aims of the American education system? What should they be? Educators have drawn up numerous lists of the educational aims for different students, different ages, and different educational programs or curriculums. In recent years these aims have been stated as types of expected behavior change that will result if the aims are realized. One statement of aims for elementary schools covers the child's physical, social, and emotional development. It includes ethical values, standards, and behavior for the child as well as reading, writing, arithmetic, art appreciation, and knowledge of the social and physical world.

Because education today attempts to achieve results in values, standards, and behavior, as well as to train the mind or to communicate knowledge or skills, its aims will be subject to controversy. Controversy will be about what and how much should be taught rather than about the need for change. Almost everyone agrees that education's aims need to be changed from time to time, although the problems of deciding upon and implementing these changes have not been resolved to the satisfaction of most educators. The compromises which have come about in American educational aims are perhaps the inevitable results of the kinds of procedures by which they are obtained. They reflect the values of a society which assumes that the quality of life is more a function of material goods than of cultivated intellect.

Some Functions of Education

In addition to considering the size and aims of the American educational system, one may well ask what its functions are. American education is related to and affected by other social institutions. For example, appointment to the school board in large cities and states is often a reward to political hacks and the average college trustee knows very little about his job. The most important agency in the American education establishment is not the school board, however, but the school itself. What are some of its functions? We have already mentioned one major function in the definition of education, namely the transmission of the culture of the society. That is to say, the school's function is to make Americans recognizable as Americans. If one of the aims of our society were to produce individualistic, independent, free men as part of a culture of men who use their freedom, then the schools would transmit the knowledge, skills, and values that go along with being a free man.

Schools have many other functions. They act as baby-sitters, allowing mothers freedom from the time-consuming and sometimes bothersome job of raising their children. High schools and colleges often have a function akin to that of marriage broker: young people can learn to know and relate to each other in order to speed up the process of mate selection. Sometimes, and perhaps most important, schools function to bring about social change. To the extent that they succeed in educating free men to seek and know truth, then the products of these schools will act to improve the society in which they live.

The different ways of looking at education are not mutually exclusive, nor are the functions of the school necessarily contradictory. Girls and boys can be interested in each other and still learn. Schools can serve as baby-sitters and still provide a good education. The point to remember is that education cannot be understood in terms of any one of its aspects alone. Functions, aims, and size must be considered as a compound.

Education as a Hope

One of the great contributions of the Enlightenment, the period that led to the rise of modern social science, was the widespread hope that if men were educated, if they knew, if they understood, then they could work together to bring about a better world. To a large extent, this hope has been fulfilled, as the achievements of science amply demonstrate. Now it is being put to a new test. The world abounds in social problems. Hanging over it like the sword of Damocles are enough atom and hydrogen bombs to kill us all a hundred times over. It has become urgent that men learn to live together and choose constructive policies. Uneducated men, acting stupidly, have up to now brought evil consequences on themselves, occasionally on others. Today it is different; madmen could destroy the world.

Johann Heinrich Pestalozzi, a Swiss educator of the eighteenth century and one of the greatest of all elementary school teachers, said, "The essential principle of education is not teaching: it is love." Education must be built on love of self and of others or there is no basis for faith in it.

EDUCATION IN THE SOCIAL SCIENCES

The important uses of social science can never be viewed in terms of a single dimension; more than one aspect of social science must come into play. In some ways science is like a well-cut diamond. You can hold it up to the light and by turning it slightly see a thousand different reflections of the light passing through.

Education as a Social Science

For a long time the great works in social science have considered education part of that discipline. Obviously the search for truth and knowledge is the aim of the educator as well as of the scientist. The educator's belief system must be the same as the scientist's. The educator believes in objective reality, time, space, relationships between symbols and reality, the possibility of measurement and comparison, purpose, reason, and causality. Is there a better observer than a good teacher? The educator describes and measures and attempts explanation. His job is difficult because he must use all the modes of explanation. He must also use more than one of the modes of prediction, typically laws, projection, structure, institutions, problems, stages, and always utopias. It would be a very restrictive definition of social science indeed that would not include education.

Education as a User of Social Science

Education is built upon the social science disciplines; it uses them in both development and practice. Education, like all social sciences, occurs in time. If we want to know why American education has its present character, we must look to history. Sociology shows education some of the ways that the groups in which we live and work are related to the rest of society. Geography, too, contributes to the educational field; differences in space and in climate both fundamentally influence the practice of educators.

The importance of economics to education is so great that it has often been taken for granted in the past. Who will pay for the school? Can education help to eliminate poverty? Do low teachers' salaries attract inadequate people to the profession? In America the public schools are political institutions governed by law, with the people who run the schools—the school boards—elected or appointed in accordance with the political process. Politics influences education as much as any other single factor. Politics kept the black uneducated in the South and built a great public college system in California. Educators, as a result of their experience with political science, can better understand what is happening and attempt to cope with it.

The student is obviously the most important part of the educational establishment. Teachers must know the minds, the souls, and the emotions of their students if they are to do a good job. Educators read psychology to learn about the relationships between students and about their behavior. Anthropology analyzes a particular culture's attitudes toward the reasons for and the goals of education and determines the roles of education in various societies. A good teacher will constantly use his knowledge of the other social science disciplines to enrich his own profession.

Although education is behind most other sciences in affluence, prestige, and perhaps even in specific and positive results, the average educator seems far ahead of most scientists in his concern for his subject and the uses to which knowledge is put. Physical scientists may have no qualms about building bombs that will kill people; biologists may develop poisons that will exterminate people; but the teacher, whether average or brilliant, rich or poor, will almost never use his knowledge and skills to harm his pupils. However, the requirement that a teacher use his knowledge first of all as a decent human being and then as a teacher means that every child with whom he deals presents a different educational problem. Of course, the teacher wants to predict and control. He wants his student to turn out to be a person functioning positively in his own right and a credit to the human race. To the extent that he can realize this goal, the teacher must try to control his students.

EDUCATION AND THE MODES OF PREDICTION

Evidence of education's complexity is found in the many methods of scientific prediction used by educators. The different kinds of prediction used by social scientists are grouped under the headings law, projection, structure, institutions, problems, stages, and utopias. Following are some examples of methods of prediction that must be used by educators.

Scientific Law

A scientific law, you will recall, attempts to state some basic and fundamental regularity of the phenomenon being investigated. Prediction according to laws simply means that the phenomenon is identified and, if it behaves regularly, a law to that effect can be stated. Social scientists have discovered few such laws, and there are fewer still that educators can use. Most of those they can use relate to child development, since the sequence of development of many kinds of behavior is the same for all children. In regard to motor control, the differences that do occur among healthy children seem to occur more in the rate of development rather than in the sequence. For example, children crawl before they run. Muscular control develops downward from the head, that is, the muscles of the head are controlled before the muscles of the trunk, those of the trunk before those of the legs. Another law is that as a child develops, his perception becomes more discriminating. It takes a baby a while before he can distinguish his mother from his father, while most young adults can easily distinguish a Ford from a Chevrolet.

How is this directly related to education? In certain fields (physical education is a dramatic example) educators study the laws of the sequence of development and mold their educational activities, such as games, accordingly. Readiness tests can be developed to see the stage of the child's development, and then the appropriate activities and learning experiences can be provided.

Predicting by Projection

Predicting on the basis of projections involves extending present trends into the future. In America almost one hundred percent of the children from the ages six to thirteen go to school. Through the use of accurate mortality tables we can tell how many children will reach various age levels at different years in the future. In the early 1960s only two-thirds of the five-year-olds were in nursery school or kindergarten and one-fourth in the eighteen to twenty-four age group were going to college. If our educational goal is for almost all Americans to go to school from kindergarten through high school, that is from the age of five to seventeen, then it is not difficult to project increases in the number of students, teachers, and costs. On the basis of projections educators can tell accurately what the situation will be like for years to come. All these projections, by the way, indicate that unless America begins to spend much more on education now, many young people will not be very well educated in the future.

Another kind of prediction is based on the structure of the educational establishment. In our country, to be a teacher one ordinarily must go to college for at least five years and go through some sort of certification process. As a result there already are shortages of qualified teachers in many fields. It can be confidently predicted that, given the same structure, shortages will continue and perhaps intensify.

Institutional Processes

Still another kind of prediction widely used in education is based on knowledge of the processes within the educational structure. For instance, in America most elementary and high-school boards are either elected or appointed, a situation which necessarily involves those who sit on the boards in politics of some sort. Since politicians are not renowned for their interest in education, the result is that amateurs in the field occupy many policy-controlling positions. Luckily this political process does occasionally produce men capable of running a school system. Nevertheless, the massive problems now facing schools, particularly in the central city, are evidence that school boards frequently are incapable of constructing quality educational systems. Educators can predict that unless the processes by which school boards are chosen are changed, no substantial overall improvement in the quality of public education can be expected.

Stages

We have already mentioned that human beings pass through certain stages in their development, stages which, when well enough known, can be stated as laws, allowing the formulation of predictions. Even when the stages of development are not precisely known, prediction is possible. For example, assume it is desirable that advanced mathematics courses be taught by a person who has a Ph.D. in the subject. Then, knowing the time and effort required to get a Ph.D. in mathematics and to become a member of a college faculty, one can predict that in most colleges advanced mathematics will not be taught by a person with a Ph.D. in the subject. Why? In America about two hundred Ph.D.'s are earned each year in mathematics, while there are about 2,200 colleges and universities teaching advanced mathematics courses in the United States. This would mean that if all those with Ph.D.'s in mathematics went into teaching, every college and university would get one new Ph.D. about every eleven years. However, about half the Ph.D. recipients in mathematics do not go into teaching, and of the half that remain many will not go to teach in small colleges and universities. Therefore, although some universities get all the Ph.D. mathematicians they want, most get less than they need.

Utopian Prediction

The utopian dream—the vision of the ideal—has been one of the main forces for improvement in education. Horace

Mann, the great American educator, devoted his life to showing the way schools could be improved; he pointed out, with examples from German schools, that effective teaching was possible without harsh discipline. He believed in "the absolute right of every human being that comes into the world to an education; and which, of course, proves the correlative duty of every government to see that the means of education are provided for all." In 1846 this idea was accepted by very few Americans. Nevertheless, educators have always worked towards a utopia where man would know more and life would be better. This is a far less scientific prediction than others we have discussed, but it may also be one of the most important in terms of possible social change.

The rest of this chapter is devoted to a discussion of efforts to reform the teaching of social science at the elementary and high-school level and the attendant problems and their complexity.

SOCIAL STUDIES AND SOCIAL SCIENCE

In 1916 the National Education Association appointed "The Committee on Social Studies of the Commission on the Reorganization of Secondary Education of the National Education Association," whose aim was to broaden instruction in social studies and focus attention on the problems of everyday life. Even then the NEA was a powerful influence, and by taking this step it made 1916 the year in which social studies became widely accepted.

Early Social Studies

The term "social studies" had been used earlier. In 1885 *Social Studies in England* was published by Sarah K. Bolton, an American who had lived two years in England. She became interested in describing for Americans England's progress in dealing with certain social problems such as providing college education for women and organizing successful women's cooperatives. Thus she related social studies to teaching young people how to solve social problems.

In 1886 R. Heeber Newton published *Social Studies,* a work also concerned with social reform, especially with the relationships between capital and labor. The use of the term "social studies" to denote efforts at social reform did not catch on in American education. The term then, as now, adhered to the committee's definition: "those studies whose subject matter relates directly to the organization and development of human society and to man as a member of social groups." Although educators today are not completely agreed on what the term should cover, it usually includes history, geography, civics, economics, and sociology. The committee did its work well—so well, in fact, that it is a safe bet that every student who reads this has had one or more courses in social studies.

By the 1950s, however, a rising chorus was heard objecting to social studies as then taught. It was held that the very use of the term indicated a condescending attitude toward the subjects covered and that the courses were too simple. Then came *Sputnik.*

Criticism Becomes Reform

When the Soviets beat us to space, public attention was first drawn to the teaching of the physical and biological sciences. Winds of reform, blowing slowly since World War II, turned into tornados by the early 1960s. Curriculums in mathematics and physics were revised; the biology curriculum was changed, as was that of chemistry. New units were put into elementary school science. Money flowed freely from government and foundations. Textbook publishers were glad to finance the writing of new texts, and, despite many false starts there is no question that progress was made.

At the same time as they were taking the new math, many students were also taking what some students irreverently called "social slops," old civic courses, often emphasizing outmoded state constitutions, and even older history courses, often poorly taught by the athletic coach. In this country, it is a fact that the overworked coach was often teaching social studies in the high school and sometimes even on the elementary level. The coach, who worked hard at school and who often needed a second job to support his family, was likely to be very poorly prepared and even less interested in social studies.

Recent Criticisms of the Social Studies

What began as neglect turned into a national scandal by the middle 1960s. Several groups of distinguished social scientists and educators made known their concern about the state of social studies. They had found that in this country social studies were taught with an overwhelming emphasis on the presentation and rote memorization of facts. Little attention was given to cause, to the use of analytical methods, or to critical thinking. Very little use of "laboratory" methods of learning had been made. Moreover, the facts themselves were deficient and were greatly oversimplified. It had apparently been assumed, wrongly, that the young mind can only tell the difference between black and white and is unable to distinguish any intermediate shades. Poverty, selfishness, conflict, evil, and death were rarely mentioned or discussed. When facts were presented, they were allowed to be shaded by public opinion and social bias, as frequently occurred, for example, in discussions of racism or communism. In addition to these failings, many social studies teachers did not keep up with new developments in their fields and consequently presented outdated material to their pupils. They also failed to separate fact from value judgment, either because they did not know the difference or because they wished to use the subject as a vehicle to instill values in the pupils.

The social studies curriculum continues to lack balance and integration in at least three ways. First, western countries and cultures are given attention far out of proportion to their size and number. Second, history and geography dominate the curriculum. In the study of history the emphasis is on the past, with little reference to the modern world. When material from other social sciences is introduced to supplement history and geography, such as government or economics, they are not presented as a part of a meaningful whole. Third, relationships between the social sciences are neither explored sufficiently nor reflected in the curriculum. There is virtually no bridge between science and the social sciences. Adequate attention is not given to the social implications of science and to the impact of technology and science on the society.

Psychologists and educators have pointed out that the sequential development of concepts or skills is largely unexplored in social studies, while those that are utilized are often unsupported by evidence. Advances in learning theory and child development have hardly affected teaching methods. The curriculum is also far behind the latest knowledge in subject matter and methodology.

Very little attention has been given to the separate needs of individual children. The child's social and economic background, as well as his ability, can affect what and how he learns. The needs of children in disadvantaged families are different from those in wealthy families. Throughout the social studies curriculum there is an emphasis on "citizenship training" that masks the fact that social science includes factual information for its own sake. The possibility of useful and interesting careers in teaching, research, or government service is not often presented.

TOWARD IMPROVING SOCIAL STUDIES

Scientists' proper response to criticisms or to demands for change is first to seek out what has been learned about the subject. With the growing criticism of the social studies curriculum, educators called together a series of scholarly conferences at which papers were presented for discussion. Further research was then conducted and it was soon discovered that a great deal of research would be needed if changes were to be made on the basis of positive knowledge. What would a teacher of social studies need to know in order to improve his teaching? What cultural backgrounds, attitudes, and information do students bring to the study of these subjects? The educators would need to know more about methods of learning as they are related to social studies. The need for research on such sensitive subjects as sex and money was clear.

Controversy Over Reform

It was easier to reach agreement on the problems and the type of research required than on the solution to the problems. Almost at the outset, sharp controversy arose among educators. The role of citizenship training gave rise to one important debate. Supporters argued that teachers and citizens have an obligation to meet the demands of the society supporting the school that certain general attitudes should be developed in the classroom. Students, they say, should not be expected to make up their own minds in the face of the authority of the classroom teacher. Therefore, the teacher should attempt to indoctrinate his students with society's values. Opponents of this position were quick to ask, "Whose values?" They pointed out that any attempt to indoctrinate requires a distortion of knowledge. The forces of science and technology, it was claimed, will destroy us if we do not learn to live together. We must make new social inventions of all kinds for which the older values cannot prepare us. Look at the state of the world, these people said. Is there any evidence that "citizenship training" has made men better citizens?

Controversy existed on several other points. Should religion be taught in the schools? If so, to what extent? This difference was resolved by the Supreme Court decision opposing the teaching of religion in public schools. Unresolved disputes still exist over issues like communism, sex education, "black power," and the role of the FBI. Social science has important things to say on every one of these subjects which every student ought to know. Ignorance of these subjects is harmful to the society.

Debate is continuing about every aspect of social studies. One group investigated American history textbooks and found that minorities, particularly the black minority, were treated very unfairly. Other groups try to improve the education of the social studies teachers by direct teaching or by writing textbooks and gathering materials. Professor Lawrence Senesh, a distinguished educator in economics, is attempting the Herculean task of preparing a text and materials for social studies at every grade level. Teaching machines and television occupy others, while some are concerned with evaluating (testing) what the student has learned. Existing tests have been proven inadequate, raising the demand for new ones. This reform movement has been in full swing since the early 1960s.

Barriers to Improvement

How did these changes affect the average classroom? Depending on one's point of view, the effect was either very little or a great deal. Certainly, private foundations, government agencies, commercial publishers, organized bodies of social scientists, and individual scholars have devoted themselves to developing new materials for kindergarten through high school. Work has been sponsored by the United States Office of Education, the American Anthropological Society, the American Sociological Society, and private foundations to name but a few. Why have most of these efforts not resulted in many materials useful for the classroom? There are many reasons.

Teaching Teachers

The teachers are one reason. The new social studies teachers have received college or university training typically in schools of education, which have not been in the forefront of reform. In one of the better schools of education, a new teacher may have learned a little more social science, but his training would not have been dramatically modified. What of the older teachers who received their training some time ago? How are they to be retrained? Often these teachers have second jobs in order to make a better living and are consequently so overburdened that they cannot spend time reading up on the latest development in social science. The problem of training the new teacher and retraining the older guarantees limited progress in reform.

Other barriers to improvement exist also. How much time is to be given to the social studies? The student's time is the scarcest of all educational resources. Is it more important to train him to read better, to learn more math, or to play a musical instrument? Where is the extra time to teach social studies going to come from? And what about the problems of grading and evaluation? Most schools seem tied to the system of marking, but every study we have of this method of evaluation indicates that marks do not mean the same from one school to another or even from one teacher to another. Without instruments for adequate evaluation, we cannot find out what the student has learned. Every discipline of social science can give some helpful insight into this practical problem of removing the barriers to social studies reform.

Using the Disciplines of Social Science

The study of history shows us how the heavy hand of the past has made reform difficult. Another discipline, economics, poses the question of who will pay for what. Education in general has been starved in comparison with automobiles or cosmetics, to say nothing of defense. Americans do not seem to understand that if they want to have good education, they will have to pay for it.

Social scientists in two other disciplines, sociology and political science, have clarified part of the mystique about local control of education as historically defined. This mystique has it that if a community votes for the members of the school board, the money to be spent, and the bond issues to build schools, it will somehow be guaranteed quality education. Studies of American education show that this is not the case. Consider the South. Few communities, generally only the wealthiest, have been willing to tax themselves for high quality education. The states are usually called upon to bear an increasing burden of expense for local education. Effective pressure has recently been put upon the federal government to increase its monetary contribution to education. State boards usually set the standards for certifying teachers. National publishers put out the textbooks that are used in every community. Local control, defined as non-state or non-national, has been the condition in which many of our school problems occur. It has been found that most commonly those who rely on arguments for local control of education do not want quality education for all. The widespread acceptance of local control as defined in terms of political boundaries is another barrier to reform in the social studies.

The law presents another set of problems in reform. Many state legislatures have set up requirements that children spend a specified time studying state history, state constitutions, and other topics of local interest. In addition, state school codes often outline in great detail what else shall be taught, and sometimes even how it shall be taught.

PROGRESS IN EDUCATION AND THE USES OF SOCIAL SCIENCE

In a social decision it is rare that an analysis focuses on a specific instance. Decision-making in education is a continuous social process carried out by a large number of complex organizations. Policies are formulated and specific solutions found by many small acts carried out by different people at different times. To understand any specific change it is necessary to know the structure and the processes of the system in which decisions are made. Because American education is so big and complex, a large number of eminent educators have suggested that we attempt first to restore the school system to a place of recognized importance and respect in American society. Here are the reforms which, in their view, would be needed if we are to remake education into a major institution for improving a future America:

1. Improved salaries and working conditions for teachers
2. Modernized certification standards for teachers
3. Better teacher selection and training procedures
4. Equal educational opportunities for all children
5. Revision of the entire curriculum
6. Removal of politics from the schools
7. Smaller classes
8. Improvement of the schools' physical resources
9. More state and federal support
10. Better health programs

11. Administrative reorganization with more emphasis on the classroom

Is it likely that American attitudes, values, and institutions will change rapidly enough for such sweeping major reforms in education to occur? Perhaps so. But more likely is a continuation of the rather fitful progress that has characterized the advance of American education up to this point. We are warned, however, by more than one responsible voice that the challenges and opportunities of our time are the greatest of all time. Education is one of man's great hopes and the key to the solution of many major problems.

Chapter 14

Social Work and the Poor

SOCIAL PROBLEMS

When the New Testament said that you always have the poor with you, it made a statement about the future that satisfied men for hundreds of years. However, times change and today most Americans are concerned, to some extent at least, with the problems of poverty in our society. This chapter, like the other chapters in this part, discusses some of the many methods social scientists use when they attempt to predict and control as they confront social problems. We will explore what social problems are and how social scientists attempt to cope with them through a discussion of poverty and social work, one of the tools employed by social scientists. It is important to remember that there are many different kinds of social problems.

Social Work and Law—Two Applied Social Sciences

Like planning and education, social work and law are applied social sciences, those that use many of the methods of the other social sciences in practice. Both fields are oriented toward action about specific aspects of man's existence. In social work the central focus is on enabling an individual to cope better with or to change the situation in which he finds himself, while law is the outcome of a society's attempts to provide order and justice for its members. Each of these is therefore concerned with social problems as they exist in the world about us. Our society has utilized both methods in attempts to cope with the problems of the poor. As social problems are often very complex, social scientists have developed special ways of thinking about them. Because the study of law is very specialized, this chapter emphasizes social work.

What Is a Social Problem?

A social problem is defined by three characteristics. The first characteristic, determined by social bookkeeping or accounting, answers the question, "What are the facts?" The second characteristic answers the question, "What does the situation mean to the society?" The third characteristic answers the question, "How do the facts affect the functioning of society?" Moreover, the social meaning and the functioning of society are interrelated: the society may or may not be acting on what it perceives to be the facts. In other words, a social problem may or may not be recognized by the society.

Perhaps some examples will make these distinctions clearer. It is a fact that American automobiles have four wheels. However, this fact has little social meaning, and no social problem can be said to exist as a result. In a different example, consider the fact that systematic and fairly successful extermination of the American Indian in the 1800s was the policy of the United States. One social meaning of the policy was that the Indians resisted. The relationship of the United States policy to the functioning of Indian societies was such that Indian culture would be destroyed. The social meaning of this fact to white Americans was quite different from the meaning it had for the Indians. For politicians at least, it meant votes from the whites and more stolen land from the Indians. The politicians set the policy, and for them whatever social problem existed could be resolved by force. The Indian, on the other hand, found resistance futile and his social problem so acute that his culture would be virtually destroyed by his failure to solve the problem.

In another example, when the Spaniards invaded the Inca Empire they were very few against millions. Had the Incas resisted, they could undoubtedly have delayed the destruction of their empire. But what social meaning did the Inca chiefs give to the invasion? They did not realize its full implications and accepted the invitation to negotiate with the Spanish leaders, who immediately killed them and left the Incas leaderless. Within a few years their society was destroyed. Had the Incas understood their social problem, they might have been able to cope with it better.

Japan furnishes a very different example. When the white man began to invade and exploit Asia, the Japanese were quick to define this as a threat to themselves and their society. In the 1600s they closed their island to foreign commerce. Except for one tightly regulated port, they were able to keep the white man out. But when an American naval expedition with its iron ships came, the Japanese were powerless to resist because of their backward economic organization. They quickly interpreted the visits of the American warship as a warning that they had better industrialize before they suffered the fate of their fellow Asians at the white man's hands. They recognized their social problem. Their subsequent rise to industrial power was one of the most rapid in the world.

Social Fact and Social Problems

Every social problem has a basis in social fact. In the most restricted sense of the meaning of social fact, a social problem can be thought about in terms of social bookkeeping or accounting, in other words, numbers. Is population the issue? Then we can know the number of people of different ages, their distribution between the sexes, where they live, and so on. Is race the problem? We can count the number of blacks or learn about typical family patterns. Is crime the problem? We can examine police records. Is slum housing the problem? We can find out about the state of the plumbing, how many people live in each room, what rents they pay. The importance of social bookkeeping cannot be overestimated when the time comes to do something about a problem, when facts are required to test an explanation and to act intelligently.

In some cases society has acted irrationally, ignoring social facts. At one time in America witches were hunted and executed. Men believed in witches and acted upon their beliefs. Their illusions were important to this social problem. Even in the twentieth century Americans have acted with little regard for social facts, as shown by the "red scares" following the two world wars or the concentration-type camps set up for Japanese-Americans during World War II.

Social problems can exist without widespread recognition of the relevant social facts, which does not mean the problems are unimportant. The attempt to find facts to support actions led to the gradual end of witch-hunts. Facts dispel illusions, however slowly. Social facts never define a social problem— but they are indispensable to thinking about and acting upon them.

In some ways, society follows the old verse, "wishing makes it so" and by not understanding social facts, creates social problems. Our society outlaws the procurement of opiates for most addicts, which forces addicts to turn to illegal underworld sources for their drugs. Because drugs from the underworld are expensive, the addict must often resort to illegal activities in order to pay for his drug. Therefore, to the uncritical there is much evidence that "drug addicts are mostly criminal." Countries differ in their attitudes toward opiate addictions; some countries consider it criminal, while in many others an opiate addict can, by following simple legal procedures, obtain the opiates he requires. The result is that in these countries the social problem of crime due to addiction differs significantly from what it is in America.

Fundamental to a social problem are the meanings a society gives to social facts. As the example of the Incas illustrates, social facts can be unperceived or misunderstood. If the social fact is important to the society, serious consequences could follow if it is thus unperceived or misunderstood. On the other hand, as the automobile example showed, some unperceived facts are of little or no importance. As the example of the witches showed, social problems can result from social meaning built on illusions.

A persistent problem of all societies is the fact that illusions about reality are common. It is the job of science to dispel these illusions—and, slowly, science is doing just that. One very difficult case, however, is that of proving the nonexistence of something believed to exist. For example, from time to time people have reported that they "saw" ghosts. When a true believer in ghosts asks a scientist to "prove ghosts don't exist," what can the scientist say? There is no way to prove that something does not exist. The scientist knows this. All he can do is ask for evidence to prove the existence collected in accordance with the best scientific methods. Pictures, tape recordings, independent evidence of disinterested eyewitnesses, writings, in fact, any reasonable evidence of ghosts, would interest many social scientists. But with ghosts as with flying saucers, it is very hard to collect reliable evidence that can be independently confirmed.

Society's Functions and Social Problems

We have seen that a social problem can be defined by the combination of social facts and social meanings. There is still another kind of social problem that comes about without society's necessarily giving any meaning or even recognition to the social facts that are the cause or result. This social problem arises when social facts show sharp discrepancies between certain present and past social functions. Such a discrepancy might result from an internal social change occurring without the awareness of members of the society. What the members of the society "see" are manifestations of the problem, with little idea as to its cause and effect. Therefore, they are unable to give social meanings to the essential facts. For example, the increasing use of the automobile brought few problems of air pollution during the first half of the century; continued unregulated expansion has now resulted in serious air pollution.

What Makes a Problem Social?

Social problems often exist long before they are recognized by the society or by individuals within it. No significant action on a social problem can occur until it is recognized by enough interested people. Perhaps the key words in any discussion of social problems are recognition and people. Recognition of a situation can result from action taken to cope with the problem, or recognition can be forced on people as a result of the problem. More than one person must be involved in the consequences for a social problem to exist.

A social problem either forces people to act or is the result of actions. In one case, the action might be the problem—remember witch burnings. In other cases, the action might be the result of the problem—for example, the Indians fighting back. It should not be hard to see, however, that a problem, social or otherwise, is not likely to be serious for a society if it neither causes nor results in any social action. This point, though obvious, is necessary to mention as a kind of social problem indicator. The social scientist has a method for determining the presence and urgency of a problem. Suppose you were told, "Americans face a terrible social problem—the men from Mars will land here in 4,000 years." In addition to wondering how this information was obtained, you might well answer, "So what?" No action need result from that information. A social problem, in other words, has either immediate or foreseeable consequences. The consequences are defined in terms of what happens to people.

There was an unlucky first person to be run over by an automobile. He had an individual problem. Today automobile injuries and deaths have become a social problem. Why? Because more people are involved and because social institutions are affected. For a problem to be a social problem, enough people must be affected so that their actions are measurably different than they were—and the society changes. Society, of course, is made up of individuals, and social problems manifest themselves in individuals. There is therefore no hard and certain line that can be drawn between individual and social problems. For example, if you are caught in a race riot, a symptom of a social problem, you also have an individual problem. Or if your parents or grandparents were unemployed during the Great Depression of the 1930s—a social problem—they also had individual problems.

However, these examples only provide the clues to the distinctions usually made between individual and social problems. An individual problem is one that affects one or a few persons. A social problem is one that affects many persons. Often a further distinction between individual and social problems is made depending upon whether the individual can resolve the problem himself. If he can adjust himself to society's standards, then he has an individual problem. If the individual or group cannot, by their own efforts, bring about a tolerable social situation, then the problem may be social.

If social problems were easy to define and understand, they would be easier to cope with, and perhaps there might even be fewer of them. Every society has a set of social norms or expectations to which persons in a given social role are expected to conform. The better the society is, that is, the more democratic and tolerant, the greater are the allowable deviations from norms. All deviations are not punished in the same way.

Society imposes different sanctions on different forms of deviant behavior. For example, our society expects presidential candidates to be married men. It does not matter if the marriage is happy, or if the candidate has a mistress whom no one knows about. If he has been divorced, the sanction invariably imposed by the voters is that he will not be elected.

A social problem also exists when large numbers of people act in ways that are different from the usually accepted social norms—without being approved by the society. The qualifier "without being approved by the society" is necessary to cover the case of a society's consciously deciding to cast aside previous norms in order to achieve some new goal—as was the case during the period of Japanese industrialization.

You may wonder why we did not simply plunge in and discuss social problems instead of starting with the preceding lengthy discussion. The answer is that too often an over simplified view has led to ineffective action. Many discussions of social problems are carried on without much concern for what social problems are. Anybody can marshal facts and declare a social problem, but intelligent action requires deeper understanding. Think of how often politicians and others promise simple answers to social problems—and how rarely the simple answers are effective. We all would like simple answers, but as social scientists we must become aware that few are to be found. The following example about the poor illustrates one way social scientists think about social problems.

THE POOR

The most important single fact about the poor is that they do not have enough money, which implies not only a small income but few or no assets as well. Economists and other social scientists often speak of an income of about $7,000 per year as providing a modest but adequate income for a family of four in a large city. Notice the explicit qualifications—"modest but adequate," "family of four." If the family were of six, then the same income would be inadequate, while it might be more than adequate for a family of one. Any monetary definition can only be a kind of shorthand expression for an average in defining "poor." In 1969, a government agency defined poverty as an annual income of less than $3,700 for a family of four. By this definition about 27 million Americans lived in poverty.

What Poor Is Not

"By any objective standard—such as calories consumed, square feet of housing space, life expectancy, health, education of children—the 10 or 20 percent of American families with lowest incomes today are much better off than the lowest 10 or 20 percent a generation ago or than the *average* family of most of the countries of the world today." Some humorist suggested that a statement similar to the one quoted be printed on little cards and given to both the poor and those concerned about the poor. His joke makes it clear that whatever truth the statement contains is likely to be of but little use in thinking about present American social problems of the poor. Our attention is also directed to the fact that being poor is in part a relative matter.

Being poor is not being lazy. If hard work alone could eliminate poverty, there would be very few poor. It is often the lowest-paid worker who does the hardest, dirtiest work, and it is not enough to say that the fact that someone's ancestors worked hard explains their wealth. For if hard work on the part of an ancestor made one rich, almost every black in America would be rich. Most poor people want to work but many cannot, either because work is not available or because they lack skills.

Neither is being poor immoral. The American culture has long disapproved of being poor. Poverty has had a connotation of "bad" or "evil" and little children have been warned against it. Very few people are poor because they are immoral or lazy, yet our culture attaches meanings to "poor" that imply personal failing and fault.

Social scientists have commented upon the curious hypocritical double standards of Americans in this respect. The Judaic-Christian tradition holds that there is nothing wrong in being poor; Christianity maintains there are virtues in poverty. Yet it is not uncommon for religious people to ignore their religion in discussing and setting policy for the treatment of the poor.

What Poor Means

Once the social scientist has freed himself from the most misleading of the common definitions of poor, he can begin to analyze the other definitions by testing for contradictions.

It is easy to see that the common language meanings are not universally true if contradictory true statements can be found.

To be poor means to be hurt and possibly to be destroyed as a decent person. The focus of this viewpoint is the direct effect poverty has on the individual and the society, including the creation of a poverty subculture.

Who the Poor Are

There are two main ways to determine the number of poor in the United States—relatively and absolutely. The relative way arbitrarily selects a percentage of the total population, for example the bottom twenty percent, and calls it poor. The absolute way defines as poor everyone who receives less than a given annual income per family size, such as $3,700 per year for a family of four. No matter which method is used, the core of poor people will continue to be included in the measurement; fluctuation will only occur among those higher on the economic scale who sometimes fall within and sometimes outside of the definition of poverty.

It is useful to think about the meaning of "poor" in relative terms. To be poor means to be worse off than most others in the society. The absolute income of a poor person is not as important as his income relative to the rest of the population. This approach takes into account the fact that there seems to be no end to the goods and services "wanted" by men in modern society. So long as there are some people who have much more than others, there will be those who "want" more. As pointed out earlier, even poor Americans consume more than most people in the rest of the world. They consume more than some people of middle income a generation or two ago in the United States. In some cases, as when they get penicillin from free medical services, they have access to goods and services not even available to the rich in the past.

Measuring poverty by considering the relative position of the poor means, therefore, that we will necessarily always have a certain number of poor. Using a third and a more social approach to the measurement of poverty, it is possible to imagine the elimination of the poor occurring only when we have eliminated social meanings attached to being poor, for example those related to schools and health. If that were to happen, then even those whose incomes were in the lower percentages would not necessarily constitute a social problem. As we have said, being poor means more than having too little income. Even if the poor had adequate incomes, and present social meanings attached to being on the bottom of the income heap remained, social problems would still remain.

Most social scientists have never proposed absolute income equality, but our society must attempt either to remedy conditions associated with being poor or give up its traditional and highly valued goal of equal opportunity.

Most government agencies today consider an annual income of about $4,000 for a family of four as borderline; individuals who receive less than $1,600 a year are considered poor. These figures, of course, are subject to disagreement. The exact financial requirements of a family of four depend on many factors: does the family live in the city or the country, in the North or in the South? Is anyone in the family chronically ill? Does the family own its own home? Obviously a family that owns its own home can get by with less income than a family that rents. Nor is income the whole story. The family's assets must also be taken into account. Not all those living on low incomes may be poor. A retired healthy couple living in Florida who own their own home and car and everything else that makes for comfortable living may find that a relatively small income meets needs quite nicely.

Why People Are Poor

A social problem, as previously stated, is one that affects many people. The belief that people are poor mainly because of their personal characteristics is not useful in thinking about a problem that involves thirty or more million people. Even when our economy produces enough for everyone, poverty will be a social problem if the amount produced is not distributed properly. During the Great Depression of the 1930s in the United States, the main social problem was that the economy did not produce enough. Since World War II the problem of the poor can be usefully thought of in terms of the distribution of income. Although our nation is very wealthy, there are those who do not get a fair share of the national income.

Being poor has little or nothing to do with personal characteristics. Practically nobody wants to be poor. A close examination of the data on those categorized as "poor" indicates some of their *personal* characteristics. Scientists have isolated five major factors. *Age*: half of the almost 20 million people who are sixty-five or older live in poverty. In their working years they were not able to save enough money to support themselves when they could no longer work. *Minorities*: there are 25 million Americans who are members of socially disadvantaged minority groups, including blacks, Puerto Ricans, and American Indians. These people are heavily discriminated against in every aspect of their lives, and, as a result, most of them are poor. *Education*: twenty-five percent of Americans over fourteen who either have a job or are looking for one have eight years of school or less. About eight million adults are "functional illiterates"—they can read or write only at the sixth grade level. With no education and few marketable skills, it is very hard to obtain employment in our society. Many of the poor were denied the opportunity to get adequate schooling. Still others who had the opportunity were forced to leave school to give immediate help to their families or for other reasons. *Health*: many of the poor suffer bad health, which makes it difficult to work regularly, and without regular work incomes are low. *Dependency*: many of the poor are women with children who have no men to support them as a result of divorce, desertion, widowhood, and different kinds of family structure.

Doing Something about the Poor

In the nineteenth century, there was a widespread belief that, as Herbert Spencer said, "Poverty purifies society." For Spencer and others, "These harsh fatalities are seen to be full of the highest beneficence. The same beneficence that brings to early graves the children of diseased parents, and singles out the low spirited, the intemperate and the debilitated as the victims of an epidemic." Andrew Carnegie, the great industrialist, felt that poverty had its advantages: "The greatest and best of our race have necessarily been nurtured in the bracing school of poverty—the only school capable of producing the supremely great, the genius."

Today we know that poverty neither purifies society nor has any great advantages to anybody. The evidence we have is quite the opposite. Being poor hurts both the individual who suffers from it and the society that tolerates it. The costs to a society that endures poverty are both direct and indirect. An example of direct costs is social welfare programs. An indirect cost is the loss to the nation of those who want to work and cannot do so. If only two million of the poor who wanted to work this year had jobs earning just $4,000, our national income would be $8 billion above what it is now. Other indirect costs result from increased social services needed in poor neighborhoods.

Important as all these costs are, the central reason for doing something about the social problem of the poor is related to the structure of values in American society. A social problem exists when values are inconsistent with the practices in the society. This is the case with the social problem of the poor. The major goals of the nation and of individuals in the nation are incapable of attainment by the poor. One set of goals proclaims that Americans should consume a lot. The poor cannot. Another set of goals makes Americans stand for freedom and justice and equality of opportunity. The poor get none of these in the same measure as their richer neighbors. Large numbers of poor constantly remind us that either our goals are wrong or that we had better work in a different way to achieve them.

A possible solution to the social problem of poverty—one we could never consider in this country—would be to adopt or modify some version of the nineteenth-century philosophy which held that there is something ennobling, perhaps even desirable or useful about being poor—not for oneself, of course. We could change the character of the social problem of the poor. A few individuals, unfortunately including some politicians, seem to use this method of solving the problem. Most Americans feel that poverty is inconsistent with American ideals and values. They do not wish to redefine these values simply in order to do away with the problem.

Another way to deal with the social problem of the poor would be to make a massive attack on every aspect of the problem. This would cost money, but if Americans spent half of what they spend on defense on the elimination of poverty, it could have been eliminated long ago. The fact is, however, that our elected officials prefer to spend on war and "defense" rather than to help the poor. Social values can be ordered in a hierarchy only with difficulty. On the one hand, most Americans do want to do something about the poor and are trying through government and private charity. On the other hand, their clearly expressed political will is to do much more in areas of defense and war than for the poor. As the country grows richer, we will be able to spend even larger amounts on death and destruction as well as on social welfare programs.

SOCIAL WORK

In 1960 the National Association of Social Workers adopted a code of ethics which begins, "Social work is based on humanitarian, democratic ideals. Professional social workers are dedicated to service for the welfare of mankind; through the disciplined use of a recognized body of knowledge about human beings and their interactions; and to the marshalling of community resources to promote the well-being of all, without discrimination."

Social work is another application of social science, regarded by many scholars as a disciplined social science. There is no sharp line between pure science and the application of science. Though the trend today emphasizes application and practice, the development of knowledge has always been one of the goals of social work. Its development of the casework method has been a major contribution to social science.

The Development of Social Work

Early in their history, Americans showed little concern with welfare problems. In the countryside as well as in small towns, each family was supposed to take care of its own. Local charity would provide for the unfortunates without resources. It was not until the late 1800s, when the United States had become urbanized and industrialized on a relatively large scale, that charity movements began. Their aim was to organize individual services for the poor. Workers visited the poor, investigated their needs, gave small amounts of help, tried to find work for those without it, and generally gave assistance through churches, employers, relatives, or friends. As public concern for the poor grew, states took stronger measures. Thus, by the 1860s Massachusetts had established a state board to assume responsibilities for "the dependent, defective, and delinquent."

By the early 1900s, those interested in social welfare changed their emphasis from helping individuals toward attempts to improve the social environment. They thought they could bring about changes in the economic and political situation which would improve the overall condition of the poor. In general, as Americans became aware of political-social problems, they developed social welfare programs to deal with each specific problem—a tendency that has continued to this day.

Social work began with concerned laymen trying to help individuals; as time passed they became highly trained professionals. To the extent that social work uses the knowledge and methods of social science, it is a social science. Samples from each of the social sciences will make this clear. Psychologists attempt to measure and predict certain aspects of human behavior such as learning. Social workers use these studies in an attempt to find effective ways to get people to change behavior. Sociologists study the way families and other social groups function. Social workers use this knowledge to change families and enable them to cope with their problems. Anthropology studies culture patterns. Social workers can use these findings when working within subcultures, such as those of the ghetto or of prison inmates. Political scientists study the distribution of power. Social workers attempt to alter that distribution. As well as benefiting from the other social sciences, the social worker contributes by being the field-tester for their theories.

Methods of Social Casework

Social casework is concerned with the interaction between the individual and his social environment. It aims to give the individual greater control over his relationship to his environment, while also often changing the effects of the environment on the individual. Casework begins with systematic observation of the individual or group and then moves on to develop a plan for desirable changes. As the plan is carried out, it is constantly re-evaluated to see that it is bringing about the desired results and to avoid incidental undesired effects. Among the many techniques available to the social worker, the following are frequently used in dealing with each case:

1. Support. The social worker attempts to support the individual (client) in his time of trouble and to encourage him toward desirable goals.
2. Clarification. Social workers attempt to make the client see his situation clearly.
3. Information. Social workers provide information relevant to the problem.
4. Interpretation. The social worker develops the meaning and implications of the client's acts and situation.
5. Development of insight. Social workers attempt to give those whom they help new understanding and insight into the situation they face.
6. Differentiation of the social worker from the individual or group. The social worker, despite his often close attachment to the people he is helping, finds it necessary to differentiate himself sharply from his clients.
7. Teaching desirable social changes. Social workers often have to give direction to their clients.
8. Activities and projects. The social worker suggests specific

ways in which the client may be able to improve his situation.

9. Utilizing available social resources. Social workers are aware of and use the services provided by public and private agencies.

Social Workers and Social Problems

Today there are too few social workers with too little available resources to solve many of the social problems of the poor. The 1960 national census reports that there were approximately 150,000 paid social workers available to help over twenty million poor people. And, of course, these social workers are not evenly distributed among the poor, so some poverty sections have many social workers while others have virtually none. Most social workers are overworked, underpaid, given inadequate facilities with which to work, and have not been able to contribute as much as they would like or could if given proper facilities. Still, social workers constitute the largest single group in our society that is consciously attempting to apply knowledge of social science to personal problems, and their contribution has been far more valuable than their numbers might suggest.

The Social Scientist and Social Problems

In a way most terminology used in discussing social problems is misleading, because it implies that there is a solution. A social problem, however, rarely is quickly "solved." History is full of examples where unsolved social problems brought about the end of the society. In a growing and wealthy society, a variety of mechanisms usually can soften the worst effects of social problems. Some are solved. In the process of growth and change, new problems of a different kind arise, but the society may be better off even with the new problems.

Coping with social problems requires that a society be able to predict the consequences of alternative courses of action or of no action. Examination and weighing of the alternatives is necessary for both individuals and societies if a better and more rational future is to become possible. Prediction is required for this process.

Chapter 15

Computers, Game Theory,
and Animal Behavior

THE RELATIONSHIPS OF THE SCIENCES

Up to this point we have stressed the relationships between the social sciences and their methods. Many of these methods, we shall remind you in this chapter, are also those of the physical sciences.

Science has many aspects. It is a means of manipulating men, machines, and nature, useful in the solution of problems. Many of the methods of the physical and biological sciences were developed with this motivation. On the other hand, science can be seen as a way to increase knowledge, motivated by curiosity, and stemming from the same sources as art, religion, and the humanities. This is, broadly speaking, the orientation of the social science methods we are discussing. This chapter examines some of the scientific methods used by social scientists which have been largely developed by scientists other than social scientists, and which tend to be oriented toward problem-solving and to be closely related to technology and control techniques. Statistics, computers, game theory, and the use of drugs and other chemicals have contributed to social science, as have biology and ethology, the study of animal behavior.

CLASSIFICATION—A BASIC METHOD

Classification is the process of grouping things, objects, and symbols according to similarities or differences. Scientists usually begin their work on the basis of a classification either assumed or explicit. For example, in social science the fundamental classification that is almost never mentioned is that which separates or groups human beings from all other groups of things, events, and states.

Many Possible Classifications

Classifications can be made in many ways. For instance, we could regroup all men, as do some of the biologists, into the classification of animals with backbones. This classification is very useful for certain purposes and represents an entirely different scheme from that of men and non-men. Classification requires that we define the objects we are attempting to classify into a broad or universal set, which then itself is defined down into subsets.

Useful information can be obtained by cross-classifying scientific data and putting the results in the form of a table or matrix. Consider the following example: a family of four, two parents and two children. This information is already classified by family which separates the four individuals from the rest of the world, by parents, which separates half the family from

the other half, and by children, which makes the same separation. The family could also be cross-classified by sex. Perhaps
one child is a male and the other a female, so that another
way to look at this group is that half of its members is male
and half female. Classification and cross-classification analyze
information. For example, the knowledge that two members
are children gives us the additional information that they are
younger than their parents.

STATISTICAL METHODS

Highly specialized statistical methods are so widely used in
science that they form part of the training of every scientist—
social, biological or physical—and they are essential to any
real understanding of modern science. They belong to the
group of methods that scientists use to discover relationships
between variables they are studying. While we cannot develop
these methods in detail here, this section covers four aspects
of statistical methods: distributions, randomness, probability,
and correlation. These terms are widely used and are essential
to the understanding of modern social science.

Distributions

In statistics, the terms *population* and *universe* refer to the
entire class that is being considered. Everyone with red hair
would be the universe of all people with red hair. Statistics
rests on the distinction between the population or universe
and observations of this population. The population is the
reality about which scientists want to know or of which they
want to make estimates. A method of observation is sampling;
the measure of a sample is a statistic.

A characteristic of a population is called a *parameter* or a
variable. These are often measured and may change according
to the problem being studied. The sample is drawn from the
population or universe and is composed of measurements or
observations of the variable—the characteristic being studied.
The purpose of statistics is to obtain reasonably good esti-

mates of the population or universe from the sample. In order to do this, statistical data are presented in mathematical formulae, tables, and graphs.

Frequencies

When all this is done we still cannot be absolutely certain that our measurements reflect the real thing. Consequently, statisticians have developed theories about frequency distributions. By *frequency* they mean the number of times a particular value of a variable occurs or is measured. For example, if every scientist who ever measured the speed of light got exactly the same answer and if there were five hundred such scientists each making two measurements, the frequency of those measurements would be one thousand. A result of this sort would give us a great deal of confidence that we knew the speed of light, but unfortunately, this rarely happens. The measurements are usually not identical but are distributed around some central point, their average. They are also usually scattered within a certain range—the highest and the lowest values of the measurement. The frequency tells how often any one measurement of the variable occurs.

When the separate values of the variables are arranged in order according to size, then we are said to have a *distribution*. When in addition to being arranged in order according to size, the frequency of occurrence is set out next to each of the measurements we have a *frequency distribution*.

Normal Distributions

One of the most common frequency distributions used in social science is a so-called normal distribution. For example, many human characteristics seem to group themselves so that there are relatively few cases at either end of the range, and most cases are in the middle.

The term "normal curve" does not mean that every kind of frequency distribution must be "normal" in the sense of an ideal distribution. "Normal" is a convenient term to describe one special kind of distribution. Having obtained frequency distributions, statisticians attempt to measure central tendencies with arithmetic means or averages, medians, modes, and many other kinds of measures you will learn about in your statistics courses. Statisticians have also learned to measure the way the data are scattered and how reliable and significant their measurements are.

Randomness

"Random" is a term that describes the process by which a sample is obtained. A *random sample* is one in which any item has the same chance of appearing as any other item. Statisticians frequently use the example of colored balls in an urn to illustrate this idea of randomness. Assume that the population is composed of black and white balls and there are two balls in an urn. If you draw both balls out you have taken a one hundred percent sample. If you assume that the population is divided equally into half black and half white balls, you would have one black ball and one white ball. Now assume that the urn contains a million black and white balls, in the same proportion of half of each. A random sample would be one in which there would be an equal chance of pulling out a black or a white ball, with no possible preference for one or the other color. Now assume that you wanted to know the proportion of white to black balls in this larger sample. How many balls would you have to take out? Obviously you could sample one hundred percent with much time and expense. Modern statistics has better ways and can tell you exactly what the chances are that you have drawn enough balls to get an accurate estimate of the composition of the urn.

Once a sample is known to be random, the mathematical laws of probability apply, and scientists can safely use the sample measurements to generalize about the whole population. It must be remembered that laws of probability work only with random numbers.

Probability

Probability is another concept central to both modern statistics and modern science. It is not a subject about which philosophers of science have reached any conclusion and, as a result, there are several definitions of probability. The two definitions that follow are, however, those most widely accepted and they will give the same results, except in very specialized cases.

One definition of probability is the ratio of the number of times a specified event would occur to the possible total number of events. In playing with two dice the chance of throwing "snake-eyes," or two "ones," is one in thirty-six. There are thirty-six possible combinations of numbers, since each dice has six sides, there are two dice, and six times six is thirty-six; but two "ones" can only occur one way, therefore the probability of throwing this combination is one to thirty-six. This approach to probability is called a *priori* because it allows the determination of certain probabilities without the necessity of actual measurement. One must know certain characteristics, such as dice have six sides, but once knowing these characteristics certain other probabilities can be deduced.

The other main approach to probability is called either a *posteriori* or the theory of frequency. This approach defines probability as the ratio of the actual number of times an event occurs to the total number of events. To continue with the dice example, a record would be kept of the number of times "snake-eyes" appear when two dice are thrown. Fortunately, and usually, the two methods amount to the same thing. Thus, repeated and long-run throws of dice have shown that "snake-eyes" do, in fact, come up one in thirty-six times.

The reason for the importance of probability is that much of modern science assumes that some events happen according to chance or randomly, but are not subject to scientific law. The law of gravity, for example, is relatively certain, compared to the probability that you will have an automobile accident the next time you drive your car.

Correlation

Scientific labors are frequently attempts to see how one or more variables are related to each other. One measure of relationship is correlation. *Correlation* measures the degree of togetherness or the closeness of relationship of two variables. Consider the following variables: *A* is the number of bottles of soda sold at a summer resort in a day; *B* is the number of people staying at the resort; *C* is the number of hours of rain during the day. Correlation analysis would give us measures of just how the numbers of bottles of soda sold were related to the number of visitors and to the number of hours of rainfall. Thus $A = 2B + CB = B (2 + C)$. If this formula is correct, when there is no rain ($C = O$), the resort sells two bottles of soda per person. But when it rains, people come inside and on the average drink a bottle of soda more per person each hour.

Correlation analysis can be used with two or more variables. When the technique works well we are able to estimate one of the variables from values of the other variables. By using other statistical techniques, such as regression analysis or multiple regression analysis, we can increase the number of variables and the number of relationships among them to determine measures of how they are related.

No correlation analysis, in fact no statistical analysis, can tell us about causal relationships among variables. For example, in the United States street lights generally go on when it gets dark; however, these two events although closely related, do not cause each other to occur. Neither mathematical nor statistical procedures, in fact any scientific method, can tell us all about cause, which is why "cause" is used so sparingly in this book.

Even though correlation cannot tell us about causality, it can draw our attention to very significant relationships that can lead to broader laws and scientific knowledge. Regression analysis is related to correlation analysis and it, too, provides understandings and measures of relationships between two or more variables.

SOME USES OF COMPUTERS

Computers have proved so useful to science that many modern scientific methods depend upon their use; they can handle large masses of data, interrelated in many complex ways and manipulated by many processes, faster than man alone ever could. As did the telescope for the astronomer and the microscope for the biologist, the computer has opened new worlds for all social scientists.

What a Computer Is

A computer is an electronic device which is able to accept information, apply certain prescribed processes, and then supply results. Almost all computers consist of input and output devices, storage or memory units, arithmetical or logical units, and processing or control units. Computers are not new; the centuries-old abacus is a computer. A more modern computing device is the slide rule, although most frequently the word "computer" refers to an electronic machine. Let us examine each of the parts of the machine mentioned above.

Input devices feed information into the computer, most often by means of electro-magnetic tape. Many computers, however, accept inputs of punched cards or typewritten or punched tape, and some of the more advanced machines now accept voice instructions, dialing (as on a telephone), writing with a light beam pencil or printed documents. The input device allows man to communicate with the computer or, more generally, the computer to communicate with the outside world. The computer can "read" holes in punched cards, electro-magnetic marks on tape, typewritten material, or voice commands. There is one very important qualification. Most computers do not speak English. Their input devices can do such remarkable things as read holes in cards, light beams, or typewriting, but all of these must be put into a specific computer language, the most popular being Fortran. This creates problems exactly analogous to translation.

The translation from human terms to computer language is called *programming*. A program is the complete sequence of instructions that the machine must have along with all the things the machine must do—its routines—in order to solve a problem. Before the computer can go to work, human beings must analyze the problem, prepare a full diagram, and generally, specify exactly what the computer is to do, in what sequence, and when. This program is then put into a storage or memory unit in the computer by the input device. Every computer stores both its instructions and its data. The usefulness of modern computers is not only a function of their speed but also of their storage of vast amounts of data, which they can reach, or retrieve, very rapidly. The larger the storage capacity of the machine, the more data it can hold and manipulate and the more complicated the instructions it can follow.

Other parts of the computer are the arithmetic or logical units and the control or processing units. The arithmetic or logical part of the machine is the one that moves the data from one part of the memory to the other, adds it, subtracts it, multiplies it, divides it, or does a multitude of other operations. It is the part of the machine that manipulates the data in ways prescribed by the control unit.

The control unit in a computer tells the rest of the computer what to do. It tells the logical unit to add two numbers together and subtract that from a fourth, and so on. It tells the computer when to listen to the outside world and when to send the results of its manipulations into the outside world.

To be useful, computers must be able to communicate with human beings or other devices—such as those they might control. This they do through their output devices. The output devices, generally speaking, are the same as the input devices. The computer may type out its message or punch out cards; it may print out messages on punched tape or on magnetic tape or it might even write out and display its results on a TV tube.

How Computers Work

A computer works by storing in its memory both the data upon which it will operate and the program which tells the computer what to do. The first command must be given to the control unit. When the first command is received, the control unit takes the second command from its memory and performs accordingly. It then proceeds very rapidly, at the rate of many millions of operations each second, through its program. Computers using combinations of discrete or discontinuous data can even change their own instructions or program in accordance with what happens to them.

Digital computers work with "bits," symbols of the presence or absence of a signal. For instance, a hole in a punched card means one thing to a computer, the absence of the hole means another thing. Modern computers can store millions of bits of information which, taken all together, can be combined into many words. The use of computers has already changed the course of development of many social sciences, and this trend can be expected to continue.

SIMULATION—BUILDING AND OPERATING MODELS

One of the most promising methods that social scientists have developed, very often in conjunction with computers, is that of simulation. The term "simulation" has a variety of meanings. In the usual sense, it means pretending or giving a false indication of something. In the biological sense, it means assuming features or structures that are intended to deceive enemies, for example insects that look like leaves or butterflies with wings that color so their enemy cannot find them.

As a social science method, however, simulation has a specialized meaning—the symbolic representation of an individual or a social process. When the social scientist simulates an individual or social process, he builds an operating model of the system, including its structures and functions. He can then experiment on this model by changing the variables and their interrelationships at will. Thus simulations have become one kind of a laboratory for the social scientist. He can experiment in a special way and extend his knowledge and ability to predict.

Models

Earlier in the book we discussed models of various kinds, mathematical, physical, and those used in the social sciences. Recall that a model is a representation which can be physical or symbolic. Simulation means that we must abstract all the features of the object that are regarded as crucial for the purposes of the study. What is abstracted from reality depends entirely on the purposes of the model.

We have pointed out earlier that models can be constructed in several different ways. Until the advent of behavioral sciences, models in social science were words, pictures, or diagrams, with some use of mathematical models. Most of these models did not function but were more like pictures. With simulation scientists can use models that actually move, that involve process, and that reflect operations of actual systems of human behavior.

Some Purposes of Simulation

When John F. Kennedy ran against Richard Nixon, part of his campaign was simulated with very useful results. Small group behavior and economic behavior have been simulated. Simulations have studied the workings of the mind, as in problem solving, and have been used to test theories in economics and political science. They have been used to train pilots and astronauts. Situations of all types have been simulated and from these simulations we have gotten much valuable information.

All-Men, Men-Machine, Pure Machine Simulations

Games of the kind we discuss later in this chapter are an example of all-men simulations. Game playing is considered by some authors as a form of simulation usually emphasizing competitive situations. Men-machine simulations are those in which human beings acting as decision makers affect the situation being simulated. Pure machine simulations are those in which human actors play no role in the model being discussed. A mathematical model is an example of a pure machine simulation.

Simulation as One Kind of Experiment

Simulation offers several advantages to the model's operator or builder. He can work the model as many times as he wants. He can study nature, social processes, and individuals in ways that are impossible otherwise. He can modify his model as he wishes and change its values. He can use different time sequences.

Those who have held that social science could not be scientific because it could not experiment now call simulating "pseudo-experimentation" and admit that simulation can often provide an acceptable substitute for the model kind of experiment usually carried out in the physical or biological sciences.

Simulation and Prediction

Simulation is very useful in testing hypotheses and predictions. The scientist can use simulation to make what are called contingent predictions which answer the question "what would happen if?" Large-scale simulation was not possible until the advent of high-speed computers with very large memory capacity.

Other Advantages of Simulation

In simulation social processes can be simplified through the elimination of all unimportant factors. The social scientist is forced to formulate accurate and precise statements about variables and how they are to be related as he builds and operates his model. Simulation then allows the confrontation of a given theory with actual behavior. The theory is programmed into the model and the computer and then compared with the actual behavior of the individual or group. Hypotheses can thus be tested. Simulation can also be useful in studying relatively infrequent processes, such as types of social upheaval. Indeed, simulation can be useful in studying numerous situations.

Simulating Thinking

Political scientists are not the only ones who are using simulation. Psychologists use it too. An early and still continuing research project that psychologists are working on with computer simulations concerns thinking processes. Psychologists have attempted to simulate and analyze human thought and behavior. One of the early simulations attempted is the way people solve problems. In this area there obviously are big differences between computers and human beings. Computers never forget; human beings do. Computers can memorize almost any amount of data; human beings cannot. Therefore, the important thing that the psychologists had to put into the computer's memory was what they thought human beings who would be asked to solve the same problem would contain in their memory. In this case the computer was not made to contain large amounts of data. Notice that this model emphasizes process.

How a Human Being Works

One of the problem-solving exercises the computer was given was a series of geometry problems. The psychologist broke each of the major steps in the computer program into sub-processes in order to determine what would happen if various combinations or other variations of the process were used. How does a human being try to prove a theorem in geometry, for example, the Pythagorean theorem that the sum of the squares of the sides equals the square of the hypotenuse of a right triangle?

The geometry student tries to find ways to go from what he knows to a proof of the new theorem. Somehow the human learner finds a way of transforming and combining definitions and rules until he is able to prove the theorem. The machine that does geometry is set up to operate in a similar fashion. It, too, is given definitions, fundamental principles, and rules for manipulating the symbols. Then it is given the new theorem to prove. First the machine tries several simple-minded ways, equivalent to trying rules of thumb. Essentially, this means running through what it knows and seeing if there is a possible application. For example, in the case of the Pythagorean theorem, the machine tried to build an area, a square, on each of the sides of the triangles to see how big the squares were and if they added up correctly.

If the machine can find a way to prove the theorem quickly and easily through one of the rules of thumb it knows, then it, like a human, has few problems. But if the machine cannot find such a simple rule of thumb, the model requires that somehow there be another way of proceeding out of the very great number of possible ways of proving things. And, of course, just like a bright high-school student, the machine does not always get every answer right. Its mistakes, surprisingly enough, are often like those of a human being. In this simulation an attempt was made to find out how humans solve problems. By putting into a machine the ways that humans are thought to solve geometry problems, a test was made to see if, in fact, the processes are analogous.

Machine Learning and Pattern Recognition

This kind of simulation also directs our attention to the fact that, contrary to what many people think, we often get more out of computers than we put into them. As a computer program gets more complicated, more and more combinations and variations become possible, leading to results which a human being would find impossible.

In working like this it may happen that in order to build the model and have the computer work properly the psychologist has to make assumptions about the processes he is investigating. Sometimes he then can look back at the human situation to see if there is not an analogous assumption that may work in the human process. Human beings learn from their mistakes and improve through practice. So psychologists have simulated this. They have built models that give better results as the models do better or "learn."

Thinking also involves recognition of patterns, such as the triangle, square, or circle. Computers have been taught to recognize all kinds of abstract patterns and, as many of you know from experience, even to recognize and read handwriting. Simulations have also been constructed so that computers can play games. Although computers still cannot play championship chess games, they can beat the average player. They never lose at such games as tick-tack-toe and they play a pretty good game of checkers. The checker-playing computer teaches itself to play better and better games because it can memorize all the good positions and all the losing positions of the checkers. In the early stages of computers it surprised the people who played against the machine to find out that it soon was able to play a better game of checkers than the men who actually programmed the machine.

Other Simulations

Other experiments in thinking are being carried on by computers. Psychologists are investigating cell organization of the brain, concept learning, and strategies of learning through simulation. In every case, the social scientist is forced to be very precise about the way he formulates the process and the data he is building into the model. With successful simulation, the theories that the model embodies automatically have a predictive power, since it is easy to see whether or not the model does the things it should be able to do. If, for example, the computer carries out a specified thought process in the same way as would a human, it is likely that the same processes will be very useful and efficient predictors of what the effects of changes would be on people.

It now appears that certain processes cannot be studied in any other way than by simulation. We must not overlook a prosaic use of computers and simulations in the analysis of existing data. With the information explosion in the social sciences, properly conducted simulations give us an increasingly efficient way to handle this information.

GAMES AND THEIR USES

You must not think that the word "games" refers only to parlor games like poker or bridge. When used in science the word has the much broader connotation of situations in which choices exist, for example when there is a conflict of interest between individuals. Even the "between individuals" is broadly interpreted so that it could mean a situation in which a person is trying to outguess nature or figure out what the best chances are for him in a given situation. In other words, game theory is concerned with situations in which more than one outcome is possible and where the individuals have choices to make that will affect the possible outcomes.

Game theory and the method associated with it have been developed mainly since World War II, although there were a few theoretical papers and studies on the subject before that time. The fact that the theory is largely the work of mathematicians means that it requires a fair amount of mathematics to study, understand, and apply. But that has not severely limited its use, for it has been applied in many fields with very useful results.

The Assumptions of One Kind of Game Theory

One kind of game theory assumes that all the players know all the possible outcomes of the game. For example, if the game is flipping coins with two players, both know what the possibilities are. It is further assumed that each player knows what he prefers. Thus in coin flipping the player who calls heads obviously prefers that a head will appear. A third assumption is that all the variables that control the possible outcomes of the situation are well specified. Game theory further assumes that the individuals who play know what will make them happy. If they are playing for money, they know that the more money they win the happier they will be; but if they are playing poker and like to bluff, then they know that more bluffing is not necessarily correlated with their winnings. Sometimes this is taken to mean that game theory assumes players are rational.

Several methods of game playing have been developed for games involving two persons playing opposite each other; but game theory involving more than two persons, while somewhat explored, is quite complicated and is not yet fully developed. The two-person zero sum game stipulates that one person's winnings are equal to the other's losses. Another two-person game allows that one person's winnings do not necessarily equal the other person's losses. Games have also been developed in which the participants cooperate.

Game Theory and the Social Scientist

Generally speaking, social scientists have not found game theory by itself applicable to a great many situations. Although such applications are increasing, game theory has usually been most helpful when combined with other methods. The difficulties of the theory mean that it must undergo further development. Social scientists are particularly interested in game theory because it is one of the first examples of detailed and elaborate mathematical developments applicable to the social sciences alone. In the past, new mathematical developments have usually been confined to problems in the physical and biological sciences. But social science is increasingly calling upon new mathematics to help solve its problems and this appears to be the trend for the future.

Terms in Game Theory

When you read about game theory you will frequently encounter words associated with "certainty." Something is said to be certain if each action leads always and inevitably to one specific outcome. For example, it is certain that cutting a man's head off leads to his death. "Risk," however, means that every action leads to one of a number of known possibilities. For example, flipping a coin leads either to a head or a tail or standing on its edge. Risk is used then, when the outcome must be one of a certain number of possibilities. The term "uncertainty" is used when an action has a set of possible outcomes, the probabilities of which are unknown. The first move in chess is an example of uncertainty. The point of game theory is to develop a strategy, a plan so complete that it takes account of every possible alternative and gives the best possible result in the face of these alternatives. Put another way, a player gets as much out of the game as he can, assuming as an opponent someone who tries to play the game to get the most out of it for himself.

An Example of Game Theory

Game theory's most important method is constructing a payoff matrix. A payoff matrix is a table which tells the value of winning for each of the players, and how payments will be distributed when the game is over. By analyzing the payoff matrix, game theoreticians can tell the procedures and principles which should govern the way the players behave. Game theory, thus, is a basis for making decisions or choices. To get an idea of how this works, think of the game of matching pennies. Each player puts a penny on the table; if both pennies are the same, that is both heads or both tails, one player takes them; if they are not the same, the other player takes them.

Let us assume George and Mike are playing this game. To construct a payoff matrix, we first list all the possible outcomes. Let us assume that George wins if the pennies are the same while Mike wins if they are not. The table which is constructed from George's point of view shows all the possibilities that can occur in this game. This is a two-person zero sum game—one person's winnings are the other person's losses, so that when George loses, Mike obviously wins and vice versa. All the possible outcomes of the game are in the payoff matrix. In this simple example we have a game of pure chance and few choices need to be made. By understanding and manipulating this matrix, game theory can tell us what the odds are and what the best moves in very complicated decision-making situations will be.

The methods of game theory are successful methods of analyzing the situations in which there are conflicts or, more generally, decision-making situations. The value of choices can be calculated. The theory can help economists with bargaining, sociologists with small groups, and psychologists with problems of choice under conditions of conflict. By forcing social scientists to think precisely about strategy, goals and the makeup of players in different situations, the role of chance in the outcome of human affairs, and the value of given actions to the actors, gaming has given social scientists another important method of analysis and solution.

BIOLOGY AND MAN

We have repeatedly emphasized the overlapping use of methods from one discipline to another within the social sciences and between them and the physical and biological sciences. It should be no surprise that in studying man many of the methods of biology, chemistry, and other physical sciences are very useful. We will discuss a few of these methods as they apply to human behavior—the uses of electricity from the physical sciences, chemicals from the chemical sciences, and drugs from the biological sciences.

Electricity, Behavior, and the Brain

Electrical activity of one kind or another occurs in many parts of the human body. It varies widely depending upon the part of the body, the behavior of the individual at the time the measurement is taken, and the state of the individual. For example, brain waves are different while sleeping than while waking, and they are not the same for healthy and damaged brains. It was not, however, until the advent of the computer that major breakthroughs were made in understanding these waves. The computer can take many different kinds of signals and analyze them in different ways, and in particular it can sort out signals from what scientists call "noise" by means of sophisticated mathematical techniques.

Scientists place electrodes—instruments for detecting the brain waves—on the human head. These are then connected to computers and the human being is stimulated or told to do something. The resulting brain waves are recorded and analyzed. Experiments have been made using sounds, light flashes of various kinds, colors, smells, and touch. With these techniques, we are learning much about the brain, about sleep, about the complex activities that go on in the brain, and about which part of the brain is responsible for which parts of our behavior.

Early in these studies scientists began to wonder if electrical signals could actually control behavior. From experiments on patients undergoing surgery it seems likely that this is the case for certain kinds of human behavior. Studies of animal brain waves further show that electrical stimuli control certain kinds of behavior. The experiments are conducted by applying electrical stimulation to certain regions in the brain stem of the animal. If enough is known about the normal behavior of the animal, the effects of the electrical stimulation can tell us much. For example, one researcher working with cats found that he could make them do things that they would ordinarily not do, such as try to eat something inedible. Chickens have been made to flee in fright from imaginary objects.

Many other uses for methods involving electricity are found in social sciences. Experiments in color vision and pain suggest that almost all of our perceptions come in signal form from outside the body. Included among such external signals are chemical, temperature, and pressure signals. These get translated into electrical signals which in turn mean something to the human being. Within the human body, pain is apparently transmitted along a series of nerves by some kind of electrical mechanism. By using proper electrical stimulation at specific points in the brain, scientists can discover which part of the brain is responsible for which perceptions.

Drugs and Behavior

Because man is also a chemical system, aspects of his behavior can be studied both as a result and a cause of chemical processes. We knew long ago that drugs influence human behavior. For almost all of recorded history, alcohol has been known to produce effects upon human beings, and studies of its influence are the best of all studies on drug effects. Recently the drug LSD has been the subject of intensive study. Medicine has long been concerned with the question of physical reaction to drugs.

Other chemical effects are also very important to social scientists. Less than a hundred years ago a large percentage of patients in mental hospitals were sick because of specific drug deficiencies. If a human being does not get enough nicotinic acid in his diet he can develop a mental illness that has symptoms called *paranoia*. Certain vitamin deficiencies can result in mental illness. Have you noticed that thiamine, Vitamin B_1, is included as an additive in many of your foods? If you go without this vitamin long enough you may suffer peripheral palsies and insomnia, delirium, anxiety, loss of memory, and confusion. Throughout history people have been considered insane who simply did not have the right diet. A whole host of methods have been developed to study the effects of drugs on human beings. By understanding these effects and the processes through which the drug exerts its influence we can learn much more about human behavior.

ANIMAL BEHAVIOR AND HUMAN BEINGS

Ethology is the scientific study of animal behavior. Most ethologists see themselves working in an area between biology and the social sciences linked by behavior. The study of animal behavior has contributed to the social sciences in many ways. The behavior of dogs, cats, monkeys, and many other animals has always interested man. Animal lovers have held that their behavior is in many ways like human behavior. Psychologists have used rats for testing purposes, to confirm or deny hypotheses and to suggest human analogs. Sheep and goats have been made neurotic and have thereby contributed to our knowledge of mental problems. The social lives of wolves, baboons, fighting fish, ants, bees, and birds of all kinds have also been studied. The methods used by ethologists typically involve close observation followed by the standard scientific methods used in the physical and biological sciences, namely experimentation, hypothesis, and verification or disproval of the hypothesis. Many of the findings and hypotheses suggest a great deal about human beings. For example, ethologists have found that certain kinds of behavior, called species-specific, are peculiar to one and only one species. This behavior is important because of the light it casts on certain questions relating to what people can learn. To certain social scientists interested in the nature of human nature, the concept of species-specific behavior has encouraged research into what aspects of human behavior are specific to our species.

ALL SCIENCES ARE RELATED

This chapter has shown you that the sciences are related through their methods. It has also introduced to you some of the frontiers of the social sciences and some terms that you will encounter as you continue your study. By using methods from other sciences and adapting them, social scientists have already made enormous advances. There is no doubt that this process will continue, leading to an ever-increasing rate of growth for the social sciences.

Part 4

Social Science
and its Future

The last three chapters are devoted to putting social science into a broader humanistic frame of reference. Social science is man's creation and must be useful to and good for him. Some issues related to this are discussed.

Chapter 16

The General Outlook of Social Science

METHODS AND SOCIAL SCIENCE

Social science is much more than its methods. It is an activity of living men, and like any such activity it is constantly growing and changing. Social science is identifying and solving significant problems or simply attempting to do so. It is theories, their construction, and their utilization. Social science is beauty, both in the older sense of something pleasing to behold and in the intellectual sense of an elegant, powerful demonstration. It is the knowledge of the science itself embodied not only in libraries but also in the smooth functioning of societies and the lives of individuals. It is both the scientific attitude and the viewpoint that social scientists have when they study men and society. And, very important, it is the uses of social science, whether by governments, private interests for gain, or individuals for their personal satisfaction. But most of all, social science is utopias, sometimes explicitly spelled out and sometimes embodied in the dreams of the men who are building with science.

Social science stems from man's desire to know himself and his world. Almost every conceivable combination of the branches and methods of social science have been used to increase our knowledge. Much of what is good in the world has been the direct result of these efforts. But man is never satisfied. In order to make his life better, he builds and utilizes social science.

One cannot point out one part of social science as the most important. Is the heart more important than the brain, or the spine than the stomach? Like the human body, the whole of social science is more than the sum of its parts. To show you how some of the parts are related to the whole living body of social science is a purpose of this chapter.

Utopias of Social Science

The word *utopia* (from two Greek words meaning "no place") was used first by Sir Thomas More in the sixteenth century as the name of an imaginary country in which ideal social conditions existed, and social theorists and philosophers have used the term ever since to describe an imagined or hoped-for ideal world. Throughout history most people have been fundamentally optimistic about the future, but it is a sign of the times that, rather than utopias, our generation has been influenced by a pessimistic imaginary country, the totalitarian state of George Orwell's *1984*. It is not hard to understand this pessimism, because it has been apparent for some time that science and society are out of joint. Science has given mankind the richest life it has ever had, with even greater possibilities for a better life to come; but science has been grossly misused and abused. Worse, it now threatens all mankind with Armageddon. The Soviet Union and the United States alone have enough atomic power and poison to kill every human being on this earth at least ten times. Ignorant politicians, greedy individuals, selfish, stupid, and grasping nations, would-be dictators, policemen and censors of every sort have used the knowledge of science for the most debased ends. But still man hopes.

Because man wants to live better, most social scientists have an optimistic view of the future in the long run. Social scientists have to assume, as their history has shown, that in the long run we can defer man's death and that at least some of our hopes for the future will come true. Social science itself plays an important role in forming these optimistic views. Indeed, we have little other basis for our optimism except the optimism of science, despite a widespread distrust and hatred of it because of its abuses.

These optimistic views—utopias—are important because they formulate a vision of the future. Visions of the future to a large extent determine the daily activities of men. Science in its role as a creator, not a destroyer, is the principal reason that men are dissatisfied with the world as it is. Almost every man knows that science has the power to give us what we need if we will but use it properly.

Implicit in much of the rebellion we see around us, whether expressed in the rebellion of the blacks against their ghetto conditions, in the alienation of the intellectuals, or in the rising expectations of the underdeveloped parts of the world, is the conviction that we can do better. And the hope and the promise are realistically based. Utopias have as one of their foundations the promise of the proper uses of science. Science alone provides the possibility for billions of people to inhabit this earth, each man with his material needs met and able to live a peaceful, self-fulfilling life in harmony with his neighbors.

Science thus shapes utopias, and utopias shape the uses of science. The physical and biological sciences along with the technology they have developed now could make it possible for Americans to live at their present standard of living if they worked only ten years of their lives. Today, in America at least, much work is necessary only to provide something for people to do because we lack the vision of a life without work. Within the very near future it will be possible for us to produce all the physical goods and services we need with but a small fraction of the people now at work.

Scientists of all kinds are concerned with giving new directions to technology, directions that yield greater human satisfactions rather than simply more production. Even now we can imagine a society building a new highway around a beautiful forest rather than through it or spending money to build safer, quieter, more comfortable aircraft rather than bigger, noisier, and slightly faster ones. Utopias link social improvement with scientific development. They impress upon us the fact that the ways we utilize science through outmoded political institutions are now inadequate. And they hold before us the vision of a more satisfying and richer life.

How Shall We Use Scientific Progress?

Thus the fundamental question raised by progress in science is what we shall do with it. Biologists are on the verge of finding a way to eliminate senility, which may make possible a human life span averaging a hundred years or more. They are close to being able to control reproduction and direct the process of evolution. But towards what end? Without scientific utopias—utopias developed by men who know science—suggestions for improving the future quality of life will range from the frivolous to the horrendous. Take for example the proposal by certain biologists to "repackage" the human race through genetic restructuring of populations by mobilizing favorable genes, which soon we will be able to do. When a biologist proposes "genius factories," where talented people would be mated with other talented people, he reveals his ignorance of the fact that in our present state of knowledge (and probably for all time) the definition of genius is socially given. A genius at one time and in one place may not necessarily be a genius at another time and place. Each society has its own definition of genius, and so breeding only geniuses as defined by one society at one time would be no guarantee at all of progress in the future. The early geniuses who discovered and developed language might easily be backward in today's world. There is even no guarantee that the great Greek thinkers such as Aristotle, Plato, and Euclid would be geniuses if they were alive today. Thus it is important that many kinds of utopias be discussed for clarifying the goals of a human science, since no man or group of men alone possesses a "true" vision of the future.

How Shall Man Serve Himself?

One of the reasons science has grown so fast in the last centuries in the West is the viewpoint, rooted in the Judaic-Christian tradition, that nature exists only to serve man, and that man exists only to serve God. But the evolution of this tradition has now raised another question, "How shall man serve himself?" The development of science has given man the power to do almost anything: create or destroy, cure or roast people alive with napalm. In other words, science has provided man with a broader range of possible answers to the question of how he can serve himself. Utopias are that part of science which strives to answer that question.

It is a commonplace that life has changed more in the last hundred years than it did in the previous thousand. Social change breeds more change, and we can expect the pace of change to grow even faster in the future. Even such an elementary thing as extending the guaranteed annual income from only the very rich who have it now to all people would cause unprecedented and complex social change. What will happen when most men find income and work divorced, when they will not have to work to survive? How will our society define success and failure? How will men fulfill themselves? One elementary change could bring about all kinds of repercussions in the economic, social, political, and value structure of Americans. These changes will be uncertain and unpredictable, chaotic and complex, so that no master plan or computer could foretell the consequences. And this is but one of the many changes we can look forward to.

We are now in the midst of minor changes. There are already signs of some social disorganization that affect many Americans, as is evidenced by the universal observation that this affluent society is not a happy one. With more change likely, the symptoms of trouble are certain to increase. What then can give us hope? On what shall we base our optimism? The only answer most modern men accept is science. Utopias give us a vision of the best possible uses of science in the service of man. The economist Kenneth Boulding has said, "If we can learn how to be clever we can learn how to be good. We can learn how to be loving and fearless and to have windows on the Infinite." Utopias open some of these windows.

FINDING IMPORTANT PROBLEMS

Finding and solving important problems is a part of science only ambiguously related to methods. The ambiguity stems from the fact that, while powerful methods prove themselves through the uses they have had in dealing with past problems, as science grows new problems are posed for which past methods are not adequate. Consequently there are no well-developed methods for finding and solving important problems. Identification of such problems is also difficult because the definition of importance varies from scientist to scientist.

Well-established methods can often be used to solve problems within the established framework of science more easily than those problems on the frontiers. Many men in addition to Newton were wrestling with the problems he was resolving so brilliantly, but, although the problems were reasonably well defined, the methods of the time were not adequate for their solution. Newton's invention of calculus enabled solution of certain immediate problems and provided the method for solving many in the future. Existing methods often can be used to solve problems not yet formulated, just as many problems can be formulated in the absence of methods which lead to their solution. Methods, in other words, provide no clear guide to the finding and solution of scientific problems.

Pure and Applied Science—Two Ways to the Future

In the past, two very different kinds of emphasis determined important scientific problems. One was the product of the scholar primarily concerned with the search for knowledge itself and but little concerned with its uses or application. The other was the product of the reformer or technician whose primary concern was with the uses of social science and who was less concerned with more abstract knowledge. These two divisions are somewhat arbitrary, reflecting extreme differences rather than the fact that almost all social scientists are interested in both pure knowledge and its applications. Yet few social scientists have been like John Stuart Mill, concerned in almost all his work with both aspects.

Arbitrary though this division may be, it is still useful in order to discuss the differences in emphasis and especially the differences in the definition of importance that the two groups make. For the sake of convenience, let us designate these two groups as the scholars and the reformers.

Scholars and Reformers

For the scholar, time moves slowly. Careful, precise, unhurried work is his ideal. A scholar like Talcott Parsons, the great American sociologist, for instance, will construct theories with little concern for their immediate application. Nor are values his central concern. Social scientists such as Max Weber were able to conceive of an important part of the body of science as being value-free.

The reformer, on the other hand, has a different time scale. He sees social science as required for dealing with immediately pressing social problems. He knows that whether or not a social scientist participates in the solution of social problems, somebody, probably relatively ignorant, will make decisions. Public policies will be established regardless of the presence or absence of scientific knowledge. The scholar is predisposed to wait until all the data are in before he makes a pronouncement; the reformer knows that the politician or businessman will make decisions with or without knowing the data.

The reformer is less concerned than the scholar with knowledge for its own sake and often tends to be somewhat distrustful of theories made without the possibility of immediate application. The reformer sees important problems for which theory is inadequate and prefers to develop theories to deal with pressing current problems. The reformer points out that although value-free social science may be possible in the minds of the scholars, the uses of social science always reflect values. Thus the knowledge the scholar has developed that may be value-free for him is not so when used by men for their own purposes. Very sharp differences exist in defining what is an important problem in social science.

Knowledge for What?

In answer to the question, "Knowledge for what?" one group says "for its own sake" and the other group says "for the sake of its uses." For one group of social sciences, a study of the classificatory kinship relationships among Australian aborigines is as important as testimony before the Supreme Court on the absence of racial differences as they affect or might affect equality of educational opportunity. Both subjects, of course, are the business of anthropologists. There is no reason to have to choose between these two extremes. The life of science has been enriched by both. The point of mentioning these things is to draw your attention to the fact that differences can exist among scientists with regard to a problem's importance. Criteria for importance are obviously a part of science. They are not necessarily related to the study of methods.

For many social scientists the importance of a scientific problem is determined at least in part by answering the question, "Knowledge for what?" In the words of the American sociologist Robert Lynd, "The significance of problems in the social sciences is to be judged not only by their relevance to the technical demands of their subject matter, but also by their ability to implement us in getting ahead with the effective control of our own cultural reforms." How do social scientists using this approach assess the importance of scientific problems?

The definition or the assessment of the importance of a social problem is not done in the usual common-sense terms. Common-sense, current, traditional, or political definitions of social problems embody much old wisdom, but the definition or assessment of the importance of a problem must be critically examined to overcome the vast amount of error and ignorance that is also part of our common-sense tradition. Therefore, although a social scientist may begin studies of important problems from common-sense awareness, he must, at a very early stage, bring his own specialized knowledge of social science to bear. The redefinition of the problem then usually involves a statement of its importance in terms congenial to the scientist, which often includes reasons why his proposed solutions are likely to work better.

Two Kinds of Problems

A problem will be more important if its manifestations are found to be inherent in the kind of culture, and it will be less important if the troubles stem from the way the culture is working. In the case of these less important problems, internal and relatively small changes of institutions will suffice to cope with them. In the case of the more important ones, new institutions may have to be devised and new social alternatives explored, a much more difficult task.

In either case, change will be required, but small changes take place with relatively few difficulties. Extensive changes cause most social problems when they are rapid or radical, or both at once. More important problems are therefore related to more extensive changes. Thus extensive change increases complexity and chaos more rapidly than it provides human satisfactions. Criteria of importance are generated to the extent that complexity, chaos, and satisfaction can be measured.

In this framework important problems are not obviously subject to scientific measurement. Yet every social scientist knows that these important problems exist. Problems that are important are related both to utopias, looking toward the future, and to the value systems of the individual social scientist and his society, looking toward the past. Because the problems have this tension in time and are so complex, social science has never had a Newton who at one stroke could define and solve important problems. The history of social science has been that men and their societies cope slowly, or not at all, with important problems, as indicated by the extinction of many men and societies.

But this slow, difficult coping was before the time of the atom bomb. Today social science faces a new challenge to develop ways of finding and solving important problems. Using the old ways could lead to the extinction of mankind, especially if the old way of conflict resolution—fighting—continues. And, furthermore, because of the fact that science cannot now tell us much about what problems are important, an introductory text must draw attention to this gap in our knowledge. Finding, defining, and solving important problems must itself become a more important part of social science.

BEAUTY AND INTELLIGIBILITY

Another part of science about which methods have little to say but which has been an important consideration to scientists is beauty and intelligibility. Beauty here is taken in its broadest sense as meaning "a pleasure to behold." It covers not only the structure of scientific theories but also the reality that men build in terms of their physical artifacts, their personalities, and the lives they lead. Intelligibility, as it is used here, means understanding of men's purposes, of society, and of men's lives. Science aims to increase both beauty and intelligibility.

Supporting Science

One of the requirements for the growth of science has always been that other people have some understanding of what science is all about. Science must be intelligible to others than scientists because scientists need support to do their work. The mass of mankind, and indeed even some of those who directly support the work of scientists, often are satisfied with simply understanding that the results of scientific work are useful and do not try to gain a deeper awareness of what science is all about. The hazards of supporting a science on the basis of its results alone are twofold. Support may be available for trivial or relatively unimportant kinds of results while basic science is neglected. If the results of science are abused too frequently, as they have been, one response on the part of those who control support—government agencies, for example, and ultimately those to whom the agencies are responsible, the public at large—might be simply to refuse further support. But there is another important positive reason that science, and especially social science, needs to be understood and supported on the basis of a broader understanding.

Science Must Be Tested

Natural and physical science is in some ways a self-propelling engine in that each advance generates further advances. Once begun, its development can be slowed down, but it is very hard to stop. It is also an engine relatively difficult to control, so that "Where is science taking us?" has, for a long time, been a very important unanswered question. Social science, however, is an engine of quite a different kind, if indeed, the analogy holds at all. Each advance only potentially generates further advance, because unless a social science theory is tested it cannot be confirmed. Advances in social science raise the more important question, "Where do we *want* to go with the help of social science?" Most societies have been content with where they were, leaving change to random forces or to powerful men's visions, for better or worse. But as men have become more rational, they have become ever less content with this approach to the future. Seeking to understand the present situation in order to plan for a better future has always given the chief impetus to social science.

Theoretical advances in social science, to the extent that they give the possibilities for future directions or application, will therefore stop unless they are tested. This is one of the major reasons for the slow development of social science all over the world. The engine of social science always runs slowly and, if the society is content with backwardness, never gets built or is easy to kill. The very fuel of the social science engine is supplied by the society and is, up to now and except for a few societies, externally supplied and dependent primarily on rationality and future-time orientation of the society. In order to grow, science must be supported and used; in order to be supported and used, science needs to be understood. There are few methods for making science intelligible other than better schools and broad education.

Science Increases Beauty

Beauty is both a characteristic and an aim of science. Scientists often refer to outstanding works as "beautiful." Mathematicians, the most abstract of scientists, frequently refer to "elegant" proofs and theorems. When the work of a scientist is cumbersome or awkward, other scientists do not hesitate to comment on this fact. The principle of simplicity is widely used in science. Jargon and infelicitous language are sometimes required, but usually regretted even in these cases.

Beauty, like some other characteristics of science, is hard to define. Beauty has few rules for its creation and few methods for its development. Clear, spare yet rich descriptions are not uncommon in science. Grace, charm, fitness, form, proportion, arrangement, all terms used in the discussion of beauty, can also be applied to scientific theories, explanations, and laws. Science in this sense has aesthetic elements of very broad and deep appeal.

So fundamental are some of these aesthetic elements that many scientists write about art when they write about science. Art and science are both aspects of man's development and expressions of himself. They bring order and beauty into his life. Even when they are manifested in material things, they move men in emotional or spiritual ways. With these shared characteristics, it is not surprising that the boundaries between science and art are often ill-defined and that each one of man's chief activities sometimes overlaps into the other.

Creative work in art is characterized by few or vague rules. In those parts of science where rules are vague or nonexistent but where results are observable, art and science are alike. In science, however, as distinguished from art, scientists are very self-conscious about their rules or lack of them. Usually artists are not. Thus science can be distinguished from art by differences in self-consciousness about method.

THEORIES AND SCIENCE

The attentive reader has probably noticed that the word "theory" has scarcely been used to this point. "Theory" is so badly misunderstood by most people that its early usage in an introductory course in science almost always entails a very considerable amount of time to clear away the everyday misconceptions. Now that you know something about science, it will be much easier for you to understand this important part of science, its theories.

A theory is a general statement that either explains or connects a group of other more specific statements. A theory can be about any phenomena. The term is not confined to scientific usage, which accounts for much of the common confusion about it, for there are theories in theology, literature, and music, to name just a few fields not necessarily scientific. Theories in these other fields often use principles quite different from those employed in science. A scientific theory is rather specialized.

Properties of a Scientific Theory

A scientific theory must have seven specific qualities or properties: (1) It must be a statement from which other statements can be deduced or inferred. (2) It must employ clear and unambiguous concepts. (3) The main concepts of a theory must be either objective and empirical or operationally defined. By objective, we mean that the statements refer to verifiable phenomena. Empirical means the data of the real world. An operational definition means that the term or concept can be defined in terms of the performance of some act or other operation. (4) It must be specific. It or the propositions deduced or inferred from it can be applied to some well-specified thing, state, person, or event. (5) The theory must be testable, either directly or potentially by testing the deductions or inferences from it. (6) It must be logical in the sense that what the theory says should happen is plausible according to the rules of logic. (7) The theory must be important or meaningful in some generally agreed upon scientific sense. A sound scientific theory should have all seven of these characteristics. Of course, some theories in social science do not have them all, and to the extent they lack them they are less sound scientifically.

Where, you may ask, does one draw the line between a scientific and a non-scientific theory, in the light of the fact that not all scientific theories have every one of the above seven characteristics? The most that can be said is that scientific consensus evaluates any given theory at any one given time. The history of science validates the theory in the long run. Indeed, no theory can hold for a very long time in science when progress is being made. As knowledge increases in any given field, theories of the past are likely to yield to new theories.

A scientific theory relates a group of concepts together in a certain way and then relates the terms or constructs of the theory to the real world. These relationships are tested, extended, and developed by means of hypotheses. Scientific knowledge grows through the development of hypotheses, which provide an important link between theoretical speculation and verification in the real world.

Hypotheses exist on several levels of theoretical abstraction. One kind—often called a descriptive hypothesis—states the existence of empirical regularities. "Every human group provides for the education and rearing of its young" is such a regularity. It simply states relationships or facts that are commonly known. For example, Newton's hypotheses about gravitation accounted satisfactorily for the motion of all the planets except Mercury. A slight deviation from that theory led scientists to search for the reason. This deviation influenced Einstein's development of a new theory. Descriptive hypotheses are also useful for predicting things that are not yet known but which must exist if the theory is correct. The discovery of the moons of Pluto was a consequence of theory, predicted before Pluto was seen in a telescope.

Here then is one relationship between data-gathering, description, and hypotheses. The gathering of data is often undertaken specifically to confirm or disprove a given hypothesis. On the other hand, if data are gathered without any explicit hypothetical framework in mind, it is always possible to deduce a hypothesis on the basis of the new data. This second approach to descriptive hypothesis is common only in the exploratory stages of study because it is a less rigorous scientific procedure. It does show, however, that no scientist can work without either explicit or implicit hypotheses.

Another kind of hypothesis is called analytical. Analytical hypotheses try to discover relationships between variables— in what ways different degrees of change in one variable affect another variable or variables. These are not the only kinds of hypotheses, but simply the most widely used. Since hypotheses are deductions from theories, it is clear that there are many other possible kinds of deductions.

Methods and Theory

All of the methods of science are related to scientific theories and often in more than one way. Look over the list of the seven characteristics of a good theory. Every one of the scientific methods you have been introduced to has the characteristic of being testable and related to the real world. Each is also specific, plausible, and meaningful. While the hypotheses state the relationships to the real world, the methods of science verify those relationships. Thus the methods are used to test the hypotheses. Confirming or disproving the hypotheses tentatively confirms or disproves the theories from which they were deduced.

There is an important elementary distinction between methods and theories that may help to clarify their relationships. By themselves, methods cannot be tested for being true or false, and in that respect, they are like definitions. Theories can be tested. Methods and definitions, however, must be evaluated, in terms of their usefulness in relating hypotheses to reality. Of a scientific theory, it can be said that it is either confirmed or disproved. Of a scientific method it can be said that it is useful or not useful.

Now perhaps you can also understand why we devoted so much attention to scientific methods of explanation. One of the primary aims of science is explanation. Theories provide important frameworks for explanation. The method of explanation that a scientist uses will depend upon his own theoretical framework. Thus methods are independent of the theory, but without methods for explanation, for testing hypotheses, theories would be untestable and hence useless.

Limiting Infinite Regress

Throughout this book it has been emphasized that scientific inquiry involves the asking of limited and specific questions. Scientific methods only provide answers to well-specified questions. But many men are not satisfied with specific answers to specific questions—they always want to know more. Attempts to get down to "fundamentals" or always to ask one question beyond what the data specify create an unending process. No matter what explanation is given for a phenomenon, it is always possible to ask further questions. Early religious philosophers got around this difficulty by quickly referring to God. Modern science goes at it another way. Methods are used to confirm or disprove hypotheses. Hypotheses in turn are deductions from theories. The methods and their uses are sharply delimited in terms of their functions and the questions they are intended to answer. These limits are drawn in terms of the theory that is being discussed. Scientific inquiry thus breaks its problems into manageable proportions. Always allowing for the fact that additional questions can be asked and further truth known, scientific activity limits its inquiry to the well-specified. Methods that are expected to provide answers within these specifications are then chosen. Thus the problem of infinite regress, as it is sometimes called, is resolved in science.

THE SCIENTIFIC ATTITUDE

Another part of the scientific system of inquiry is that characteristic of scientists often referred to as the scientific attitude. The scientific attitude, perhaps, begins with a dedication to reason in the sense of having a passion for learning and seeking order and regularities. Scientists, according to their own testimony, find their chief delight not so much in knowing but in seeking. They are thrilled when they make a discovery, but this rarely happens in the life of even the greatest scientist. What keeps them going is their constant love of learning.

Disciplined Imagination

Another characteristic of the scientific attitude is a certain kind of disciplined imagination. There are no rules for constructing a theory and few rules for inferring hypotheses or choosing methods appropriate for testing them. Therefore, scientists have to use their imagination or intuition to help them gain insights. A visualization of connections and imagining of relationships, the object of which is explanation and order, are other characteristics of the scientific attitude. Included is the disciplining of strong personal feelings, biases, and prejudices. The controversies in science and the biographies of scientists testify that scientists differ from most other men in that wherever their scientific work is concerned they set aside these personal feelings at least to the extent that they can utilize the objective methods of science. Whether they do their work because of or in spite of their personal feelings and value judgments, they are able in their scientific work to stand aside from their subjective feelings.

Skepticism

Skepticism is also part of the scientific attitude. The scientist is self-critical of his own work and critical of all science. He accepts nothing on faith or authority. Neither the age of an idea nor where it came from influences his critical judgment. The scientist accepts no premise or idea as beyond the possibility of questioning or investigation. He is constantly testing and retesting accepted facts. He often doubts. Every idea, his own included, must be subjected to the rigors of demonstration. The scientist is never satisfied. This attitude implies a very high tolerance for change, conflict, and intellectual insecurity. The history of science illustrates that what is true today may well be partially so tomorrow and false the day after that. Many cannot tolerate the mental and emotional insecurity seemingly caused by changes in their beliefs and knowledge, but a scientist must be willing to change, for he knows that the truth he is seeking is never absolutely attainable, only more closely approachable. He is satisfied to be constantly reaching for a goal he can never touch.

These are some of the characteristics of the scientific attitude. Most who have cultivated it have found their lives more satisfying. When they were industrious and lucky, they were able to push our knowledge forward. Having the scientific attitude does not make a scientist, but few scientists have been successful without it.

Methods are just one part of science, as are the laws that express regularity, the descriptions, the classifications, and all the facts that scientists have discovered. Knowledge is largely achieved through the use of methods. As the methods prove their power they become part of the body of knowledge, and as the knowledge grows new methods have to be developed. Thus methods are necessary but are not a sufficient condition for knowledge. Sometimes methods come before knowledge, sometimes with it, and sometimes after it. But no matter what the time relationship, the body of science is developed only through the use of methods, and that is the significant relationship. The entire body of scientific knowledge is mankind's most prodigious feat and his most striking achievement. His ability to conquer space and disease, to master himself and nature, all stem from this knowledge. No man can know it all, but all men can use and benefit from it. This knowledge gives us a confidence in the future not based on faith alone.

Chapter 17

The Uses and Future
of Social Science

MAIN USERS OF SOCIAL SCIENCE

Why does our society push the rapid development
of the physical and biological sciences and neglect
the social sciences? Why is much of the knowledge
of social science under-utilized? How does politics
affect the development of social science? What are
some of the basic issues in the use of social sciences? Questions like these are often asked by those
who are concerned with individual and social problems in our society and realize that social science
will undoubtedly play an important role in their

solution. What, then, are some of the major factors conditioning the uses and future of social science?

In America today the users of social science fall into three
main classes. First, and by far the largest in terms of size, number, and influence, are the various governments in the United
States. The local levels of government provide the main support for the elementary and high schools. Our public schools
are influenced by social science both in the methods of teaching and in subject matter taught, especially the social studies.
But, sad to say, this is a worn out and ineffective use of social
science, principally because the application lags far behind
current knowledge. This lag means that most children are
being educated in accordance with social science ideas of long
ago. The fact remains, however, that local governments are
large users of social science knowledge in the schools alone.
And of course they use it in many other ways, such as in planning for the growth of cities and suburbs.

State governments appear to use social science very little.
There is little doubt that the power of state governments is
steadily decreasing, the centers of power shifting to Washington and the large metropolitan areas. Whether it has been the
unwillingness or the inability of the states to solve problems
as they grow, the fact is they have not been able to do so, and
this may be related to their very slight use of social science.
Of course, state governments support institutions that do use
social science, most notably the university structures and
mental hospitals. But even here they have not done a good
job. The greatest universities in the country are still dispropor-
tionately the private universities, and practically nobody who
can afford private care goes to a state mental hospital because
of the often inadequate treatment they are likely to receive
there.

The federal government is so vast that simple characteriza-
tions about its uses of social science are difficult. Of the three
main branches of the government—legislative, executive, and
judicial—the judicial branch seems to employ the findings of

social scientists most frequently. The legislative branches often utilize the knowledge of social science in a formal way through records and hearings, but direct utilization in effective government as reflected either in the laws or the budget is still low. Legislation and the economy are influenced more by low-level "politicking," special interest groups, and log-rolling than by higher goals of increasing the general quality of life for Americans and offering positive leadership to other nations of the world.

Since World War II, presidents have used social science advisors with increasing frequency. Although their influence is noticeable in some legislative recommendations and presidential vetos, politics is still more important. But there is an interesting paradox in all of this. Despite the relatively slight use the three main branches of government make of social science, many of the departments of the government are among the leaders in the employment and development of certain branches of social science. The Department of Defense, for example, has one of the most effective teaching structures in the world. By using modern social science methods, this department has shown that you can teach large numbers of men almost anything quickly and at relatively low cost. The Department of Defense uses social science in the screening and selection of personnel. The Central Intelligence Agency, the Rand Corporation, and the Department of Defense utilize social scientists when they attempt to subvert the governments of other countries. Economics is used by many departments of the federal government. Witness the president's Council of Economic Advisers, the members of which are usually skilled economists.

In summary, then, governments in the United States are the largest users of social science, but this usage is sporadic and very commonly, as in the case of the public schools, based on old-fashioned and outdated knowledge. Knowledge of social science is not sufficiently utilized in the solution of certain central problems of our society, those of improving the quality of life, increasing democratic participation in government, and peace-making.

Individual Uses

Individual and private use of social science is quite common, but the knowledge used is not the most recent and all too often it is directed towards private, rather than public, gain. One of the most visible usages of social science is in the field of mental health. Over half the hospital beds in the United States are occupied by people with mental problems. Almost everybody in the United States will require professional help for a mental problem at one time or another. In this situation, it can reasonably be said that individuals use the knowledge of psychology.

Individuals also use the knowledge of social science that is built into our institutions and absorbed by common sense. But once again this kind of knowledge is rarely up to date because of the time lags for social science knowledge to be absorbed into common sense or a social institution. For example, most parents nowadays do not punish their children by means of beatings. This, however, is a relatively recent development despite the fact that social scientists knew about the harmful effects of physical punishment long ago.

It is worthwhile to distinguish individual uses, that is to say, uses of social science for specific individual purposes, from private uses, where individuals or groups of individuals use social science knowledge for their own ends on other people. American business, particularly the five hundred largest companies which do more than half the business of the United States, are big users of social science knowledge. They use the latest findings in their attempts to manipulate human beings for corporate ends, such as in advertising and labor relations. Advertising agencies and marketing departments of corporations use social science knowledge in order to mold the preferences of the buyers of their products or to come to terms with other preferences. Departments of labor and industrial relations use the knowledge to ensure high production from their workers. Other private groups also use it for their own ends. Charitable organizations, for example, use it when they employ social workers. Candidates for public office use polling techniques to find out how the voters respond to their appeals and what they should tell them.

The hallmark of this usage of social science is often private gain rather than public or individual welfare. There is no invisible hand operating which ensures that private uses of social science knowledge for private gain guarantees the public welfare. In fact, the opposite is often the case.

The brief survey above of the uses of social science has shown that there is no systematic employment of this knowledge. No private or public agencies attempt to use the knowledge or even significant parts of it in any massive effort to improve the quality of our lives. Contrast this with the situation in the physical sciences. The transistor is discovered and within a few years electronics is revolutionized and every one of us benefits. Or in the biological sciences, when polio destroys and cripples, a systematic attempt is made to discover a preventative for it. By pouring resources into the search, vaccines are developed. Within a few short years the menace of polio is virtually eliminated from our society.

Why is social science not used and developed in this way? There is no simple answer, but it is worthwhile to explore some of the factors that might be involved. Almost every scholar who has paid any attention to this problem agrees that men cannot realize their fullest potential without the development of more adequate social institutions. And social science knowledge will undoubtedly be important in the development of these.

THE GROWTH OF SOCIAL SCIENCE

The development and utilization of social science requires money. This central fact has conditioned every aspect of the modern history of social science. It accounts for the fact that well-to-do amateurs continue to make important contributions to it and for its very distorted development. For example, the history of social science, which promises few immediate returns in dollars, is almost completely neglected, while much is spent in the field of testing, where more adequate personnel selection for jobs or pupil selection for schools makes or saves millions of dollars. It accounts for the fact that most social scientists are connected with either universities or governments, where institutional policies sometimes bear heavily on them, to the virtual neglect of the individual, independent scholar.

Needed—New Institutions to Support Social Science

The recent development of social science took place in the West, where most countries have a mixed free enterprise economic system. In this kind of system, private gain is the main motive for the spending of money. Until recently, there was little prospect that the development or the utilization of the social sciences would lead to private gain. This explains much of the past neglect. But even today there are few prospects for making much profit from its development. Therefore, if it is to be developed and used, social institutions will have to be devised for its support without the goal of private profit but rather for the public good.

Do not be surprised by this suggestion. Most western societies support churches with no hope of private gain but only of public good. And all societies support so-called defense establishments where the motives of private profit are often less important than those of a somewhat distorted sense of public good. Our society supports schools and hospitals and many other such institutions.

Costs Against Benefits

In a society accustomed to thinking of spending money for which specific measurable returns are obtained, proposals to increase the amount of spending on social science are almost always met with the question, "What will we get for it?" The question is a reasonable one, and the social scientist is hard put to answer in his own terms. What will society get in dollar terms for recording remote languages which are now spoken by two hundred or fewer people and which will soon be extinct? What will society get if it develops the history of social science? The calculation of dollar values and returns does not always work in such cases. Other values need to be appealed to. Until more men understand social science and its potential, probably the dollar calculus will also hold in the future.

A grave difficulty in persuading people to spend money on social science is the failure to understand it. Most men think they know more than scientists accept. They "know" that "men have stronger sexual drives than women," or "you get what you pay for," or "spare the rod and spoil the child," or "human nature is the same everywhere." But scientists don't accept common-sense knowledge unless it is verified, and therefore they have to spend large amounts of money testing and retesting such statements. When they do this, they often find that common-sense knowledge is wrong. And then the "Monday morning quarterback" may reply that he knew it all the time. So failure to understand the need for testing accepted ideas remains an obstacle to the funding of social science.

Different Ways of Formulating Problems

Another obstacle to the development and use of social science lies in the different ways of formulating problems. Very often the men who want to use social science ask questions that social scientists find inappropriate. Robert Merton, the distinguished American sociologist, writing on this subject, has said, "Characteristically, the problem is so stated as to result in the possibility of the researcher being seriously misled as to the 'basic' aspects of the problem which give rise to the contemplated research. The practitioner, or man who wants to apply social science, often feels frustrated, therefore, when he tries to get a social scientist to help him. And sometimes the feeling is mutual." The social scientists may think that the practitioner does not know what he should be doing. This kind of gap has undoubtedly created many difficulties.

SOCIAL SCIENCE AND PUBLIC POLICY

By its very nature, social science will not develop more rapidly without changes in public policies. The fact is that knowledge is increasing in the field, the numbers of social scientists are increasing, and the quality of their training is improving. Therefore, we can expect social science to grow more rapidly in the future. But the question is whether it will grow rapidly enough and in useful enough ways to allow it to deal more effectively with our individual and social problems.

Public Policy-making Issues

Generally speaking, policy-making is the setting of a course that will be followed in the future. So far as the federal government is concerned, the reasons for supporting social science are the same as for supporting any kind of scientific research—almost everyone agrees it is good public policy to have more and better scientists. But the central reason for government support is that the results can be reasonably expected to help in the solution of public problems. Once before in man's history—during the Industrial Revolution—social science provided much help during a period of rapid and far-reaching social change. The social sciences were very young then, but few policy-makers doubted their usefulness. Now change is more rapid and far-reaching and the consequences for man are much greater, perhaps even annihilation. There is little reason to doubt that the social sciences could help us even more now.

But what does policy formation involve? It involves increasing scientific creativity or providing for a continuing stream of fundamental knowledge and it also involves planning and formulating scientific policies for the utilization of the knowledge gained. Whatever policies are formulated either on the creative or useful level, they must later be executed. Who will do these things? Where will the scientists and other planners and administrators come from? What should their training have been? The men and women who formulate and execute the scientific policies of the federal government will have to have a broad scientific competence enabling them to understand the questions they will face and to be respected by the persons with whom they will deal. Such people now are rare. Social scientists who are interested in better government policies would do well to start thinking about the men who help formulate them.

Making and executing government scientific policies are not only intellectual processes; they are also very complicated social processes more like bargaining or negotiation than logical decision-making or logical problem-solving. Fortunately social scientists are studying the processes of government decision-making, and, as we learn more about these processes, perhaps more intelligent government support for social science will be forthcoming.

Ineffective Support in the Social Sciences

Because the government officials and politicians seem to understand social scientists even less than social scientists understand them, it is saddening to observe that very often federal support and even foundation support for social science has impeded rather than helped to develop social science. This stems primarily from the way social science support is given. Because there are so many worthwhile social science projects, or simply because the work of many social scientists requires substantial support beyond the individual researcher's or his institution's means, social scientists make many requests for funds, which take a great deal of time and energy. However, foundations and government agencies are able to fund only one-tenth to one-twentieth of all the requests they get. With so many people trying to get so little money, it is not impossible that there is waste of social science manpower just in drawing up requests for support, time resulting in very little gain to the social science community. If all the time spent in drawing up requests were taken into account, in some cases the total time preparing requests for which social scientists were not paid would be worth the amount of money finally given to one scientist or group of scientists.

But this not the end of the story. The requests for funds are typically gone over by a committee of prominent scholars in the field. These scholars often do the initial screening and sometimes have the final word on who gets the funds. Thus it happens that most of the money spent on social science research goes to a very small handful of scholars in a very few of the nation's 2,200 colleges and universities.

But the sad story does not even end there. Many agencies of the federal government that give funds for social science research do not insist upon widespread dissemination of the results. Of course, many scholars do research and publish the results voluntarily. But they do not often publish *negative* results, and this failure to publicize the negative results leaves other scholars free to make the same kinds of mistakes. The failure to insist upon widespread dissemination of government-supported work in social science shields agencies and committees that gave the money from criticism for work of little value. In science there is no room for this kind of protection.

Finally, many scholars feel that governments control research activities too much through a series of rules, poor administration, and cumbersome procedures. For instance, most government agencies will not support the work of individual scholars but insist that the money go to some institution and through the institution to the scholar. This imposes two sets of controls on the scholar before he can get his money. Sometimes these controls are a problem. One result has been that individual scholarship in America, that is, the man who wants to work alone on his own ideas, is now virtually extinct in social science.

It should not be assumed that the federal government is alone in its inefficient, cumbersome, and controlling methods of supporting social science. The great foundations follow many of the same policies and seem to be unduly influenced by fads, often using their funds to push certain narrowly defined kinds of social science. For example, one of the greatest foundations in the country poured tens of millions of dollars into one field during the 1950s. It stimulated large numbers of able people to enter the field and to begin elaborate research projects. It then suddenly stopped its contribution and, as one social scientist put it, "sterilized" the field by disappointing able people and stopping them in the middle of their projects, thus wasting much of their time and discouraging further efforts.

Politics and Dollars

Certain scientific fields have recently been as close to the hearts and pocketbooks of congressional spenders as defense. To understand why medical research, for example, has obtained large and increasing funds of money while problems of chronic unemployment, urban mass transit, education, drug usage, and even reform of certain backward American medical practices, have been neglected, is to understand how politics determines where scientific support is granted. In the last few years, Congress has given about a billion dollars, or almost one percent of the national budget, each year to medical research. Why do congressmen behave this way? One reason is that they are mostly well-to-do. Their ability to live away from or buy their way out of the problems of our society makes them less aware of these problems. But they all know about appendicitis, cancers, and mental illness. Moreover, they feel there is a certain democracy in illness because it strikes Republicans as well as Democrats, members of all faiths, and both farmers and city dwellers. Social scientists could tell them that is not so. In fact, many illness rates are closely correlated with income. In any case, this mistaken belief in the democracy of illness does not seem to carry over to social problems.

The American Medical Association has been called the mightiest trade union in the world. It has succeeded in restricting entry into the medical profession so that in recent years the number of doctors per thousand persons has actually gone down in the United States, while their incomes have increased substantially. The medical profession as a whole supports its association and the association's lobbyists very handsomely. But there are no lobbyists for the poor—none to entertain congressmen while telling them about the evils of air pollution, none, in fact, for most of the pressing problems of our time. Of course some groups do work on Congress, but usually they are volunteer, part-time, and generally lack the resources of the mighty special interest lobbies.

These factors alone do not explain why medical research gets so much money. One must also look to the nature of congressional leadership. Some of the strongest advocates of medical research among the most influential congressmen are in key positions on appropriations committees. Thus a combination of factors, none of which hold for social science, has insured large appropriations for medical research. The point of this example is not that appropriations for medical research should be cut, but that political factors, with a big element of chance or luck, combined with special interests are what principally determine the amount of money appropriated for various aspects of science. For social science, the sums are pitifully inappropriate to the demands of today. Although money would not automatically guarantee the uses and development of social science, without it social science will definitely grow more slowly.

THINKING ABOUT THE FUTURE

Progress depends, at least in part, on the goals that men have. Indeed, a central problem for social science is that of a self-fulfilling prophecy—a situation in which what men think about the future causes that very future to come about. For example, if everybody in the country thought there was going to be a terrible depression beginning next week, it would be perfectly reasonable for them not to spend their paychecks on Friday. But this massive withdrawal of money from the economy might easily bring about the very depression they fear. Science and its promise, by influencing the goals of men, has already greatly affected man's future.

Many men, however, do not know science, cannot use or understand it, and will not support it. A large number of the world's people live in developing areas, including many in America. Poorly educated, although they may have finished high school or even college, thinking about science in terms more appropriate to their grandparents, fearful, superstitious, it is almost as though they lived in another world or another century. One of the things that is required for more and better uses of social science is to increase the understanding of it and release those of our citizens who are ignorant or fearful or superstitious from the bonds imposed by these relics of the past. One way to do this is by blueprinting the future. Using the best social science we now have, we must set forth a vision of what might be; then men could work more intelligently to bring a better future about. Lacking such a vision, progress will be slower.

Shifting Values in Social Science

As we have seen, social science, like all of science, is pervaded by a basic optimism that assumes man has a future and that this future will somehow be better as rationality and science grow. But this fundamental optimism is more an article of faith widely shared than knowledge widely verified. The most common fate of leading nations and peoples is for history to pass them by. And this could even happen to us. If the lower motives present in our society were to overcome the higher ideals of science, it is not impossible that history could pass us by, too. This is not likely now, yet there are signs observed by social scientists that have put them on their guard.

Up until about World War II, the principal reward for the social scientist was professional recognition. Communication was very important to him. He was a dedicated individualist and usually worked either alone or in relatively small groups. He was not entirely motivated by worldly gain and was interested primarily in basic research. Today, for some at least, professional recognition is less important than world prestige, power, and money. Now, instead of communicating for criticism and recognition, communication is often thought of as a means to private gain. Individual research is less valued, and in certain fields, discouraged. Large anonymous teams are the vogue in many fields, and in some of them basic research is played down in favor of applications which give power, money, and influence to individuals or private groups. This kind of shift in basic social science values may not now be of much importance, but if it continues it will surely threaten the older, well-established goals of science.

At this point, some of you might be asking, "Is not the author being inconsistent in just warning us about the uses of social science for individual and private goals when all along he seems to have been urging more use of social science?"

There is no inconsistency involved. All of science is public property. The ideal of science is that whatever knowledge is produced should be for everyone to the largest extent possible. This viewpoint is not inconsistent with some uses of science for individuals and private groups. The central distinction is that individuals and private groups should not use the knowledge of science for their own benefit *at the expense of others*. This would be a travesty of science. Individuals and groups who use scientific knowledge for their own benefit without denying these uses to other people and without using the knowledge against other people are within the ideals of science. The greatest uses of science are those which benefit the greatest numbers.

Science has placed immense powers in the hands of men. Now largely freed from want, illness, and early death, man already has most of the powers to remake himself and his world as he thinks best. But simply possessing this power does not guarantee its sensible use. As Bertrand Russell has said, "Science enables the holders of power to realize their purposes more fully than they could otherwise do. If their purposes are good, this is a gain; if they are evil, it is a loss."

The aims of men are largely determined by their education, not only in science but also in the humanities, literature, art, and music. The institutions and processes of government elevate men to the positions where they can use power. Thus is science linked to humanism and democracy. Without the highest ideals drawn from humanism, what aims might men choose for the uses of their new power? Without a democratic, self-realizing society, what use will social sciences have? The methods of social science open the door to the future by providing reliable knowledge. Man's future will be determined by how this knowledge is used.

Contents of Appendix A

Appendix A

How to Find It
in the Social Sciences

The purpose of this appendix is to help searchers for social science knowledge find the published information they seek. One of the most important characteristics of science is the cumulative nature of the knowledge it produces. Each advance takes account of what is already known. Thus, whether you are a sophisticated researcher or a beginner, it is necessary to find out what is already known about the subject under investigation. This appendix tells you where to look.

There are few libraries so small that they do not include a very large percentage of social science knowledge. The trick is to find what you want. This appendix gives you many ways to find social science knowledge.

HOW TO USE THIS APPENDIX

The first rule about finding information is to state as clearly as possible what you are looking for. Perhaps it is a very specific question, such as "When did Adam Smith publish the *Wealth of Nations?*" Perhaps it is a very general one, such as "What is political science about?" No matter what the nature of the question, you have to state it in such a way that when it is answered you will have found out what you want to know.

You might consider three aspects of a problem in the initial stages of a search for information. These aspects are: the man or men who worked on the subject; the subject itself; and the appropriate discipline of the social sciences. Rarely does an investigator know everything about each of these three at the beginning of his search. You have to begin with what you do know. First, make sure you know the meaning of the terms you are using, starting with the dictionaries. Then you may want to check the encyclopedias and handbooks for quick summaries of knowledge. Alternatively, you may find the surveys and other guides to the literature useful for general overviews. As your search progresses, you may then turn to the indexes and abstracts for more specialized knowledge. From them, when you want the most detailed and up-to-date information, you can look into the scholarly journals. There are many other patterns for searching for knowledge; as you work, you will discover the specific one that suits you best.

The material in this appendix is divided into eight parts:

Guides to Library Use
General Bibliographic Aids
Dictionaries
Encyclopedias and Handbooks
Surveys and Other Guides to the Literature
Indexes, Abstracts and Bibliographies
Where to Find Facts and Biographies
A Selected List of Journals in Social Science

These sections are prepared for those just beginning an investigation. One can then go as deeply as desired into any part of social science. Most libraries will not have all the sources listed. However, the selection of sources was made with the average library in mind, and most libraries will have many of them. The sources are restricted to publications in English, although good works in social science are not limited to English. The entries emphasize the United States despite the important work done elsewhere.

When relevant, the headings listed above are further divided into the disciplines of the social sciences, as follows:

Anthropology
Behavioral Science
Economics
Education
Geography
History
Law
Planning
Political Science
Psychology
Social Work
Sociology

This list has been chosen for its usefulness. There is no consensus among scholars about which disciplines make up the social sciences or about the subject, content, or methods within each discipline. The first *Encyclopaedia of the Social Sciences* included three classes: the purely social sciences—politics, economics, history, jurisprudence or law, anthropology, penology, sociology, social work; the semi-social sciences—ethics, education, philosophy, and psychology; and the sciences with social implications—biology, geography, medicine, philology or linguistics, and art. The recently published *International Encyclopedia of the Social Sciences* has two major classes, the sciences of human behavior—anthropology, economics, history, political science, sociology, and psychology; and those which deal only in part with human behavior—geography, law, psychiatry, and statistics. (See Appendix B for a definition of "behavioral science.")

In this appendix, references to psychiatry and psychotherapy are included under "psychology." No separate listing is made for "statistics," for two main reasons. Each of the disciplines of social science has its own approach to statistics; and the mathematical preparation required for modern statistics is such that each person must seek knowledge according to his own level of training. Therefore general references are likely to be of little use.

The material under the previously mentioned headings progresses from the general to the particular. The procedure is to begin with works that cover broad subjects and then deal with the more specialized information. Perhaps the best way to use this appendix is to read it over quickly. Then, after you have some idea of the variety of material available, you will be able to select those materials useful for your own projects. When you acquire this general overview, you will discover that "index," "encyclopedia," and "dictionary" mean different things in different disciplines. A general knowledge of what is included under each type of source is necessary if you are going to use these materials.

GUIDES TO LIBRARY USE

You will save yourself much time, effort, and frustration in looking for information if you are familiar with the organization and procedures of your library.

The book below has a good section that tells you how to use libraries. College textbooks from the first English course may also include a section on library use.

> TURABIAN, KATE L. *Student's Guide for Writing College Papers.* Chicago: University of Chicago Press, 1963.
>
> Chapter II of this paperback contains an excellent introduction to the library.

Many libraries have published their own booklets which describe their libraries and give the rules for use of books. See if your library has such a booklet. When in doubt about any aspect of library use, ask your librarian.

GENERAL BIBLIOGRAPHIC AIDS

This listing includes reference books which themselves contain many references to other books. A reference book is read in order to find specific knowledge and is not designed for continuous reading like a novel. A bibliography is a selected and organized list of materials that sometimes includes critical comments. The general bibliographic aids that follow are intended to help you find the place where the information you seek is located. Bibliographies appear in very many of the works cited in this guide. The ones covering the broadest subjects are included in this section. Those that are more closely organized around a given subject area appear in the section "Indexes, Abstracts and Bibliographies," under the appropriate discipline. Be warned, however, that there is little uniformity of definition in the classification of social science literature. What is called a dictionary, for example, may in fact be a bibliography.

When problems of classification arise, the procedure that has been followed is to put the item under the heading that the author of the work designated but with a comment about where else it could fit conceptually or a cross-reference.

> WINCHELL, CONSTANCE M. *Guide to Reference Books*. 8th ed. Chicago: American Library Association, 1967.
>
> The best single source on reference books in general, with a section on social science. It is kept up-to-date by supplements.

The next book is less authoritative, but easier for some to use.

> MURPHEY, R. W. *How and Where to Look It Up: A Guide to Standard Sources of Information*. New York: McGraw-Hill, 1958.

The next two are the best overall bibliographic indexes. They are both classified by subject, but note well that "subject" includes place names. These two bibliographies are not specialized in social science and include much more, but they do have a great deal about social science as well.

Bibliographic Index: A Cumulative Bibliography of Bibliographies. New York: Wilson, cumulated with semi-annual additions from 1938 to present.

Under each subject, the entries are by author.

BESTERMAN, THEODORE. *World Bibliography of Bibliographies and of Bibliographical Catalogs, Calendars, Abstracts, Digests, Indexes and the Like.* 4 vols. 3rd ed. Geneva, Switzerland: Societas Bibliographica, 1955–56.

The entries under each subject are chronological with earliest publication first.

The United Nations Educational, Scientific, and Cultural Organization (UNESCO) publishes much that is useful for the social sciences. The general listing covering everything follows.

General Catalogue of UNESCO Publications and UNESCO Sponsored Publications, 1946–59. Paris: UNESCO, 1962.

There are references to such publications as the *World List of Social Science Periodicals, A Selected Inventory of Periodical Publications* which includes major documentation and bibliographic services in the social sciences, and the *International Bibliography of the Social Sciences* which is especially useful—a series in the fields of economics, sociology, political science and social and cultural anthropology, with volumes published annually.

The United Nations Department of Public Information publishes a complete catalogue of the printed documents published by the U.N.

Ten Years of United Nations Publications, 1945–1955: A Complete Catalogue. New York: United Nations, 1955, with annual supplements.

The most comprehensive bibliographic resource for the social sciences is:

WHITE, CARL AND ASSOCIATES. *Sources of Information in the Social Sciences: A Guide to the Literature.* Totowa, New Jersey: The Bedminster Press, 1964.

This is the best single-volume guide to the literature of social science, covering history, economics and business administration, sociology, anthropology, psychology, education, and political science. It does not include behavioral science, geography, law, planning or social work as separate categories, although it has some references to these subjects. Valuable references to geographical literature are included in the section on history. Social work is covered to some extent under sociology. The index is a good one for finding works by author and title, but not by subject. When looking for material on a subject, first use the table of contents to find the chapter most likely to include the subject. Then glance through the chapter to find what you want. For example, suppose you are interested in modern Europe. Look up "history" in the contents. The chapter begins on page 63. As you go through the chapter you will find on page 77 a paragraph entitled "Modern Europe" which gives two annotated references. Henceforth this is referred to as White, *Sources.*

More specialized bibliographies are given in many of the reference works cited in this guide.

DICTIONARIES

This listing covers dictionaries which give the meanings of terms. If you are not sure of the meaning of a term, look it up.

Webster's New International Dictionary of the English Language. 3rd ed. Springfield, Mass.: G. and C. Merriam Co., 1961.

This should be used first when you want recent word usage. Use abridged dictionaries only when the unabridged is not available or for finding the meanings of common words briefly stated. Be cautious about using the current dictionary for words used in works published before the dictionary, since the meanings can change. When you look up words from works published in the 1950s or earlier, you will want to check the meanings given in Webster's second edition, sometimes even in the first edition. The third edition dropped 150,000 terms that the second contained.

To trace the history of a word use one of the following dictionaries.

CRAIGIE, SIR WILLIAM A. and JAMES R. HULBERT, eds. *A Dictionary of American English on Historical Principles.* 4 vols. 2nd ed. Chicago: University of Chicago Press, 1960.

American English is not the same as English English. This is the best work on our distinctive usage.

The next is the best overall work.

MURRAY, SIR JAMES A. H. *et al.* eds. *A New English Dictionary on Historical Principles.* 13 vols. Oxford: Oxford University Press, 1888– 1933.

With its supplements, this is the best single source for tracing the development of word meanings. It is commonly called the *Oxford English Dictionary.*

Even good general dictionaries are not sufficient guides to how authors use special terms. In addition, every science develops its own jargon as it grows. For these reasons a number of dictionaries specializing in the social sciences have been published. The following two attempt coverage of all the social sciences but without complete success.

GOULD, JULIUS and WILLIAM L. KOLB, eds. *A Dictionary of the Social Sciences.* New York: The Free Press of Glencoe, 1964.

This was compiled under the auspices of UNESCO. Generally speaking, the entries, written as short essays and covering 1,022 terms and concepts, are well done and give references to the basic works on the subject. The work does not cover, except incidentally, education, geography, history, law, planning, psychology or sociology. There is no entry for "behavioral science." If you are interested in recent, more specialized, usage of social science terms this is a good first place to look.

ZADROZNY, JOHN T. *Dictionary of Social Science.* Washington: Public Affairs Press, 1959.

This includes about 4,000 terms covering mainly economics, sociology and political science, with some on anthropology, history, law and psychology. The entries are less authoritative, shorter and therefore developed less, than those in the UNESCO work. An older dictionary that covered many terms as they were used before 1900 in anthropology, economics, psychology and education is Baldwin's, described more fully under the psychological dictionaries.

No discipline in the social sciences exists by itself. Therefore, all the specialized subject dictionaries contain some terms used by all the others. Sometimes different disciplines use the same work to mean different things. If you suspect this, use two different dictionaries from the many disciplines of social science that have them.

Anthropology

WINICK, CHARLES. *Dictionary of Anthropology.* New York: Philosophical Library, 1956.

This is a general dictionary of terms used in the field but must be employed with care. Some experts claim it has "many errors of fact or interpretation." It was the first dictionary of its size and scope in English. There are others in process. Check to see if your library has them.

Behavioral Science

There is no dictionary of terms in behavioral science. If you want to find the meaning of a term in this field, try to find out, or guess, what discipline might use it, then look it up in one of the dictionaries covering that discipline.

Economics

HIGGS, HENRY, ed. *Palgrave's Dictionary of Political Economy.* 3 vols. New York: Macmillan, 1923–26.

This is the standard dictionary covering older uses of economic terms. It was first published in 1894–96 and later reprinted and expanded, but it is not up-to-date. It is most valuable for finding out what terms meant to about 1920. Many terms used by early political scientists are included in it. It has good bibliographies for the terms it covers.

HORTON, BURNE J. et al. *Dictionary of Modern Economics.* Washington, D.C.: Public Affairs Press, 1948.

Modern, as you can see from the date, means up to the late 1940s. For the period from that covered by Palgrave to the late 1940s, it is possible to get some idea of what terms meant. For later usage see the next work.

SLOAN, HAROLD S. and ARNOLD J. ZURCHER. *A Dictionary of Economics.* 4th ed., rev. New York: Barnes and Noble, 1961.

Neither the Horton nor the Sloan dictionaries cover economic terms as deeply and as well, or as they are currently used as does the UNESCO dictionary, but they both cover more ground. See also the *McGraw-Hill Dictionary,* listed under the section "Encyclopedias and Handbooks."

Education

There is one very good dictionary of more than 20,000 terms used in education.

GOOD, CARTER V. *Dictionary of Education.* 2nd ed. New York: McGraw-Hill, 1959.

Geography

A recent authoritative dictionary for geography exists.

MONKHOUSE, F. J. *A Dictionary of Geography.* Chicago: Aldine Publishing Co., 1965.

The next dictionary is older but widely available and has clear short definitions.

MOORE, WILFRED G. *A Dictionary of Geography: Definitions and Explanations of Terms Used in Physical Geography.* 3rd ed. Harmondsworth, Middlesex: Penguin Books, 1963.

Stamp's is good for all around use, more advanced and detailed, and the best by far.

STAMP, L. DUDLEY, ed. *A Glossary of Geographical Terms.* New York: Wiley, 1961.

It covers older as well as current usage and is also the most authoritative work.

History

Historians have a relatively small technical vocabulary which is not well-covered in any dictionary, even in Webster's. By and large, however, historians use language appropriate to their subject, and therefore when a term is unfamiliar, try first a general dictionary. If that is not satisfactory, then try a more specialized subject dictionary. Dictionaries in history are not dictionaries in the usual sense of the word.

For the period 1789–1945, a good reference follows.

> PALMER, A. W. *A Dictionary of Modern History, 1789–1945.* London: Cresset Press, 1962.

For looking up terms in American history see the next book.

> ADAMS, JAMES T., ed. *Dictionary of American History.* 5 vols. and index. 2nd ed., rev. New York: Scribners, 1942.
>
> This was brought up-to-date by *Supplement I, 1940–1960,* or Vol. 6, published in 1961. It has been called an encyclopedia because it includes many brief articles on a large number of topics.

A shorter dictionary follows.

> COCHRAN, THOMAS and WAYNE ANDREWS, eds. *Concise Dictionary of American History.* New York: Scribners, 1962.

Many of the special fields of history also have dictionaries. If you want to find out when an event occurred, the next work, although called a dictionary, is a tabular listing with a good index.

> PUTNAM, GEORGE P., comp. *Dictionary of Events.* New York: Grosset, 1936.

Law

English common law, the basis of much American law, is built on precedent. This means that accurate word meanings must be established by use and in courts in order that all users of the law may know what it means. Law has, in addition to a large specialized vocabulary, a general concern with precise word meanings. The pitfalls of sloppy language are very great, and the beginning student should not venture far into legal investigations without experienced help.

BLACK, HENRY C. *Black's Law Dictionary, Definitions of the Terms and Phrases of American and English Jurisprudence, Ancient and Modern.* 4th ed. St. Paul, Minnesota: West Publishing Co., 1951.

This is a standard, good dictionary, but it is still best to try Webster's first.

The following is an older dictionary.

BOUVIER, JOHN. *Bouvier's Law Dictionary.* Edited by William E. Baldwin. Baldwin's Student Edition. Cleveland: Banks-Baldwin, 1934.

This is intermediate in difficulty between Webster's and Black's.

Next is a newer dictionary but not so comprehensive as the other two.

RADIN, MAX. *Law Dictionary.* Edited by Lawrence G. Greene. New York: Oceana Publications, 1955.

Planning

There is no dictionary of planning. If you are in doubt about a term found in this discipline, first check Webster's. If that will not do, then try a specialized subject dictionary. Many newer planning terms are drawn from economics, older ones from art and architecture.

Political Science

Political scientists use the vocabulary of law very often. Therefore, for some terms a law dictionary will help. They also use the language and jargon of government, politics, and politicians. For these uses, see Webster's or one of the following.

SMITH, EDWARD C. and ARNOLD J. ZURCHER. *Dictionary of American Politics.* 2nd ed. New York: Barnes and Noble, 1967.

This has about 3,000 entries.

WHITE, WILBUR W. *White's Political Dictionary.* New York: World Publishing Co., 1947.

Both of the above are useful for the general reader. A bit broader than a dictionary, but useful for more recent world affairs, inexpensive, and up-to-date is:

ELLIOTT, FLORENCE and MICHAEL SUMMERSKILL. *A Dictionary of Politics.* Rev. ed. Baltimore: Penguin Books, 1957.

The background of American political terms with quotations illustrating their use is given in the next work.

SPERBER, HANS and TRAVIS TRITTSCHUH. *American Political Terms: An Historical Dictionary.* Detroit: Wayne State University Press, 1962.

Psychology

For the usage of terms in psychology and related social science fields before 1900, Baldwin is excellent and authoritative.

BALDWIN, JAMES M., ed. *Dictionary of Philosophy and Psychology.* 3 vols. in 4. New York: Macmillan, 1901–1905. Also reprinted in 1949 and 1960.

Baldwin is also good for bibliographies. Many famous social scientists contributed to it. Keep its date in mind, however.

For the meaning of terms as used during the period between 1900 and the early 1930s use the later but still not up-to-date dictionary given next.

WARREN, HOWARD C. *Dictionary of Psychology.* Boston: Houghton Mifflin, 1934.

For more recent usage three very good dictionaries are available.

ENGLISH, HORACE B. and AVA C. ENGLISH. *A Comprehensive Dictionary of Psychological and Psychoanalytical Terms: A Guide to Usage.* New York: McKay, 1958.

This is probably the best if you know a little about the subject.

DREVER, JAMES. *A Dictionary of Psychology.* Baltimore: Penguin, 1964.

Perhaps the beginner should start with this first for the concise, clear definitions.

HINSIE, LELAND E. and ROBERT J. CAMPBELL. *Psychiatric Dictionary.* 3rd ed. New York: Oxford University Press, 1960.

Good, but a bit more advanced than Drever or English and English. Use them first.

Social Work

The best dictionary, although somewhat dated, still is:

YOUNG, ERLE F. *Dictionary of Social Welfare.* New York: Social Science Publishers, 1948.

Social work uses terms from many fields, so if Webster's does not give a satisfactory definition, try one of the special subject dictionaries.

Sociology

The field of sociology does not have any good modern dictionaries.

FAIRCHILD, HENRY P., ed. *Dictionary of Sociology.* Totowa, N.J.: Littlefield, 1962.

A good reference for material up to the middle 1940s.

Not quite a dictionary, but a place where you can get more up-to-date meanings is given next.

MIHANOVICH, CLEMENT S. *et al. Glossary of Sociological Terms.* Milwaukee: Bruce Publishing Co., 1957.

For a more recent definition of fifty-two important sociological concepts you might look up the next journal article.

BOGARDUS, EMORY S. "Selected Sociological Concepts for Beginning Students in Sociology." *Sociology and Social Research*, vol. 64 (Jan.-Feb., 1960): 200–208.

ENCYCLOPEDIAS AND HANDBOOKS

Both encyclopedias and handbooks contain large amounts of knowledge. Encyclopedias usually have more information, and they are usually organized more tightly and in a more scholarly way. They are always written by more than one person. At their best, they are attempts to put together large amounts of knowledge in an orderly fashion. Handbooks, in contrast, contain information that workers in the field like to keep nearby for frequent use. They are set up so that the knowledge is in a more practical form. Both are likely to be organized into entries headed by topics which are then alphabetized. Use encyclopedias and handbooks after the dictionaries which you have consulted to make sure you know what the terms mean.

> *Encyclopaedia of the Social Sciences.* 15 vols. New York: Macmillan, 1930–1935.
>
> Henceforth this will be referred to as ESSI. It is the first encyclopedia of its kind, a great work, summarizing social science knowledge up to the 1930s. Look here to find knowledge on a subject as it existed up to that time.

> *International Encyclopedia of the Social Sciences.* 17 vols. New York: Macmillan and The Free Press, 1968.
>
> This work should be examined early in any search for recent knowledge. Henceforth it is referred to as ESSII.

Covering much more than social science but very useful because of its emphasis on older thought about classical topics is the *Syntopicon.* Use it to find out, for example, what Aristotle thought about love or what Freud thought about angels. The *Syntopicon* is organized topically. Each topic has an article summarizing western thought on it, followed by references to authors who have written about it.

> ADLER, MORTIMER J. *et al. The Great Ideas: A Syntopicon of Great Books of the Western World.* 2 vols. Chicago: Encyclopedia Britannica, 1952.

Anthropology

There is no encyclopedia for anthropology but the following two books, taken together, come very close to being one.

KROEBER, ALFRED L., ed. *Anthropology Today: An Encyclopedic Inventory.* Chicago: University of Chicago Press, 1953.

TAX, SOL, ed. *An Appraisal of Anthropology Today.* Chicago: University of Chicago Press, 1953.

These two works summarize the knowledge of anthropology as it existed in the early 1950s. In 1955 another volume appeared which carries the summary from 1952 to 1955.

Yearbook of Anthropology. New York: Wenner-Gren Foundation for Anthropological Research, 1955.

Still not an encyclopedia, but encyclopedic in scope are the various publications of the Human Relations Area Files.

MURDOCK, GEORGE P. *Outline of World Cultures.* 3rd ed., rev. New Haven: Human Relations Area Files, 1962.

MURDOCK, GEORGE P. et al. *Outline of Cultural Materials.* 4th rev. ed. New Haven: Human Relations Area Files, 1960.

These two volumes present the classification schemes for all the available data for all known cultures in the world. They are also a guide to the data in the Human Relations Area Files.

Behavioral Science

No encyclopedia of behavioral science exists. Much material on behavioral science is included in ESSII.

Economics

No encyclopedia of economics exists; see the ESSI for information through the early 1930s. The general encyclopedias found in most libraries are, however, reasonably good for the more common topics studied in economics. Be careful to use a recent edition or recent yearbook of the encyclopedias if you want to be sure to be up-to-date.

A handbook containing 1,300 definitions of modern economic terms, about 200 descriptions of economic agencies, and other references to sources of information follows.

> GREENWALD, DOUGLAS *et al. The McGraw-Hill Dictionary of Modern Economics: A Handbook of Terms and Organizations.* New York: McGraw-Hill, 1965.

Education

No good modern encyclopedia on education exists, but for the period to about 1910 there is an excellent one.

> MONROE, PAUL, ed. *A Cyclopedia of Education.* 5 vols. New York: Macmillan, 1911–1913.

For research in education that is more current see the next item.

> HARRIS, CHESTER W., ed. *Encyclopedia of Educational Research.* 3rd ed. New York: Macmillan, 1960.
>
> This work specializes in surveying the research in education.

Next is a one volume encyclopedia of rather general nature that sometimes helps for the period since Monroe.

> RIVLIN, HARRY N., ed. *Encyclopedia of Modern Education.* New York: Philosophical Library, 1943.
>
> SMITH, EDWARD W. *The Educator's Encyclopedia.* Englewood Cliffs, N.J.: Prentice-Hall, 1961.
>
> This is a practical guide to how schools are run.

Two good handbooks follow.

> GAGE, NATE L., ed. *Handbook of Research on Teaching.* Chicago: Rand McNally, 1963.
>
> FOSHAY, ARTHUR W., ed. *The Rand McNally Handbook of Education.* Chicago: Rand McNally, 1963.

Geography

No up-to-date encyclopedia of geography exists. However, one volume comes close for the period up to the early 1950s.

JAMES, PRESTON E., ed. *American Geography: Inventory and Prospect.* Syracuse, N.Y.: Association of American Geographers, 1954.

History

The works that follow are not encyclopedias in the sense that they cannot present either all, or a synthesis, of knowledge in history. After all, the subject is so large that one could hardly expect an encyclopedia of the usual kind. Most of what are called encyclopedias of history in America are date-books or chronological listings of facts, like those given below. They are a handy source of dates, terms, and facts.

CARRUTH, GORTON, ed. *The Encyclopedia of American Facts and Dates.* 4th ed. New York: Crowell, 1966.

LANGER, WILLIAM L. *An Encyclopedia of World History: Ancient, Medieval and Modern, Chronologically Arranged.* 3rd ed., rev. Boston: Houghton Mifflin, 1952.

MORRIS, RICHARD B. *Encyclopedia of American History.* rev. ed. New York: Harper & Row, 1965.

Law

No encyclopedia or handbook can exist for American law, which is based on precedent. The facts of the law, in other words, exist largely in the previously decided cases—and there are thousands of volumes of these. Research in law is highly specialized so do not venture far without help. A reference to a guide on how to do research in law is given in the section on law in the next part of the appendix, "Surveys and Other Guides to the Literature."

Planning

No encyclopedia or handbook of planning exists. You will have to guess what disciplines a planning subject comes under, and check the reference there.

Political Science

Only short encyclopedias and handbooks exist in political science. An old but very useful work for the period to about 1914 follows.

> McLAUGHLIN, ANDREW C. and ALBERT B. HART, eds. *Cyclopedia of American Government*. 3 vols. New York: Appleton, 1914.
>
> Its title is descriptive.

For the United Nations, the U.N. Department of Public Information puts out the following work which, although not an encyclopedia, might loosely be called a handbook.

> *Everyman's United Nations: The Structure, Functions, and Work of the Organization and its Related Agencies.*
>
> For example, the 7th edition covers 1945–1962 and was published in 1964.

Psychology

> HARRIMAN, PHILIP L. *Encyclopedia of Psychology*. New York: Philosophical Library, 1946.
>
> This is a short work, of uneven quality.

Not quite but almost an encyclopedia, and more modern and useful than Harriman, is Koch.

> KOCH, SIGMUND. *Psychology: A Study of a Science*. 6 vols. New York: McGraw-Hill, 1959–1963.
>
> This series, a seventh volume of which is promised, is an attempt to survey the field of psychology. The later volumes contain very good discussions of the relationships of psychology to the other disciplines of social science.

The following is an excellent handbook written by experts, and widely quoted.

> LINDZEY, GARDNER, ed. *Handbook of Social Psychology*. 2 vols. Cambridge, Mass.: Addison-Wesley, 1954.

There are four good handbooks covering different psychological subjects that you might find useful.

ARIETI, SILVANO, ed. *American Handbook of Psychiatry.* 3 vols. New York: Basic Books, 1959–1966.

CARMICHAEL, LEONARD, ed. *Manual of Child Psychology.* 2nd ed. New York: Wiley, 1954.

FRYER, DOUGLAS H. and EDWIN R. HENRY, eds. *Handbook of Applied Psychiatry.* 2 vols. New York: Rinehart, 1950.

STEVENS, STANLEY S., ed. *Handbook of Experimental Psychology.* New York: Wiley, 1951.

Social Work

The field of social work is covered by a good encyclopedia.

LURIE, H. L., ed. *Encyclopedia of Social Work: Successor to the Social Work Year Book.* New York: National Association of Social Workers, 1965.

Sociology

Encyclopedic works exist in several special fields of sociology, for example: marriage and the family, organizations, population, and social gerontology. There is none for the whole field. The same is true of handbooks. The following work is excellent for the concepts it covers.

OGBURN, WILLIAM F. and MEYER F. NIMKOFF. *A Handbook of Sociology.* 4th ed., rev. London: Routledge and Kegan Paul, 1960.

An earlier American edition is *Sociology*, 3rd ed., rev., Boston: Houghton Mifflin, 1958.

A more up-to-date reference that covers 27 topics with good bibliographies follows.

FARIS, ROBERT E. L., ed. *Handbook of Modern Sociology.* Chicago: Rand McNally, 1964.

SURVEYS AND OTHER GUIDES TO THE LITERATURE

Included in this section are books or articles which are intended to introduce the writings in a particular area of the social sciences. A good survey or guide critically discusses a well-selected and organized sample of materials. A survey or guide differs from an encyclopedia in that it attempts to cover more of the subject in less space and detail. In contrast to the usual journal article which is very specialized, the survey or guide will include a large amount of material that has been put into a systematic arrangement with the aim of giving a broad overview. Science makes progress both with the small specialized contributions and the large-scale attempts to synthesize. Use the surveys and guides for looking over and getting introduced to the whole field. Two widely available works provide excellent introductions to social science and contain many further references.

> BECKER, HOWARD and HARRY E. BARNES. *Social Thought from Lore to Science.* 3 vols. 3rd ed., expanded and rev. New York: Dover, 1961.
>
> Organized on historical principles with references to almost every major figure in social science, it also has sections on various countries. Be careful about using the indexes; both volumes 1 and 2 have indexes for volumes 1 and 2 but volume 3 has only its own index. Therefore use the index in volume 1 or 2 plus that of 3.

> HOSELITZ, BERT F., ed. *A Reader's Guide to the Social Sciences.* Glencoe, Ill.: The Free Press, 1959.
>
> This fine work is a collection of articles on the main disciplines of the social sciences. The first chapter contains the best short history of the social sciences. If you had to limit yourself to one book covering the social sciences, this would have to be the one. Henceforth it will be referred to as the Hoselitz *Reader.*

Another, more elementary, view of what is taught under the name "social science" is discussed in the following work.

> EHRMANN, HENRY W., ed. *The Teaching of the Social Sciences in the United States.* Paris: UNESCO, 1954.

Still another view of social science is covered in the next work.

> JUNKER, BUFORD H. *Field Work: An Introduction to the Social Sciences.* Chicago: University of Chicago Press, 1960.
>
> This book emphasizes the acquisition of social science knowledge through study of people in the field. It is full of references.

There is no book that discusses the methods of social science in the broad sense although there is a paperback that emphasizes certain ones.

> DUVERGER, MAURICE. *An Introduction to the Social Sciences with Special Reference to their Methods.* New York: Frederick A. Praeger, 1964. (Published in French under a different title in 1961.)

I have not seen the following work, but experts refer to it.

> LEWIS, PETER R. *The Literature of the Social Sciences: An Introductory Survey and Guide.* London: Library Association, 1960.

Do not forget that a good college textbook is also an excellent way to see what a field is all about. To find a good textbook you can look up the course number of the basic course in the catalog of a college near you and then get the book from the college bookstore. Libraries do not usually acquire texts.

Anthropology

Where good surveys and guides to the literature are lacking, one can often learn much from the history of the field. For an idea of how anthropology came to be what it is, in other words, for a good historical introduction, see one of the three standard histories, although they are all dated.

> HADDON, ALFRED C. *History of Anthropology.* rev. ed. London: Watts, 1934.

> LOWIE, ROBERT H. *History of Ethnological Theory.* New York: Holt, 1937.

PENNIMAN, THOMAS K. *A Hundred Years of Anthropology*. 3rd rev.
ed. New York: Humanities Press, 1965.

For a broader, more detailed, and up-to-date survey, see
the volumes under "Anthropology" in the encyclopedia and
handbook section of this book. The Hoselitz *Reader* has a fine
introduction to the subject.

Behavioral Science

One fairly comprehensive and up-to-date survey exists in
this field.

BERELSON, BERNARD and GARY STEINER. *Human Behavior: An Inventory of Scientific Findings*. New York: Harcourt Brace & World,
1964.

The book contains a series of propositions about behavior with
references to the research that supports them.

More elementary is another book which contains twenty
chapters. One group of chapters is on the present interests of
anthropology, psychology, and sociology as these disciplines
relate to behavioral science. Other chapters cover various aspects of the behavioral sciences with some references to other
works.

BERELSON, BERNARD, ed. *The Behavioral Sciences Today*. New York:
Basic Books, 1963.

Before using the next publication, keep in mind that all who
call themselves behavioral scientists do not agree on what
behavioral science is. The discipline is too young yet to have
well-defined subdivisions.

*The ABS Guide to Recent Publications in the Social and Behavioral
Sciences*. New York: The American Behavioral Scientist, 1965, with
annual supplements.

This basic volume includes more than 6,500 citations to selected
literature, published from 1957 through 1964.

Economics

The American Economic Association has published a series of volumes surveying some of the important subjects of economics and republishing important articles. The series runs to more than ten volumes. You usually will be able to locate them if you find the first two:

> ELLIS, HOWARD, ed. *A Survey of Contemporary Economics.* Homewood, Ill.: Irwin, 1948.

> HALEY, BERNARD, ed. *A Survey of Contemporary Economics.* Homewood, Ill.: Irwin, 1952.

The essay on economics in the Hoselitz *Reader* referred to at the beginning of this section is an excellent short overview.

Education

Two practical and high quality guides to the literature of education are available.

> ALEXANDER, CARTER and ARVID J. BURKE. *How to Locate Educational Information and Data: An Aid to Quick Utilization of the Literature of Education.* 4th ed., rev. New York: Columbia University Press, 1958.

> PARK, JOE, ed. *The Rise of American Education: An Annotated Bibliography.* Evanston, Ill.: Northwestern University Press, 1965.

Far more elementary, but clear and well written, and a good source of general information is a textbook.

> HARTFORD, ELLIS F. *Education in These United States.* New York: Macmillan, 1964.

Geography

The best guide, although now dated, to the literature of geography follows.

> WRIGHT, JOHN K. and ELIZABETH T. PLATT. *Aids to Geographical Research: Bibliographies, Periodicals, Atlases, Gazetteers, and Other*

Reference Books. 2nd ed., rev. New York: Columbia University
Press, 1947.

There is a good chapter on geography in the Hoselitz
Reader. Maps are an important part of the study of geography.

WHYTE, FREDERICH H. *Whyte's Atlas Guide.* New York: Scarecrow
Press, 1962.

This is a subject index to twenty standard atlases.

History

Two useful guides to the literature of history are authoritative and comprehensive.

AMERICAN HISTORICAL ASSOCIATION. *Guide to Historical Literature.* New York: Macmillan, 1961.

HANDLIN, OSCAR et al. *Harvard Guide to American History.* Cam-
bridge: Belknap Press of Harvard University Press, 1954.

In 1967 a paperback edition was published by Atheneum.

The Library of Congress has published what it calls a guide
but most people would call a bibliography. It is a very complete topic listing with annotated references.

U. S. LIBRARY OF CONGRESS. *A Guide to the Study of the United
States: Representative Books Reflecting the Development of Amer-
ican Life and Thought.* Washington: U. S. Government Printing
Office, 1960, with a supplement in 1966.

The Hoselitz *Reader* provides a good short statement of
what history is about with references to some important works.
Another useful guide follows.

HEPWORTH, PHILIP. *How to Find Out in History: A Guide to Sources
of Information for All.* Oxford, Pergamon Press, 1966.

Law

There are few overviews of important legal developments
that are not written in legalese. A good one that can be understood without needing a law degree is:

> *Annual Survey of American Law.* Dobbs Ferry, N. Y.: Oceana Publications, annually since 1942.

The next is written for the law student.

> SURRENCY, E. C. *et al. A Guide to Legal Research.* 2nd ed. New York: Oceana Publications, 1966.
>
> This is a fairly clear statement of how to do research in the law.

For an up-to-date overview of an important part of current law the American Civil Liberties Union publishes a useful annual report.

Although neither a survey or guide in the strict sense, the next work can help you to orient yourself in the field of law.

> PRICE, MILES D. and HARRY BITNER. *Effective Legal Research: A Practical Manual of Law Books and Their Use.* Englewood Cliffs, N. J.: Prentice-Hall, 1953.

Planning

There is no very useful guide to the literature of planning, nor any useful survey of the field. If you want a quick overview of the kind of activities in which some planners engage see:

> *Urban Research News,* a fortnightly newsletter.

Political Science

There is a good short survey of political science in the United States.

> WALDO, DWIGHT. *Political Science in the United States of America, A Trend Report.* Paris: UNESCO, 1956.

A longer and more recent work also surveys the field.

> HYNEMAN, CHARLES S. *The Study of Politics: The Present State of American Political Science.* Urbana, Ill.: University of Illinois Press, 1959.

A good short guide is the article in the Hoselitz *Reader.*
The work that follows, although not brought up-to-date, is still a useful guide to the literature of political science.

> BURCHFIELD, LAVERNE. *Student's Guide to Materials in Political Science.* New York: Holt, 1935.

Psychology

A very good guide to the literature of psychology follows.

> DANIEL, ROBERT S. and CHAUNCEY M. LOUTTIT. *Professional Problems in Psychology.* Englewood Cliffs, N. J.: Prentice-Hall, 1953.

A good survey source for part of the literature follows.

> *Annual Review of Psychology.* Stanford, Calif.: Annual Reviews.
>
> The problem is that it only surveys certain topics each year so you must be sure about the topic and find the proper volume for it.

The Hoselitz *Reader* has a good chapter on psychology.

Social Work

There is no good guide or survey of the literature on social work. Some of the beginning texts might be useful for certain problems.

Sociology

There is no useful guide to the literature of sociology but a good survey of part of it exists.

> GITTLER, JOSEPH B., ed. *Review of Sociology: Analysis of a Decade.* New York: Wiley, 1957.

Once again see the Hoselitz *Reader* for a good short overview of the subject.

INDEXES, ABSTRACTS, AND BIBLIOGRAPHIES

This section of the guide includes indexes, abstracts, and bibliographies not mentioned elsewhere. An index is a listing of publications—articles and books—usually according to subject, title, author, or kind or date of publication.

An abstract or digest is a summary, the aim of which is to briefly describe what the whole publication contains. By reading the abstract, it is often possible to tell if one should go to the trouble of reading the whole book or article. The best abstracting practice includes the preparation of indexes for the abstracts and combines the functions of indexing and abstracting. Therefore when you find a good abstracting service, you will usually have an index.

A bibliography is, like an index, a listing of items in some order, usually alphabetical, with an indication of where the items can be found. For most purposes, the central distinctions between indexes and abstracts in the social sciences lie in the selection of materials from which they are composed and the details and format of the reference. An index is typically more restricted in terms of the sources of its items. The index is most likely also to stress where the item can be found, while the bibliography is likely to describe the item more fully.

Most users of the library need not concern themselves about these and other matters of definition so long as they understand that all three, indexes, abstracts, and bibliographies, may have to be consulted in order to find information.

Indexes

For general use on current subjects or for how and when a subject was reported in the press, use the best newspaper index.

> *New York Times Index.* New York: New York Times.
>
>> Except for the year 1859 and the period 1906–1912, it covers from 1851 to the present.

If you are lucky enough to be searching for information about which a good doctoral dissertation has recently been written, you will be saved much time. The book that follows is primarily an alphabetical list of authors by year. The subject classifications are very broad, so you must know the author to use it expeditiously.

> *American Doctoral Dissertations.* Ann Arbor, Mich.: University Microfilms.

More useful, since it is classified by subject, is the following abstracting service.

> *Dissertation Abstracts; A Guide to Dissertations and Monographs Available on Microfilm.* Ann Arbor, Mich.: University Microfilms. Bimonthly.

Usually it is not a good idea to use even the general indexes until you know something about your subject. This is because the indexes mainly include journals. The principal journals of social science are indexed in many different places. Therefore you may have to use several indexes as you probe more deeply for knowledge. This part of the guide is set up so that you can find out a lot about a subject quickly. Begin by using the subject index in either of the two indexes given below and then let it lead you to the appropriate journal.

The best single index for the social sciences and the first one to check is:

> *Social Science and Humanities Index.* (Formerly the *International Index*) Published four times each year, with annual cumulations.

As an example of the coverage of this index, the following journals are among those indexed.

> *American Anthropologist*
> *American Behavioral Scientist*
> *American Economic Review*
> *American Journal of International Law*
> *American Journal of Sociology*
> *American Political Science Review*
> *American Sociological Review*
> *Current Anthropology*

Economic Geography
Geographical Journal
Geographical Review
Human Organization
Journal of Politics
Journal of Political Economy
Social Casework
Social Service Review
Southwestern Journal of Anthropology

Another very useful index follows.

PUBLIC AFFAIRS INFORMATION SERVICE. *Bulletin*.

Often referred to as the PAIS index, it lists by subject many publications on topics of interest in social science. In recent years, over 1,000 periodicals have been indexed by subject.

Indexes in Related Disciplines

Following are some other indexes and one abstracting service which cover social science subject matter.

Applied Science and Technology Index
Art Index
Biological and Agricultural Index
Business Periodical Index
Biological Abstracts

Once in a while you will find it interesting to see what has been said of a book by those who reviewed it.

An Index to Book Reviews in the Humanities.

This title could be misleading. Many reviews from social science journals are indexed alphabetically by the author of the book.

There are three ways to use the indexes to find out what has been written about a subject. One, discussed above, is to look first in the general indexes. The other two ways, discussed more fully below, are to check the indexes for the disciplines or to go from the journal list back to the indexes, and then into the journals again.

The next listing is more specialized. It includes those indexes, abstracts and bibliographies not mentioned elsewhere that are focused on social sciences. Use this section when you know the discipline that includes the subject in which you are interested.

You will notice that not every discipline has an indexing or abstracting service. When this is the case, look up the main journals in the field (see later section) and then check White *Sources* to see in what publication they are indexed. Then you can use the more general index and often find what you need. Even if your library does not have certain special indexes or abstracts, you can almost always use one of these techniques.

In using the following list of indexes and abstracts, note carefully that even when a discipline does not have an index or abstract of its own, many of the leading social science journals are cross-indexed. That is, journals in one discipline are indexed in the indexing services of some other discipline.

Anthropology

No general index of anthropology exists. The abstracts that are available are organized to cover special subjects such as "New World Archaeology," "Africa," or "Acculturation."

A fine international bibliography exists for anthropology.

> *International Bibliography of Socio-cultural Anthropology.* Chicago: Aldine, annually, 1955– .

Behavioral Science

No index exists. The journal *American Behavioral Scientist* publishes *New Studies: A Guide to Recent Publications in the Social and Behavioral Sciences*, a monthly reference service.

Economics

The American Economic Association has published a fine series of volumes which indexes every article that has appeared in English in the major economic journals of the world from 1886–1959 with later supplements.

> AMERICAN ECONOMIC ASSOCIATION. *Index of Economic Journals.* 7 vols. Homewood, Ill.: Irwin, 1961–1966.

The same association publishes *Economic Abstracts* four times a year, which abstracts all the articles in the major journals.
The discipline also has an excellent bibliography.

> *International Bibliography of Economics.* Chicago: Aldine, 1952– . Annually.

Education

One of the best indexes in the disciplines of social science is:

> *Education Index: A Cumulative Subject Index to a Selected List of Educational Periodicals.* New York: H. W. Wilson, 1932 .
>
> It appears monthly with cumulations yearly and every three years.

No general abstracting service is available, although the U.S. Office of Education is developing a computerized information retrieval service for some subjects under the Educational Reference Information Center (ERIC) program, and UNESCO publishes *Education Abstracts.*

Geography

There is no general index or abstracting service covering only geography or all of it in English, although fine sources exist in other languages, especially French.

An excellent classified and annotated bibliography currently being up-dated follows.

> CHURCH, MARTHA, ROBERT HUKE, and WILBUR ZELINSKY, eds. *A Basic Geographical Library.* Commission on College Geography. Publication No. 2. Washington, D.C.: Association of American Geographers, 1966.

History

BOEHM, ERICH, ed. *Historical Abstracts: A Quarterly Covering the World's Periodical Literature, 1775–1945.* Santa Barbara, Calif.: Clio Press. 1955– . Quarterly.

This is an attempt to cover what has been written about the period 1775–1945, since 1954.

The subject of history is too broad to be covered by any one index, abstract, or bibliography. The following bibliography is the best however.

International Bibliography of Historical Sciences. New York: Wilson, 1930– . Annually. Publisher varies.

Because of the special nature of history and the need for social scientists to use primary sources of information, the following four works are also given. The first two can be especially useful because they list various manuscripts and some other collections available in the United States. These collections are so scattered about that almost everybody is near one. You may easily be able to get the thrill of working with original sources by finding those near you.

National Union Catalog of Manuscript Collections: Based on Reports from American Repositories of Manuscripts, 1959–1962. 3 vols. Hamden, Conn.: Shoe String Press, 1962–1964.

HAMER, PHILIP M., ed. *A Guide to Archives and Manuscripts in the United States: Completed for the National Historical Publications Commission.* New Haven: Yale University Press, 1961.

Two other valuable locators of primary source material follow.

KAPLAN, LOUIS. *A Bibliography of American Autobiographies.* Madison: University of Wisconsin Press, 1961.

MATTHEWS, WILLIAM. *American Diaries; An Annotated Bibliography of American Diaries Written Prior to the Year 1861.* Berkeley: University of California Press, 1945.

Law

A good digest service covering international law is available.

> *International Law Reports.* London: Butterworth. 1938– . Annually.

For the United States, the Library of Congress publishes the following:

> *Digest of Public General Bills with Index.* Washington: U. S. Government Printing Office, 1936 to present, about 8 issues for each session of Congress.

The basic index follows.

> *Index to Legal Periodicals.* New York: H. W. Wilson, 1908– .

There is much overlap in some of this material. See also the reference to Edwards below.

Planning

Neither a comprehensive indexing nor an abstracting service exists for the field of planning. The best publication is steadily broadening its coverage.

> *Research Digest.* Published semi-annually by the Bureau of Community Planning of the University of Illinois, Urbana, Ill.

Political Science

There are no comprehensive indexing and abstracting services in the discipline of political science. The following indexes cover only a part of the field.

> EDWARDS, RICHARD A. *Index Digest of State Constitutions.* 2nd ed. New York: Legislative Drafting Research Fund of Columbia University, 1959.

> *Background on World Politics: An Inter-Disciplinary Digest.* 1957– . Quarterly.

The two best book-length bibliographies of political science are:

> HARMON, ROBERT B. *Political Science: A Bibliographical Guide to the Literature.* New York: Scarecrow Press, 1965.

> WYNAR, LUBOMYR R. *Guide to Reference Materials in Political Science: A Selective Bibliography.* Denver: Bibliographic Institute, 1966.

The international bibliography is comprehensive.

> *International Bibliography of Political Science.* Chicago: Aldine, 1952– . Annually.

A good bibliography on foreign affairs is published annually.

> *Foreign Affairs Bibliography: A Selected and Annotated List of Books on International Relations.* New York: Bowker, 1933– .

Psychology

Two excellent abstracting services are available in psychology.

> *Psychological Abstracts.* Washington: American Psychological Association, 1927– . Bimonthly.

> *Child Development Abstracts and Bibliography.* Lafayette, Ind.: Purdue University, 3 times a year.

Social Work

The field of social work has neither a long established index nor a comprehensive abstracting service. The following British publication is often useful.

> *Bibliography of Social Work and Administration: A Classified List of Articles from Selected British Periodicals, 1930–1952.* London: Joint University Council for Social and Public Administration, 1954 with annual supplements.

A classified bibliography, harder to use than it should be because it lacks an index, follows.

TIGHE, LEO W. *A Classified Bibliography for the Field of Social Work.* Santa Clara, Calif.: Premier Publishers, 1959.

Sociology

Sociology is another one of the disciplines of social science with an excellent abstracting service.

Sociological Abstracts. New York. Nine times a year.

International Bibliography of Sociology. Chicago: Aldine, 1951– . Annually.

The following annotated bibliography covers all aspects of population problems.

Population Index. Princeton, N.J.: Office of Population Research, Princeton University, and the Population Association of America, 1935– . Quarterly.

WHERE TO FIND FACTS AND BIOGRAPHIES

Facts of one kind or another are to be found in all the materials previously referred to. As it is used here, the term "fact" means mainly statistical data with emphasis on sources of current information and biographical information. Once you have decided what facts you want to find, the following publications can help you locate them.

The federal government is the largest producer of statistics. The books below can help you find your way to them.

ANDRIOT, JOHN L. *Guide to U.S. Government Statistics.* 3rd ed., rev. and enlarged. Arlington, Va.: Documents Index, 1961.

SCHMECKEBIER, LAURENCE F. and ROY B. EASTIN. *Government Publications and Their Use.* rev. ed. Washington: Brookings Institution, 1961.

UNESCO also publishes many facts and figures. To see what they are, refer to the General Catalogue fully cited in the earlier section "General Bibliographic Aids." As a sample you will find:

> *Basic Facts and Figures: International Statistics Relating to Education, Culture and Mass Communication.* Published annually since 1952.

The U. N. Statistical Office publishes a *Statistical Yearbook and a Compendium of Social Statistics.*

The handiest single source of government-produced data useful to the social scientist follows.

> U. S. BUREAU OF THE CENSUS. *Statistical Abstract.* Washington: U. S. Government Printing Office. Annually.

For facts about the United States in the past there is an excellent volume:

> U. S. BUREAU OF THE CENSUS. *Historical Statistics of the United States.* Washington: U.S. Government Printing Office, 1965.

The U. S. Bureau of Census also publishes much other data, including the following:

> U. S. BUREAU OF THE CENSUS. *Eighteenth Decennial Census of the United States, Census of Population: 1960, United States Census of Housing: 1960,* and the *County and City Data Book, 1966.*

The best source of vital statistics follows.

> U. S. NATIONAL OFFICE OF VITAL STATISTICS. *Vital Statistics of the U. S.* 2 vols. in 3. Washington: U.S. Government Printing Office, 1939– . Annually.

There are two excellent books for finding facts about business.

> COMAN, EDWIN T. *Sources of Business Information.* rev. ed. Berkeley: University of California Press, 1964.

> ALEXANDER, RAPHAEL. *Business Pamphlets and Information Sources.* New York: Exceptional Books, 1967.

This is a guide to currently available pamphlets, reprints, and paperbacks in the field of business, and to organizations and government agencies which are sources of business information, arranged by subject.

For a quick way to find facts about current events, see the following.

Facts on File, A Weekly Digest of World Events with Cumulative Index. New York: Facts on File, Inc., 1940– .

Any good reference book can guide you to all kinds and vast numbers of facts. For example, the following excellent short reference book has a section "Books of Curious Facts, Customs, Folklore and Mythology."

BARTON, MARY N., comp. *Reference Books, A Brief Guide for Students and Other Users of the Library.* 6th ed. Baltimore: Enoch Pratt Free Library, 1966.

Biography

Biography is a much neglected aspect of social science. If you are interested in learning about those who made the social sciences, first see the *Encyclopedia of the Social Sciences* and *International Encyclopedia of the Social Sciences* in the encyclopedia section of the library.

Then check your library card catalog, White, *Sources*, and the various indexes.

For more detailed biographical information, use one of the following, depending on your needs.

Current Biography.

This is a monthly publication about people in the news with references to other publications that tell more about the person.

A more detailed and comprehensive source is:

Biography Index: A Cumulative Index to Biographical Materials in Books and Magazines.

For the best single source of information about Americans of the past see the following:

The Dictionary of American Biography. 20 vols. New York: Scribner, 1929–1959, with an index and two later supplements.

Each reference has further bibliography about the person.

For brief information about living Americans, look into one of these:

The Directory of American Scholars
Who's Who in America
Who's Who of American Women
American Men of Science

Directories of scholars which exist in almost every field of the social sciences are often published by professional associations and are sometimes useful.

A SELECTED LIST OF JOURNALS IN SOCIAL SCIENCE

Journals are the place where scholars publish the results of their research. They are the up-to-date sources of specialized information about a subject. In the early stages of research, you are not likely to find them of much use. They are valuable after you have learned a fair amount about a subject. Increasingly, articles in some journals are being written in mathematical language.

Do not forget that one way to acquire a broader knowledge about a subject and related subjects in a discipline is to look up the publication in White, *Sources*, and read the appropriate section. A way to find out how a subject is related to other subjects from a multi-disciplinary point of view is to find out in what general index or abstracting service the journal is covered and then look up that subject there.

Given here are the titles of some of the main American journals in the social sciences. The listing is selective—there are many other journals. The indexes, abstracts, guides, etc., will lead you to more specialized journals and complete references if required.

Anthropology

American Anthropologist
American Journal of Physical Anthropology
Current Anthropology
Human Organization
Southwestern Journal of Anthropology

Behavioral Science

The American Behavioral Scientist
Behavioral Science
Journal of the History of the Behavioral Sciences

Economics

American Economic Review
Journal of Political Economy
Quarterly Journal of Economics

Education

American Educational Research Journal
Journal of Educational Research
Journal of Educational Sociology
Phi Delta Kappan
Review of Educational Research and the Research Bulletin of the National Education Association
Teachers College Record

Geography

Association of American Geographers, Annals
Economic Geography
Geographical Journal
Geographical Review

History

American Historical Review
Current History
A Journal of American History
Journal of Modern History
William and Mary Quarterly

Law

American Journal of Comparative Law
American Journal of International Law
Harvard Law Review
Law and Contemporary Problems

Planning

Journal of the American Institute of Planners
Town Planning Review
Urban Affairs Quarterly

Political Science

American Political Science Review
Political Science Quarterly
Proceedings of the Academy of Political Science

Psychology

Contemporary Psychology
Journal of Abnormal Psychology
Journal of Applied Psychology
Journal of Psychology
Journal of Social Psychology

Social Work

Smith College Studies in Social Work
Social Casework
Social Service Review

Sociology

American Journal of Sociology
American Sociological Review
Rural Sociology
Social Forces
Sociology and Social Research

Appendix B

A Working Definition
of "Behavioral Science"

Behavioral Science: a part of social science; social science, in turn, being a part of science.

1. (a) *aims*: Behavioral science has as its primary aim the explanation of human behavior. It is thus only a part of social science, which studies man, and distinct from those sciences which study animal behavior, or the behavior of things.

(b) *methods*: Any scientific method that seems to be helpful in the study of a behavior problem is used. Behavioral science is usually more willing to adapt other truth seeking methods than are the older social science disciplines.

(c) *scope*: The precise boundaries of the science are not well defined. Practically, the scope is set by the conditions of the problem under investigation. These problems often lie beyond the scope or overlap the boundaries of the older social science disciplines.

For example, findings from biology (animals) and medicine (drug effects) may be used to clarify aspects of human behavior.

(d) *theory*: The main body of theory has been adapted from social science although significant parts have been taken from other fields, such as computing and engineering.

(e) *methodology*: In the sense that methodology studies the principles of method, little has yet been developed.

(f) *content*: Because of its novelty and despite numerous studies, little generally accepted content in terms of the structure of a scientific system has yet developed. Despite this limitation, many studies have been put to practical use by institutions, e.g., hospitals, business, and governments.

(g) *relationship to social science*: In addition to those pointed out above, behavioral science stresses rigorous definition of both its experimental and theoretical terms and is concerned with the structures of its theory and rules of correspondence.

(h) *practitioners*: Anyone whose scientific problems fit the aims, methods, and scope above can be involved in behavioral science. In practice these are most often psychologists, social psychologists, and political scientists.

2. *Archaic*: "Behavioral science" is a term often used interchangeably with the older term "social science" mainly by members of the behaviorist school of psychologists to designate the newer social science they hoped to construct. This practice fell into disuse by the early 1940s, and the term was abandoned until the late 1940s when several widely different groups redefined it variously for their own, often non-scientific, purposes. It then became a designation for different combinations of scholarly disciplines, subject matters, aims, theory, methods, and practitioners until it had lost all precision except among those members of a given group that shared the definition.

Index

2. BY NAME